The Sex Lives of Cannibals

The Sex Lives of Cannibals

ADRIFT IN THE EQUATORIAL PACIFIC

J. Maarten Troost

Broadway Books ∽ New York

PRINTED IN THE UNITED STATES OF AMERICA

Visit our website at www.broadwaybooks.com

First edition published 2004

Book design by Elizabeth Rendfleisch

Library of Congress Cataloging-in-Publication Data
Troost, J. Maarten.
The sex lives of cannibals : adrift in the Equatorial Pacific / J. Maarten Troost.— 1st ed.
p. cm.
1. Ethnology—Kiribati—Tarawa Atoll. 2. Tarawa Atoll (Kiribati)—Social life and customs. 3. Tarawa Atoll (Kiribati)—Description and travel. 4. Tarawa Atoll (Kiribati)—Humor. I. Title.
GN671.K57T76 2004
306'.099681—dc22

2004040768

ISBN 0-7679-1530-5

10   9   8   7

DISCLAIMER

This book recounts the experiences of the author while he lived in Kiribati. A few names have been changed, either because the author, who is very bad with names, couldn't remember what they were, or to protect their privacy. Also, since we're disclaiming here, the author wishes to acknowledge that in a few incidents recounted herein, he has played a little fast and loose with the space-time continuum. He has done this for you, the reader.

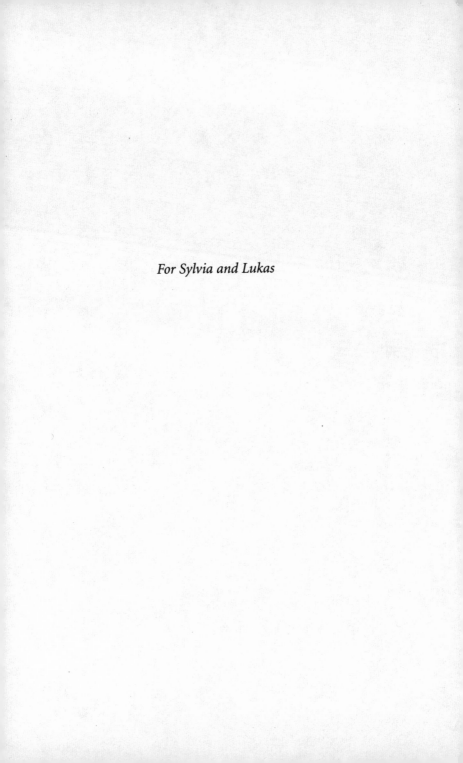

For Sylvia and Lukas

wear thy Mother Hubbard, never mind the heat), and Modern Administration (Queen Victoria knows what's best for you), which has resulted in a Colonial Legacy, as evidenced by the continued use of the Fathom as a unit of measurement.

Chapter 20

IN WHICH the Author discusses the Foreign Aid Industry, whose emissaries, the Consultants, arrive monthly, air service permitting, peddling Models of Sustainable Development, which have worked very well in Africa, followed by some thoughts on the Red Menace on Tarawa, the sinister agents from China, whose Evil Plottings were Subverted at every turn by the Author's Beguiling Girlfriend, who engaged in the Black Arts of Spy Craft, the Perilous Game, a game that she did not master, which led to some false information being sent to Washington, possibly leading to Unforeseen Consequences in U.S.-Sino relations.

Chapter 21

IN WHICH the Author shares some thoughts on what it means to Dissipate, to Wither Away, Dissolute-like, and how one becomes perversely Emboldened by the inevitability of decay, the sure knowledge that today, possibly tomorrow, the Body will be unwell, which leads to Recklessness, Stupidity even, in the conduct of Everyday Life.

Epilogue

In which the Author expresses some Dissatisfaction with the State of his Life, ponders briefly prior Adventures and Misfortunes, and with the aid of his Beguiling Girlfriend, decides to Quit the Life that is known to him and make forth with all Due Haste for Parts Unknown.

One day, I moved with my girlfriend Sylvia to an atoll in the Equatorial Pacific. The atoll was called Tarawa, and should a devout believer in a flat earth ever alight upon its meager shore, he (or she) would have to accept that he (or she) had reached the end of the world. Even cartographers relegate Tarawa either to the abyss of the crease or to the far periphery of the map, assigning to the island a kindly dot that still manages to greatly exaggerate its size. At the time, I could think of no better destination than this heat-blasted sliver of coral. Tarawa was the end of the world, and for two years it became the center of mine.

It is the nature of books such as these—the travel, adventure, humor, memoir kind of book—to offer some reason, some driving force, an irreproachable motivation, for undertaking the odd journey. One reads, *I had long been fascinated by the Red-Arsed Llama, presumed extinct since 1742, and I determined to find one*; or *I only feel alive when I am nearly dead, and so the challenge of climbing K2, alone, without oxygen, or gloves, and snowboarding down, at night, looked promising*; or *A long career (two and a half years) spent lever-*

aging brands in the pursuit of optimal network solutions made me rich as Croesus, and yet I felt strangely uneasy, possibly because I now own 372 (hardworking) kids in Sri Lanka, which is why I decided to move to a quaint corner of Europe, where I would learn from the peasants and grow olive wine. And typically, the writer emerges a little wiser, a little kinder, more spiritual, with a greater appreciation for the interconnectivity of all things.

Let me say at the top here that I didn't have a particularly good reason for moving to Tarawa. There was nothing Quaker-ish, Thoreau-ish, Gauguin-ish (as you wish) about my taking a little leave from Western civilization, which I thought was fine mostly, particularly as manifested in certain parts of Italy. True, I had worries. News You Can Use, the peculiar link between consumption and identity, professional athletes who strike, Cokie Roberts, the Lazarus-like resuscitations of Geraldo Rivera's career, and the demise of the Washington Redskins as a team to be reckoned with all gave me pause and even some anxiety regarding the general course of Western society. However, these issues seemed insufficient to justify a renunciation of continental comfort. I was simply restless, quite likely because of a dissatisfaction with the recent trajectory of my life, and if there is a better, more compelling reason for dropping everything and moving to the end of the world, I know not what it is.

It was the summer of 1996 and I had just finished graduate school in Washington, D.C., which is where I'd met my girlfriend, Sylvia. Both of us had studied international relations. I focused on Eastern Europe (think triumph of good over evil), and Sylvia concentrated on Western Europe (think agricultural subsidies), for which she has been teased mercilessly. While Sylvia passed her semesters with determined ambition, I drifted through, racking up modest grades, until finally there was not an exam left to be taken, not a paper to be turned in, and I was discharged. Job offers were not forthcoming, most likely because I didn't apply to any jobs. Nor was

I particularly adept at what is called networking, which is highly encouraged among job seekers, but perhaps not entirely useful for reticent souls utterly flummoxed by what career to pursue.

Instead of getting a job I went to Cuba, which as expected was interesting, and this delayed for ten more days my entry into the ranks of the employed. I traveled there impulsively, deciding one day that Havana was where I really wanted to be, and within a week I found myself on the Malecon, the seaside avenue, saying yes to cigars and no really, I didn't want to meet their sister. In Havana, I danced in the salsa manner. I rode in a Studebaker. I had long rambling conversations with handsome, middle-aged women about the troubles in Cuba and I learned from them where on the black market in Habana Vieja I could find a chicken. I smoked a marijuana cigarette with Havana's bad element. I learned that Che is ubiquitous in Cuba, and that for most Cubans he is something more than a fashion statement. I learned much else besides, and I didn't even speak Spanish, dredging up instead a hybrid patois composed of schoolboy Latin tossed with French spoken in the accent of Ricardo Montalban.

One may wonder how an unemployed ex–graduate student with no means whatsoever was able to afford a trip to Cuba. The truth of the matter was that I couldn't afford it. However, in an act of colossal misjudgment, American Express had agreed to give me a credit card. American Express, of course, was not accepted in Cuba itself. This is because Cubans are Communists and we are not allowed to trade with Communists, unless they are Chinese Communists. American Express, however, was very helpful in obtaining the full-fare economy-class Washington–Newark–Mexico City–Havana round-trip ticket on AeroMexico, as well as one night's accommodation at an airport hotel in Mexico City, after my last twenty dollars were used to pay an unexpected departure tax in Havana. ("Mais ca dise dans la guido por visitor, no departure tax.") Since I was resoundingly broke at the time, what cash I did have came from defying the tenets of my lease and subletting my one-room apartment to an intern contributing his time to restoring values in America, which apparently lost them, probably in the sixties. He lived in my apartment for one month (cleanliness, apparently, was not a value worth returning to). Since I spent only ten days in Cuba, this left three weeks of unresolved residence needs that needed addressing, which led to an interesting conversation.

"Hi, Mom."

"Uh-oh."

"I'm going to Cuba tomorrow."

Pause.

"I'll be back in ten days, provided that Castro doesn't arrest me and the INS lets me back in. Ha-ha."

Pause.

A whispered aside. ". . . he's going to Cuba tomorrow." The family dog, a beagle, howled.

Bob, my stepfather, got on the line. "Maaaaarten," he said, which he does whenever I'm doing something unreasonable, something that will upset my mother. "You know your mother doesn't like Communists. But listen, since you're going, let me call my friends at the Agency. You could do some freelance work for them."

Offline, my mother's voice, plaintive. "Bob!"

It was Bob's method of diplomatic, benevolent stepparenting, suggesting something more outrageous than what I had devised, so that in comparison, my own reckless irresponsibility seemed suddenly like a moderate course of action. I was grateful for this. I promised my mother that I would not act on Bob's suggestion. It would be foolhardy, I said, to spy for the CIA. I assured her that I would refrain from engaging in any activities that could lead to my spending the rest of my days withering away in a Cuban gulag. In return, I received three weeks of accommodation in suburban Washington, meals included, which worked out well, I thought.

Alas, I soon discovered that a daily wake-up call from a collection agency is a remarkably unpleasant way to begin one's day. These are not warm, friendly voices delicately reminding you that your account is just a trifle overdue, but intimidating snarls threatening personal ruin, and while they didn't precisely say that they were sending Vinnie over and that I might soon have some mobility issues, it was implied. Also, these calls didn't impress Sylvia much. And so I made another phone call.

"Hi, Dad."

"Uh-oh."

"Well, it's like this—"

"No."

"It appears that this particular situation might have certain ramifications regarding—"

"I believe at this point you owe me $180,000."

A gross exaggeration, but effective. It was time, at last, to do something about my income stream, such as, for instance, obtaining one. Like many highly educated people, I didn't have much in the way of actual skills, with the notable exception of forklift operator, at which I did not excel. My lack of excellence in forklift operations, however, did not prevent the manager of the produce market–plant nursery emporium where I labored after high school from sending me forth onto Rockville Pike, one of the main arteries linking Washington, D.C., with the Maryland suburbs, where technically, forklifts should not be—as I soon learned—because when forklifts take a corner a wee bit too fast they tend to tip, which can lead to hundreds of watermelons rolling across the intersection with Montrose Road, followed by said watermelons being chased by a very embarrassed forklift operator wondering whether this, finally, would be the last straw before he was fired. Other skills included housepainting, which I could no longer continue on account of an accident that had made climbing a ladder an experience too terrifying to contemplate; and waiting tables, which I had done at numerous establishments along the Eastern Seaboard, for numerous years, and I just felt that I could no longer serve the numerous assholes that frequent restaurants in a courteous, efficient, nonhomicidal manner.

While it is true that my grasp of the situation in Macedonia and my familiarity with the Czech Republic's privatization program could, potentially, have led to a professional job, perhaps even a good professional job, I chose not to pursue employment in the field for which I had spent many years acquiring knowledge because . . . because, well, I didn't really have a good reason. It just didn't seem like the right thing to do, possibly because to obtain a professional job requires much letter writing and phone calling and boot licking, which comes suspiciously close to being a real job in itself and this I was in no mood for. Instead, beset by fiscal realities, I turned to Jenny and Debbie, kind yet firm managers of a temporary employment agency. They interviewed me, quickly discerned that I was not quite bereft of brains ("Put the following states in alphabetical order: Utah, Arkansas, Idaho, and Nebraska"), that my knowledge of software programs was scant ("But it says on your resume that you are proficient in Word, WordPerfect and Excel"), and that despite three typing tests I could never exceed twenty-nine words a minute, which was most unfortunate because the temp agency determined wages based on typing speed. And so after six years of exceedingly expensive, private school tertiary education combined with the amassment of some interesting and potentially job-relevant experiences elsewhere in the world, I became a minimum-wage temp, an experience that need not be recounted with much detail, though I will note that to be a temp is to have all the illusions and conceits of youth shattered, which was useful and necessary though disagreeable.

My temporary job assignments varied, taking me from law firm to trade association and around again, and always I would be led to the ominous file room and told with the patient civility reserved for the learning impaired that I was to make some order of the files. In the few assignments that lasted longer than a week I was offered the opportunity to enhance my skills and I would be taught how to answer the phone while others were on their lunch break, and even how to order office supplies, which I should note is usually very complicated indeed. Occasionally, I lamented my poor typing skills, but I refused Jenny and Debbie's well-meaning offers to take the typing tutorial offered by the agency, fearing that such a move would lead me inexorably toward a career that depended on my typing speed. Instead, I found myself quietly stagnating, slowly approaching the pathos of self-pity—pathos because I was twenty-six, in the full blossom of youth—until one morning I meandered away from the day's job, entered a café in Georgetown, ordered a large coffee, freshly squeezed orange juice, a poppy seed bagel, toasted, with lox and cream cheese, and read a newspaper with the mirth of one who has time to linger over the Home and Garden section. Jenny and Debbie were not pleased. "Not showing up for an assignment makes us look bad," said Debbie. "I'm afraid we're going to have to let you go."

It is an unfortunate reality for innate idlers that our modern world requires one to hold a job to maintain a sustainable existence. Idling, I find, is immensely underrated, even vilified by some who see inactivity as the gateway for the Evil One. Personally, I regard idling as a virtue, but civilized society holds otherwise and the fact remained that I still had to get a job. And so I soon found myself involved in the exciting world of publishing. I was an associate editor for a small publishing firm in Washington, where I worked on a reference book that detailed the work of lobbyists. The first half of the book, which was essentially a Yellow Pages for influence peddlers, was comprised of listings of companies and countries and who they retained to purchase favors from the guardians of democracy in the heart of the free world. The second half of the book listed all lobbying firms and lobbyists and their clients, as well as the "government relations" staff of corporations that saw the need to maintain offices in Washington. The job consisted of sending out questionnaires, following up with phone calls, confirming lobbying data at the Justice Department, and plugging in the results into a computer database that crashed twice daily. I amused myself by matching the names of the Washington representatives of the Bosnian Serbs, the Mobutu regime, various Somali warlords, and Nike with the guest list of state dinners at the White House. Remarkably, however, there were some who did not take kindly to having their lobbying activities made public, which led to some coarse language directed my way over the telephone, and I would like to say here that I wish the "government relations" staff of (*Deleted by Legal Department*) nothing but ill will, and that I have it on good authority that the ingredients of a (*Deleted by Legal Department*) include canine fecal matter.

While this job included health insurance as a little perk to compensate for its serf-like wages, there was no disguising the fact that I was still treading water in the river of life. I had some notion of wanting to write, though little inclination to actually write, which sometimes led me to believe that I should develop other notions. An obscure literary journal had just published a five-thousand-word essay I had written, and while I was pleased to have something published, the $50 and two free issues in compensation for three months of evening work seemed, somehow, inadequate. I kept sending essays, trifles, queries to national magazines, and while often the editors would respond with a kind, encouraging note, even a phone call, they still, sadly, continued to publish the petty ruminations of windbags long past their prime instead of fresh new voices with interesting things to say. (Not that I'm bitter.)

It was often suggested to me by concerned family members that I should get my foot in the door with a midsized newspaper. I rejected this out of hand. I was familiar enough with journalism to know that were I to cover a news-type event I would rapidly lose all my journalistic-like composure, discard all my faculties of reason, and descend into a stifling murk of uncertainty and fear. I knew this because when I lived in Prague I had been an actual journalist. An English-language weekly newspaper had generously agreed to assign me to real stories based on the masterpiece that was my analysis of the Saudi oil industry, a twenty-page, richly textured, subtly nuanced, carefully crafted display of plagiarism, which earned me a B+ during my junior year of college. These, obviously, were the glory years of the whole westerners-in-Prague era, shortly after the demise of that little experiment in social engineering known as communism, when hundreds, perhaps thousands, of Americans, Canadians, Australians, and other purveyors of Western ways descended upon the most beautiful city in the world and pretty much did anything they wanted to do. It was great.

My mother is Czech and as a consequence I like to think that I was not merely a seeker of the transcendently hip when I lived in Prague. I was born in the Netherlands and as a child I often traveled to Czechoslovakia to visit my grandfather, who lived in an apartment in Prague overlooking the Vltava River. The faint whiff of burning coal is enough to bring back the indolent river swans, the salty bread and sweet yogurt, the smoke-drenched rooms, my grandfather's beer glass, and the long wanderings through soot-stained passageways in a city that for a time spoke to me only of the deeds of kings. When I was seven, just after my parents divorced, my mother had my younger sister and me baptized in a small church in South Bohemia. Seven, of course, is the age when the brain is at its most fecund, when every image and experience offers portent, and so when Prague's many statues of beheaded saints, detongued martyrs, and gargoyles were all helpfully brought to my attention as being relevant in some way to my life and death, I pretty much stopped sleeping for a year, fearing the nightly intrusion of alarming images, particularly of a slender bearded man being put to death in a highly creative and terrifying fashion just so I could go to heaven one day. To further the potency of my imagination, Prague in the 1970s was experiencing what was quaintly called Normalization, which is Soviet-speak for the dread that occurs when the babicka next door is an informer, which leads to a somber and fearful state of being that is far more efficient in quelling deviation from the right and true path than the intimidation offered by Soviet soldiers.

That world, of course, was happily discarded, and with Vaclav Havel installed as a kind of philosopher-king in the great, looming castle above Prague, I moved to the city shortly after college, fortunately no longer palpitating at the sight of saintly relics, but aware that this city of spires and pubs had a way of getting inside you. There was something ephemeral about Prague in the early 1990s, and it is the only city I have known to truly have a spirit. I began writing for *The Prague Post*, or rather they used my name above articles that bore no semblance to the prose I submitted for their consideration. "A story is like a car trip," tutored my editor. "You, the writer, are the car that takes readers from point A to B to C without leaving the road." As careful readers may have already surmised, I favor the ditches of digression.

During my foray into journalism, I never really felt I knew enough about a particular newsworthy event to provide written coverage of the newsworthy event. The written word presented in a journalistic fashion is regarded by most as the indisputable truth and this just left me dumbfounded with a fear of being wrong. I am a big believer in the Law of Unintended Consequences and I imagined that my failure to capture every nuance and subtlety of a newsworthy event would lead to the collapse of governments, economic crises, and lots of hardship for the people of Eastern and Central Europe. Never mind that my stories usually appeared on page C8, and that they were written in a language few people in the region understood, and that my readership probably never exceeded four, and that those four people were, presumably, the four people I interviewed, via a translator, who would suggest—not unkindly—the questions I should be asking. Fortunately, I was both keenly interested in events in the region—march of history and all that—as well as highly opinionated, and so I began writing for the newspaper's opinion page, providing comment on the European Union's policies toward their Eastern brethren, the historical roots of the severing of Czechoslovakia, the West's dithering over Bosnia, Havel's conception of democracy, and other topics I was not remotely qualified to comment upon. This I found to my liking. It is a remarkably easy thing to do, pointing out the faults of others and suggesting remedies or courses of action in an argumentative and pedantic sort of way, and I am still amazed that there are many people in the American media who are paid very big money to do this.

Churning out 750 words on what American policy toward Slovakia should be rarely takes more than an afternoon, and so I spent a lot of time falling in love and traveling and living the life I wanted to live. I saw things that both pleased and horrified me, and in comparison America seemed a sedate and frivolous place. I traveled wherever my meager funds allowed and saw history unfold. On a trip to Poland I had the train connection from hell—arrive at Frankfurt an der Oder at 1:30 A.M., depart for Warsaw at 5:45 A.M.—and while curled asleep on the train platform I was suddenly awakened by the Russian Army. Thousands of Russian soldiers passed through the station on their way from Eastern Germany, which was once again one with Western Germany, on their way back to Russia, which I thought was just the niftiest piece of history I had ever seen. A few months later, I too boarded a train for Russia, where I had a very exciting encounter with a bear on a bridge in St. Petersburg, and where I discovered that everything one has read about vodka consumption in that part of the world is true, and now that I think about it, the bear on the bridge was probably the only sober creature I encountered during my three weeks in Russia. I took a ferry to Dubrovnik, on the stunningly beautiful Dalmatian coast, where my friends and I were accosted by a Croatian soldier who charged out of a bar upon our passing, exclaimed "Tourists!" and when we nodded, said "You are the first since the war," and then hustled us into the bar, where we spent the hours after curfew descending into a sublime melancholy on a verandah overlooking the shell-scarred old town while listening to the staccato crackling of gunfire. In Turkey, I slipped while rock climbing above a waterfall and fractured three vertebrae, which really hurt, though I did find great happiness when, lying crumpled in a gorge, I told my toes to move and they did. I also went to Bosnia-Herzegovina. I obtained press credentials through *The Prague Post* and soon found myself in Mostar, where I was deeply, deeply in over my head and utterly dependent upon the kindness of English mercenaries, and I learned there that the distance between civilization and savagery is exceedingly small and this has scared me ever since.

The point of this little excursion into events and happenings that have nothing whatsoever to do with the South Pacific is simply that I had grown accustomed to life being interesting and adventure ridden and, rather childishly, I refused to believe that this must necessarily come to an end and that the rest of my life should be a sort of penance for all the reckless, irresponsible, and immensely fun things I'd done before. Being a data-entry clerk, even though I was very, very good, just didn't compare to being an incompetent war correspondent. In Washington, I never quite knew what my ambitions were. I sensed that I should move on from waiting tables and housepainting and temping and clerking, but the idea of working in an office and doing office-type work in a committed fashion seemed like a quiet little death to me. Fortunately, with no prodding from me, Sylvia was also inclined to make a few changes. She had begun working for a nongovernmental organization that focused on international development. Suffice it to say that the Washington end of such work can be a mite dispiriting and Sylvia soon began to yearn for the field, which is international development–speak for Third World hellhole. And so we both began applying for jobs in the most miserable places on Earth.

I should perhaps pause here for a moment and mention something of my courtship with Sylvia. It was a night of possiblity. The air was redolent of wheat, hops, and barley. A kindly gentleman, his dreadlocks flowing, made polite introductions. I suavely filled her plastic cup with Budweiser. Her eyes sparkled. Soon, a few dates, some soulful conversation, several well-timed romantic gestures, a stirring hike in the Appalachian Mountains, up where eagles soared, and we moved in together, sharing a charming apartment with an enormous deck shaded by an ancient elm, on a narrow street illuminated by gaslights in Washington's hip, predominately gay neighborhood of Dupont Circle. We were smitten. We pledged to follow each other to the ends of the Earth. ("*Pphhhttt*," said Sylvia, upon reading, over my shoulder. "What drivel.")

Sylvia got the first potentially interesting, exciting, possibly dangerous job nibble. Sarajevo beckoned. She was being considered for a position as a program officer with a refugee agency. She had a phone interview and I watched, standing in our living room, silently cheering *yes, good answer!*, but, in a loss for Bosnia, she was passed over for lack of experience. Then I got the call. Tanzania this time. I was being considered for a position as a press liaison for a refugee agency that operated a camp for 500,000 Rwandan refugees. I am pretty good at compartmentalizing and I figured that I could balance the wretchedness of the camps, and the dismal fact that they contained the Hutu perpetrators of genocide, with safari-type excursions and remain sane. But the guy who had the job decided that one year of liaising between the Rwandan refugees and the world press was not quite enough and so he decided to stay for another year, which upon reflection was probably just as well. And then nothing, just a few letters thanking us for our interest in the program coordinator position in Sudan, or Angola, or Cambodia, but unfortunately, et cetera, et cetera. A change of strategy was called for. If no one was going to send us to an exotic locale then we would just go ourselves and make the best of it.

We decided to move to Hanoi. We would do this by moving out of our apartment and into the basement of my mother's house, where we would live for three months and save enough money to get going in Vietnam. My mother, inexplicably, was not opposed to this and we were about to give notice to our landlord when Sylvia called me at work and asked if I would be inclined to move to a small atoll in the Equatorial Pacific and whether I would be able to do so in about three weeks' time. She had been offered a position as country director for the Foundation for the Peoples of the South Pacific– Kiribati Office. Five seconds later I quit my job. Then I called Sylvia back.

"Kiri-what?"

CHAPTER 2

In which the Author reveals the fruit of his Research into the Strange Island Nation he has declared his new Home (which leaves much unknown), compensates for his Ignorance with his Lively Imagination (which is inadequate, very much so), and Packs (inappropriately).

The word *Kiribati*, pronounced *kir-ee-bas* on account of the missionaries being stingy with the letters they used to transcribe the local language, is derived from the word *Gilberts*, which is the name of one of the three island groups that comprise this improbable nation. Located just a notch above the equator and five thousand miles from anywhere, Tarawa is the capital of this country of thirty-three atolls scattered over an ocean area as large as the continental United States. The total landmass of these islands is about three hundred square miles, roughly the size of the greater Baltimore metropolitan area, though I believe it halves at high tide. Most of Kiribati's landmass is found on Kiritimati Island (Christmas Island), several thousand miles away from Tarawa. What remains is not much.

To picture Kiribati, imagine that the continental U.S. were to conveniently disappear leaving only Baltimore and a vast swath of very blue ocean in its place. Now chop up Baltimore into thirty-three pieces, place a neighborhood where Maine used to be, another where California once was, and so on until you have thirty-three pieces of Baltimore dispersed in such a way so as to ensure that 32/33 of Baltimorians will never attend an Orioles game again. Now take away electricity, running water, toilets, television, restaurants, buildings, and airplanes (except for two very old prop planes, tended by people who have no word for "maintenance"). Replace with thatch. Flatten all land into a uniform two feet above sea level. Toy with islands by melting polar ice caps. Add palm trees. Sprinkle with hepatitis A, B, and C. Stir in dengue fever and intestinal parasites. Take away doctors. Isolate and bake at a constant temperature of 100 degrees Fahrenheit. The result is the Republic of Kiribati.

Of course, I didn't know all this at the time. Despite insinuations otherwise ("Imagine a littered, stinking sandbar in the middle of nowhere," relayed a prior visitor to the island, "That's Tarawa"), I knew, just knew, that distant Tarawa would be the proverbial tropical paradise, where the natives were kind and noble, and the setting, undoubtedly lush and languid, would prove inspirational for ambitious endeavors of an artistic and edifying nature. I knew this because I had little else to go on, and when unaware I tend to be buoyantly optimistic. There is only so much research one can do on a place like Kiribati. It appears that for some reason no one goes there. Not even Paul Theroux bothered stopping by on his journey through the Pacific, which he wrote about in *The Happy Isles of Oceania*. When one considers how much territory Theroux, Bruce Chatwin, Jan Morris, and the other superstars of the travel-writing genre have covered, there really isn't much left for others to scribble about, except maybe Kiribati and Buffalo, New York. I've been to Buffalo, but I will graciously leave that commentary for someone else and instead present a few interesting tidbits about Kiribati. Henceforth, the facts, as gleaned from the Internet, the Central Intelligence Agency, and random sources:

Population (1996)—79, 386

Life Expectancy (male)—52.56 years

Life Expectancy (female)—55.78 years

Infant Mortality Rate—9.84%

Religions—Roman Catholic, Protestant, Seventh-Day
   Adventist, Baha'i, Church of God of North Carolina,
   Mormon

Number of Islands—33

Number of Inhabited Islands—21

Ratio of Sea to Land—4000:1

Natural Resources—Phosphate (production halted in 1979)

Independence—July 12, 1979 (from the United Kingdom)

Foreign Missions—Australia, New Zealand, the People's
   Republic of China

Arable Land—0%

Terrain—Low-lying coral atolls with extensive reefs

Currency—Australian dollar

Per Capita GDP—A $800 (US $450 approx.)

Underemployment Rate—70%

Exports—Copra, fish, shark fins

Radio—AM 1, FM 0, Shortwave 0

Television—None

Military—None

From this I discerned that if I wanted to live for longer than 52.56 years I'd best get my shots; that solid bowel movements might become worthy of some celebration; that there is something about the Church of God of North Carolina that gives me the creeps (ditto the Mormon church); that the end of phosphate production and the beginning of independence is perhaps not entirely coincidental; that China is probably up to no good in Kiribati; that with 70 percent of the country underemployed I would fit in just fine, professionally speaking; that shark fin exports suggest the presence of sharks; and that despite some snobbishness vis-à-vis my relationship to American pop culture, I might, just might, start yearning for *The Simpsons* and televised professional football games.

In those frantic three weeks, I learned little else about Kiribati and so I relied upon my imagination, which was no longer boyishly unformed, but conditioned by experience. I knew that Tarawa was a thin island and that it curved around an expansive lagoon and since I had never actually been on a thin island with a lagoon I visualized something very like Cape Cod, which technically is not an island, nor is a bay a lagoon, but that's neither here nor there. Naturally, I began to assume that we would live in a wood shingle house with white window frames just beyond sand dunes with tall grass and that the natives would be drawn toward plaid and complaints about summer people. I also knew that there were villages on Tarawa. Islands with villages conjure up the Mediterranean for me and so I imagined that there would be village squares with charming little cafés occupied by people looking fabulous in Armani and passionately arguing about coconut varieties, revealing that despite years of multicultural awareness training I still remained an ethnocentric dunderhead.

Regarding the South Pacific generally, I had seen pictures of Bora Bora and the like and knew that the South Pacific was deemed pretty and that the words *tropical paradise* were often tossed about in reference to islands in the South Pacific. I knew that the Brando kids had not thrived in Tahiti. I knew that while I was exceptionally literate in matters of geography, I had never heard of Niue, Tuvalu, or Vanuatu. I knew that periodically an island was nuked. I knew that Pacific Islanders were either Polynesian, Melanesian, or Micronesian and that I had a pretty good idea which was which. I knew that James Michener's *South Pacific* didn't tell me much about the South Pacific, but lots about the mores and predilections of

Americans in the 1940s and '50s. I knew that the islands were both good and bad for Paul Gauguin. I knew that Robert Louis Stevenson had spent some time in the region and that Amelia Earhart didn't quite make it out. (And neither did RLS, which I did not know then.) I knew the significance of Pitcairn Island and suspected that there were many bars in the South Pacific called The Bounty. I knew that the South Pacific was where anthropologists went to prove that Pacific Islanders were somehow *different*, in a fundamental violent way, only to be refuted later, though the cannibalism thing kind of lingers. I knew that the first westerner to touch upon many of the islands was Capt. James Cook. I knew that during World War II battles in the Pacific were inevitably described as "bloody," and if I had to choose, I would rather land on the beaches of Normandy in 1944 than on Tarawa in 1943. I did not know anything else.

We began packing. It was like a high stakes game of *If you were stuck on a deserted island* . . . Our only guidance was Kate, the woman Sylvia was being sent out to replace. Her advice was to bring nothing we valued. Everything will rot, she said. Nothing of value was easy enough. More difficult was my inability to imagine equatorial heat. "I don't think you're going to need those," Sylvia said, observing the wool sweaters I was packing.

"I'm sure it will be a little cool in the evenings," I replied. "Particularly in the winter."

"I see. I think, perhaps, you might be having a little conceptual trouble with the idea of living on the equator."

This was true. I'd spent my formative years in Canada. I was hard-wired for seasons. We discussed what Kate had said about the weather on Tarawa.

"Hotter than Washington in August?" I inquired.

"Hotter. *Searing* was her word."

"It's not the heat, you know. It's the humidity."

"Like a wet blanket," she said.

I decided that this was wrong, inaccurate, an exaggeration. It is well known that the stultifying weather conditions predominant in Washington, D.C., in August are the result of unique topographical and climatic conditions having to do with the jet stream and the gulf stream and the pollen situation and that it is unique to the Mid-Atlantic region and could not possibly be worse anywhere else on Earth.

I packed a sweater. "And I'm taking my jeans too," I said, defiantly.

The last few days were spent saying goodbye to friends and family. Do try to visit , we told everyone. Yes, we'll try, they said, but when they envisioned the trip we could sense the skepticism. Finally, there was only one thing left to do. I proposed to Sylvia. The proposition was accepted. And then we left, in the darkness of night, beginning the long, long journey—as such journeys should be—to Paradise.

CHAPTER 3

In which the Author and his aforementioned Beguiling Girlfriend depart the Continental World, alight briefly upon fabled Hawaii, escape from the Dreaded Johnston Atoll, and fall into Despair upon arriving in the Marshall Islands.

L ike many air travelers, I am aware that airplanes fly aided by capricious fairies and invisible strings. Typically, this causes me some concern. And so, typically, I am not shy about accepting those little bottles of wine kindly proffered by flight attendants, gratis, on international flights. However, I no longer drink when flying, having learned that being both jet-lagged and alcohol-bloated makes you feel like crap and basically establishes a poor beginning to any trip. Despite the lack of alcohol, I had been doing just fine since leaving Washington, occasionally repeating like a mantra that no one dies from a little turbulence, and if a bump combined with a mechanical groan warranted it, Sylvia would take my hand and calmly coo about the rigors of the FAA airplane certification process. Indeed, after three days of flying, I was beginning to feel abnormally at ease on an airplane. The sky was blue. The water also. I was bored senseless. Clearly, we had traveled far.

The thing about flying from a place like Washington, D.C., to an island like Tarawa is that, despite the interminable tedium of the journey, there really isn't sufficient time to make a smooth transition. And I am a transition person. I need those interludes of adjustment. I need coffee, a transition mechanism, to help me adjust from the comatose to, if nothing more, consciousness. I need Pennsylvania, a transition state, to adjust from the Mid-Atlantic to New England. But flying from the heart of the free world to the end of the world offers no satisfying transitional process. There is no spring or fall in long-distance air travel. It's straight winter to summer. One predawn moment we were inside a terminal seething with ambitious people, business travelers tramping up to New York and Boston for very important meetings, where we stood at a counter under the curious gaze of a counter person, who noted that our tickets read Washington–Newark–San Francisco–Honolulu–Johnston Atoll–Majuro–Tarawa and that they were one-way tickets, causing the counter person to exclaim "Gosh," and then after many long hours spent in a magic tube, punctuated by semilucid gate-to-gate wanderings, we found ourselves in Waikiki Beach, where we strolled among shops offering the latest from Givenchy, Chanel, and the Japanese porn industry, until we reached the actual strand—surfers bobbing, Diamond Head looming, a sun descending in crimson grandeur—and we began to laugh because life can be funny sometimes.

Soon, too soon, it was time to leave Nippon . . . er, Hawaii, and we returned to the airport, where we strolled past the gates where flights to Osaka and Los Angeles drew their passengers, and walked on to the gate where Air Micronesia awaited. Again we were flying, not to the continents straddling the Pacific Ocean, but to another, more distant island. The trip was beginning to feel like an act of willful disappearance. No one who claims this to be a small world has ever flown across the Pacific. Tick-tock, tick-tock, the hours, the days, passed with excruciating monotony. It was very blue. Celestial blue merged with aquatic blue, and it just went on and on and on, the blue did, and also the time, and then a descent began and it was still blue, and quickly now we were very near the Pacific Ocean. I felt as if I could touch the water. I saw ripples carving ocean swells. I sensed sharks lurking. There were ominous shadows, twenty-footers at least. And then fingers of coral whooshed by and we landed with a hard whomp, and then we stopped. We were on Johnston Atoll and here, very briefly, we shall pause.

Johnston Atoll is the vilest place on Earth. In the 1960s the United States used the island for atmospheric nuclear tests, which is a definite no-no in most neighborhoods. Not content to merely nuke the atoll, the U.S. then decided to poison it. This is where America stores and disposes of such wonders from the laboratory as the nerve gas Sarin and other clever agents for delivering disease and death. There are two bleak processing plants and they sit at either end of the runway, steadily burning canister after canister of poison. Between the plants are military barracks with satellite dishes protruding from their roofs, receiving signals from a world that seems very far away. There is nothing else on Johnston Atoll. Now and then, there are little accidents, leakages, small *oopsies*, and the hapless soldiers assigned here don their gas masks.

It is tempting to dash off a page or two and expound upon the philosophical implications of Johnston Atoll. The physical manifestations of humanity's capacity for great evil reside here, and for writers more ambitious than I this would be like catnip. However, sitting in an airplane watching one passenger, a civilian who had made a peculiar career choice, disembark, I was not struck by any profound ruminations. My thoughts were more along the lines of *Could someone please close the fucking door before we all turn into mutants?* Armed soldiers guarded the airplane and I just knew that they were sporting fish gills, and while I felt deeply sorry for them and their offspring, I just wished that someone would close the door and let us breathe airplane air again, which is only slightly less toxic, but still. And then someone did just that, and we were back in the air, scanning the water closely, searching for signs of Godzilla.

So maybe I'm wrong. Perhaps Johnston Atoll is the transitory island in the Pacific. The illusion-buster. The island that announces to travelers that they should cast aside their naivete, their glossy presumptions, and realize that the Pacific is a big place, a big empty place, and that some may find the emptiness useful. True, Johnston Atoll is just a rock, barren and about as distant from settlement as one can be, and so if one must nuke an island, and gas it too, Johnston Atoll does all right, never mind the fishies. Not so the Marshall Islands. Here, after ever more hours spent hurtling across the Pacific, we arrived, exhausted and crabby, accustomed to movement, and not at all prepared, after all that flying, to find ourselves in a spookily familiar place, as though we were inside a forgotten episode of *The Twilight Zone*, the one where *Dr. Strangelove* descends upon the set of *South Pacific*. We were on Majuro, the capital atoll of the Marshall Islands, a grim island group deemed useful by the United States. It is, frankly, not so good to be found useful by a superpower, particularly one interested in exploring the nuances of the hydrogen bomb.

It was in the Marshall Islands where scientists finally discovered what, in fact, constitutes a coral atoll. A coral atoll is the crest of a dying volcano. Like many explanations this one derives from Charles Darwin, building upon the work of previous naturalists. Coral only thrives until about 150 feet below the surface, but rather than assume that the coral is steadily rising atop an expanding underwater volcano, which was the belief at the time, Darwin theorized that coral replenishes itself by matching the rate of a sea volcano's dissolution. As the land far below the water surface steadily recedes into the depths, coral polyps grow from its slopes, seeking the sun, rising first to become a barrier reef, and then, as the volcano continues to disintegrate, slowly inching toward its base, an atoll is formed, the living crest balanced atop layers of dead coral and far below, the volcano itself.

Of course, it took some time to prove this theory, since one had to dig awfully deep to find the volcano below. Attempts were made, but it was not until 1952, more than a hundred years after Darwin first proposed his theory, when a drill bit was pushed 4,610 feet into Eneewetak Atoll in the Marshall Islands and struck volcanic rock, that Darwin's theory was proved correct. It was incidental, however, to the purpose of the drilling. Enwetak was being canvassed as a sight for testing the hydrogen bomb and the drilling indicated that the atoll was suitable for obliteration. Shortly after dawn on November 1, 1952, a bomb called Mike was detonated, and an island, a home, an ecosystem was blown up, irradiated, and poisoned, leading many to wonder what is the point of having Nevada.

This was hardly the only apocalyptic event in the Marshalls. I just happen to enjoy the weird symbiosis between discovering the nature of an atoll and blowing it up. Dozens of tests occurred in the 1940s and '50s and '60s and one would think that nuking the Marshall Islands over and over again would be enough punishment to inflict on the country for one epoch, but the U.S. Department of Defense thinks otherwise. Every year, the United States targets the Marshall Islands with its intercontinental ballistic missiles. These weapons are fired from California, using missiles randomly selected to ensure that if the green light for Armageddon is ever given, what follows will go smoothly. The ICBMs are aimed at Kwajalein Atoll, the catcher's mitt, where research is also conducted on several missile defense systems, including for some years the Strategic Defense Initiative, and more recently, a humbler defense system (THAAD—Theater High Altitude Defense) that requires missiles to be fired from two other atolls in the Marshalls. Access to two-thirds of Kwajalein is restricted to American soldiers and those who supply them with their weaponry, which in addition to the four islands already poisoned by radiation—Bikini, Eneewetak, Rongelap, and Utrik—results in five islands lost to the U.S. defense industry. With the Bush

(II) administration's decision to discard the ABM Treaty, even more testing will be conducted in the Marshall Islands. For a country with a total area of less than 120 square miles, the loss of five islands is not insignificant. And so payments must be made.

The Marshall Islands had received $800 million of American "aid" over the previous ten years, which amounted to $14,300 for every man, woman, and child in the country. The vast majority of this money was sent directly to the government of the Marshall Islands, which, of course, is the best possible way to instill corruption, inefficiency, and a dependency mentality in Third World governments everywhere. Not only did all this aid fail to significantly improve the health and welfare of the Marshallese, it introduced new afflictions. Hypertension, diabetes, and high blood pressure are now serious problems as a result of the local diet being supplanted by food imported from the United States. Alcoholism and suicide, particularly among the young, have taken root in a society no longer held together by traditional bonds. And Majuro, an atoll not more than two hundred yards wide, is besieged by traffic jams, mountains of garbage, aimless youth fashionable in their East L.A. ghetto wear, and a population as a whole that has already moved beyond despair and settled into a glazed ennui. It is a miserable place where coconut palm trees have disappeared, replaced by concrete and tin.

And there are cockroaches. Enormous cockroaches. I began to wonder. What precisely had caused the cockroaches on Majuro to become so enormous? They trolled like sinister remnants of the Pleistocene era, when everything was bigger, meaner, and just generally more voracious (or was that the Cambrian era?), and because I was fairly well informed about the activities of a certain superpower on these islands I immediately began to think about radioactive fallout and where, exactly, did it all go? Which way was the wind blowing in the 1940s, and the 1950s, and the 1960s, because there are some scary cockroaches on Majuro. In the back of a taxi, they scurried across our feet. They emerged from every nook and cranny in our hotel room. In a restaurant, they rushed across the table and asked, really, if we were going to eat that.

This did not please Sylvia. She's good with spiders, indifferent to snakes, and unmoved by mice. But cockroaches? They are, in her word, *eeuuwh*.

Surely, we thought, there must be something else to see on Majuro besides the impressive roach population. We were staying at the Robert Riemer Hotel, a modest haven for consultants, and I mentioned to the stout woman more or less attending to us that we fancied a walk, and since this was our only day on Majuro could she recommend a destination. Someplace interesting, worth seeing, touristy is fine.

"You want to walk?" she said. She seemed aghast. She heaved in her flower-print dress. "There is nothing to see." A cockroach scurried across the counter.

Eeuuwh.

We walked out and turned left, which we discovered was one of only two directional options on an atoll, but after some time wandering we were forced to concede that she was, indeed, correct. There is nothing you would want to see on Majuro. There is a filthy fringe of beach that recedes into soppy mud before disappearing into a lifeless lagoon. On the ocean side of the atoll there is a gray and barren reef shelf stained with what from a distance look like large, whitish-brownish polyps that on closer inspection turn out to be used diapers, resting there under the high sun while awaiting an outgoing tide. On dry land, there are decrepit two-story apartment blocks and garish prefab houses. The road was one long traffic jam and alongside it were the fattest people I had ever seen, wan and listless, munching through family-sized packets of Cheetos. As we passed, nodding our greetings, they offered in return quiet contempt, and it was not long before I became sympathetic to the spleenish air of the Marshallese. This ghetto/island has none of the romantic sense of dissolution found elsewhere in tropical urban areas succumbing to age and wear. Majuro wasn't built to slowly, grandly crumble. It was built with the ambition of a strip mall, a place for America to traffic trifles to a people who in a generation exchanged three thousand years of history and culture for spangled rubbish and lite beer. New pickup trucks passed by. Every government minister had a chauffeur-driven Lexus. A store offered the latest in washing machines. A video shop displayed the most recent features from Steven Seagal and Jean Claude Van Damme. Teenagers loitered in $100 sneakers and trendy baggy shorts. There was money on Majuro, but the overwhelming sense was one of immense poverty.

We were not happy. Pretty close to despair, actually. Tarawa was supposed to be similar, but poorer. It occurred to us that this might not be such a good idea after all, that moving to an atoll at the end of the world is really nothing more than an act of romantic delusion, and it was tempting to succumb to negativity, but we resisted, and instead yielded to a simmering anger, anger at the United States for obliterating a nation, just for practice, and anger at the Marshallese for behaving like debased junkies, willing to do anything for another infusion of the almighty dollar. This included removing the population of one island so that a Korean resort and casino could operate unhindered by the sight of poor, dark-skinned people who presumably dampen the tourist's gambling instinct, and allowing an American firm the use of an uninhabited island to store the radioactive waste generated by reactors in Japan and South Korea. For a country already so traumatized and polluted by radiation, encouraging the importation of more radioactive waste can only be called pathological.

But for us things did get more negative. In our room, which was not a bad room, I spent much of the night like a taunted monkey in a cage, lurching from wall to wall flinging my sandals at the insidious creatures, and when my tally reached five dead cockroaches (five!), I thought it safe to attempt sleep. And then I felt it. It was scrambling up my back, a sharp pitter-patter with razor fur burning my skin. I knew that very soon I would have a cockroach in my ear. Instinct took over. I emitted a primal scream and bounced out of the bed. Sylvia did likewise. She does not like to be woken up suddenly. I calmly explained the situation and she was thoughtful enough to summon with some urgency several higher-power characters in Christian theology. We found the cockroach lurking behind the headboard and so I shoved the bed hard against the wall and there it remained, and it is probably still there today, emitting a soft green glow.

CHAPTER 4

In which the Author finally sets foot on Distant Tarawa, where he is led by the Evil Kate, who seeks to Convince him that Tarawa is not what it seems; and, Conceding that it is indeed Very Hot on the Equator, he Bravely overcomes his fear of Sharks and encounters something Much, Much Worse.

We were to have awoken at 5:30 A.M., courtesy of the wake-up call thoughtfully provided by the staff of the Robert Riemer Hotel, but their subservience to the American Way was not yet so complete as to follow through on the promise of a wake-up call, and so we arose at 6:10 A.M., ten minutes after the minibus that was to take us to the airport was scheduled to depart. This left us a trifle ill-tempered. We scrambled out of the hotel, bent double like hungry coolies underneath the weight of all our possessions, and boarded the lingering minibus, which contained a gaunt blond Australian man. "About bloody well time," he said in a voice that suggested his larynx was not what it should be. I acknowledged Sylvia's look and resolved to quit smoking sometime very soon and then we both gave him piercing dagger eyes. He was wearing shiny white shoes.

We were expected to arrive at the airport two hours before our flight, which seemed inexplicable to me. It isn't as if Majuro International Airport receives a lot of air traffic requiring complex organizational procedures to ensure that passengers and baggage arrive and depart as intended. It has one runway built upon a reef. It has one single-story dilapidated building that contains customs and immigration and a hole in the wall for baggage to be tossed through. The waiting area is the curb outside. Here, during the one hour and fifty-seven minutes that remained after we checked in for our flight on Air Marshall, we met a friendly Marshallese woman who commented on the amount of luggage we were lugging. We explained that we were moving to Tarawa.

"Tarawa is like Majuro was thirty years ago. There's nothing there," she said, betraying in her voice a distinct air of superiority, as if any island not yet awash in the detritus of Americana must be very primitive indeed. Finally on this journey we felt something like elation, a sense of hope that on Tarawa we would find, if not an Edenic paradise, at least an island not yet so distant from the Fall—an optimism that was dampened only a little bit by the plane we would fly, a plane that didn't allow you to stand up straight, a plane where the pilot rearranged the passengers because of weight and balance issues. That kind of plane. But it would take us elsewhere, away from the American Pacific, the blasted, forgotten periphery of empire, and that was all that mattered.

The day was very blue, not sharp Autumn blue, but faraway tropical blue, languorous, timeless. The northern Gilbert Islands, our first glimpse of Kiribati, passed below and the islands seemed not like islands, but suggestions of islands, emerald crescents rising from the depths, as if there was something provisional about existence. And then Tarawa appeared. We flew over the northern part of the island, a ribbon of land topped with palm trees and bisected by channels feeding the ocean into the lagoon. The tide was in and the lagoon seemed incandescent, a startling fusion of greens and blues. On the ocean side of the atoll, white streamers of broken waves rushed toward barren beaches. Villages of thatch appeared and faded away. We were very low now. Beside us there was no more sky, but a wall of coconut trees. Any moment we expected contact, the hard bounce of the wheels on the runway. And then . . . something was wrong. My inner ear was confused. My stomach lurched. The engines screamed. Sylvia's hand gripped my arm, seeking comfort, finding none. We raced over the tarmac like a careening hovercraft, not quite making contact with the ground. Still flying. And then we began to ascend. Tarawa gone. The blue ocean. The blue sky. Again. The pilot spoke: "Ah . . . sorry about that. There were pigs on the runway. We'll just swing around and try again."

The pilot's voice revealed nothing. No tremor. No gulping for air. No crackling of the chords to indicate that we had very nearly met a most pathetic end, the unknown void, courtesy of errant swine. We made a second approach, landed, and in the rush fleetingly saw children on the side of the runway, as if they had been playing in a suburban cul-de-sac and had given way for a passing car. I absorbed this. We had departed a country where children are swaddled in helmets and body armor, and only then allowed to ride a Big Wheel in a carpeted living room, and now we had arrived in a country where children play on active runways.

We emerged from the plane and were immediately stricken by the heat. It was astonishing, a wonder of nature, a blazing force that left us awestruck. As we walked—slithered actually, slowly melting, panting—across the tarmac, hundreds of people, dressed in the brightest of hues, observed us from behind the steel fence separating the two barnlike structures comprising the departure and arrival areas of Bonriki International Airport. The fence, clearly, was there for decorative purposes only. The runway had been reclaimed by children playing soccer. A shirtless man pedaled serenely across on his bicycle and was swallowed by a tangle of coconut palm trees. A dog was in urgent pursuit of five squealing piglets. Go, dog.

There were two other planes on the tarmac. This would be the

Air Kiribati fleet. One looked like a sickly dragonfly with a thin fuse-lage—was that tin?—and spindly wings. Each passenger had their own door. The windows were made of plastic sheeting with snap-on buttons. It was less an airplane and more a treacherous carnival ride. Could the pilots be carnies? The other airplane must have been the runt of aviation. It had a complex geometrical shape, as if it were a seven-sided box, and wings that did not seem to align. Shirtless men, the mechanics presumably, sat in the shade underneath the crooked wings, pondering the Air Marshall plane, a Saab 2000 turboprop, which suddenly seemed enormous, and it was not an enormous plane. One pointed at the Air Marshall plane, and I could see him thinking, *You see. I knew the wings had to align.* I could think of only one circumstance that would compel me to fly Air Kiribati. I won-dered if there was any crack on the island.

With trepidation, we approached the immigration desk. We didn't have visas. The Republic of Kiribati doesn't exactly maintain an impressive diplomatic presence abroad. It owns no imposing embassies. It does not have a fleet of black sedans immune from parking laws. It does not send forth trained cadres of expert conver-sationalists skilled in the usage of acronyms. Kiribati was not, in fact, even a member of the United Nations. There was no place to go to obtain visas. But there were procedures, and we followed them closely. We had letters from the District of Columbia Police Depart-ment stating that after an extensive search it was determined that we did not have criminal records. And we had letters from doctors asserting that after comprehensive examinations it was found that we did not have any communicable diseases. Being very broadly informed of the health situation in Kiribati, I speculated that the country was seeking healthy host bodies through which to transmit a little bit of Kiribati to the rest of the world.

We handed over our letters and passports to the immigration official and explained that we wanted to live in his country and so far we had found it very lovely indeed. The immigration official had tattoos on his forehead. He looked at the papers and asked if we had onward tickets. No, we said. "Okay, no problem," he said. I was pleasantly stunned. There is *always* a problem. He took out a cigarette. I lit it for him. I have learned to be deferential in these situations. I contemplated a kind remark about his tattoos, green stains that folded and bounced on his crumpling brow, but before I could inquire about his gang allegiance, a tall, rail-thin American woman appeared beside us. Here was our Kurtz.

"You must be Sylvia," she said, coolly appraising her successor. "And you must be her husband."

Oh, that's right. I had forgotten. We were going forward with the marriage ruse for certain bureaucratic reasons mainly having to do with health insurance and also because we weren't sure how a simple living-together arrangement would be received in Kiribati. But this was the first time I had been referred to as a husband and I suddenly felt a little older, more mature, content, though desirous of children. I patted Sylvia affectionately.

The angular woman was Kate, the person Sylvia was sent out to replace. She was about fifty years old, and from the picture we had seen of her in Washington, she typically appeared years younger. One year on Tarawa, however, had aged her considerably, quite likely because she was suffering from malnutrition. She had the hard features of a bird of prey. Kate admitted this. One year on Tarawa, she calculated, was like five years elsewhere. She was leaving Tarawa mid-contract because, as she cryptically put it to Sylvia, "I just can't take it anymore."

Kate turned to the immigration official. "I have letters here from the Ministry of Foreign Affairs and the Ministry of Health indicating that Sylvia will be the new country director of FSP and that her visa and residency permit should be processed immediately. These letters were forwarded to the Department of Immigration but I gather you did not receive them." She stared at him hard.

"Okay, no problem," said the official.

"And um . . . I'm Sylvia's husband," I added helpfully.

The immigration official stamped our passports. I was pleased to see that it was a modest little stamp, unlike most developing countries, which seemed to have decided that if they couldn't be Great Powers, they could at least have Great Stamps, ornate displays of grandeur occupying a full passport page, sometimes two. The more irrelevant, troubled, dictatorial the country, the larger the stamp, and so the small ink stain made by the immigration official seemed to bode well, as if Kiribati was declaring *We are small. We are content. We have no illusions.*

But we had a few illusions and no one, certainly not Kate, a walking spout of bilious bile, was going to deprive us of what we wanted to see. We had traveled far, uprooted our lives, moved to the end of the world, and there was no way we were going to concede that we had made a mistake. The proverbial glass would be half-full today. We gathered our bags and emerged into Tarawa proper, where we were immediately enveloped by neon munchkins. Dozens of little ones gaped and giggled and twittered as we walked through, and all of them pointed and repeated the same word over and over again. *I-Matang.* Meaning what? I asked Kate.

"One who comes from the land of the gods," she hissed, Brando-like.

Cool.

Around us, entire extended families were gathered on mats weaved from pandanus leaves. It seemed as if they resided here in a swirling display of color. The women were attired in a bewildering kaleidoscope of primary colors displayed on wraparound lavalavas, crude sarongs featuring orgasmic flowers and melting sunsets, matched with extreme discordance with sleeveless tops that made each woman seem particularly buxom. The men seemed impossibly fit and weathered, bulging muscles and deep lines, tattoos and festering sores. These were outer islanders awaiting a rumored flight to their home island. A woman of prodigious girth did a brisk trade selling coconuts. She, I gathered, was the airport café.

We put our bags in the back of a pickup truck and drove off with Kate, our eyes on the shimmering lagoon and the palm-topped islets that stretched and stretched until absorbed by an ambiguous horizon where lagoon and ocean and sky touched and were seamlessly fused into a blue-green oneness and the whole scene was one of such calm and tranquil prettiness that I couldn't help but sputter about the beauty of the lagoon and that this sight right here was what the romance of the South Seas was all about.

It's polluted, said Kate.

The homes we passed were traditional structures of wood and thatch, small stages raised on platforms with walls of flapping mats. These homes seemed well engineered, sensible, and cool.

If you don't mind rats, dogs, and prowlers.

There was a vitality in the villages we rumbled through, not the brooding stillness we found on Majuro, but a sweet familiarity, a sense of playfulness that we sensed in the smiles and laughter of people trading and gossiping.

The I-Kiribati are like children, and you must treat them as such.

The island was awash with fish. Alongside the road, women were selling their families' catch out of large coolers.

Most fish are toxic.

Boys clambered more than fifty feet up coconut trees rich in nuts, where they sang and worked to extract toddy, the nutritious sap.

They should be in school.

Small children played with ingenious toys made of sticks and string.

Most children have chronic diarrhea and there are indications that cholera has returned.

Tarawa was the loveliest place I had ever seen. The water, the beaches, the palm trees, the colors, the sky, and the hovering silver-blue clouds bisected by the horizon.

Tarawa isn't a disaster waiting to happen. It is a disaster.

We drove on. I was hoping we could be deposited at our new abode, wherever it might be, and have a cup of coffee and absorb atmosphere for an hour or two. But there wasn't any time, we were assured. We would have a full schedule today.

Besides, there is no coffee to be found on this island.

A tic seized my eye.

Our first mission would be to obtain driver's licenses at the Bikenibeu Police Station, a humble two-room cinder-block building with a tin roof. A barefoot policeman snoozed on a bench outside. In front of the station was a doddering pickup truck with a cage in the hold. The paddy wagon, presumably.

"You do have a driver's license, don't you?" Kate asked me.

"Oh yes . . . though it's a little expired."

A withering look. We weren't getting along very well. I found her to be a contrarian.

The policeman, however, didn't seem much bothered by the fact that I was not legally entitled to drive anywhere on Earth. He opened up a dusty logbook that looked to predate the twentieth century. He entered our names with a careful scrawl and then went to a type-writer that would probably fetch a good price at an auction for col-lectible antiques. Slowly he hammered out our licenses on pink paper. Our licenses read Mrs. Sylvia and Mr. Maarten, respectively.

The police are incompetent.

Easygoing.

Onward to the power station, which was a diesel generator in a small tin warehouse capable of meeting the electricity needs of, optimistically, three average Americans, provided that they didn't use a refrigerator and a hair dryer concurrently. We waited patiently for the clerk, who was lying prone atop the counter, to arise from his slumber. He lay there like an offering until a chorus of throat clearing elicited unembarrassed consciousness.

Kate rolled her eyes. *You see what it's like here.*

Relaxed.

Kate wanted to change the electricity bill for the house that FSP had rented into our name. This proved impossible. The bill was filed under *M* for Mary. Only Mary could change the name on the bill. Kate explained that Mary, who was a former director of FSP, had left the country four years ago.

"Well, she can change the bill when she comes back," said the clerk, very patiently, I thought.

And so it went. We continued madly driving up and down the atoll, swerving perilously around children, pigs, and dogs on an epic quest of errand fulfillment. I understood Kate. She was Washington, D.C., personified: a humorless bureaucrat, a taskmaster, a results-oriented person with long experience at the U.S. Agency for International Development, whose functionaries are best known for roving from one embassy cocktail party to another in deluxe SUVs, liberally sprinkling million-dollar checks on pliable dictators. Kate was accustomed to long, fruitful days spent writing memos and executive summaries, followed by a G and T or two on the verandah at the Club. On Tarawa, however, she had found an unrefined, crude little hellhole, an island that wanted little and strove for nothing, and this drove her well beyond exasperation and just shy of madness. I was not blind. I could see that Tarawa was a raw place. There was, for instance, no coffee on the island. Kurtz, let it be said, adapted. While it is true that he didn't adapt very well, at least he tried. Kate, it seemed to me, refused to adjust, and I took note of this. I resolved to start drinking tea.

Eventually, we pulled into a dirt road with cavernous potholes that led toward the ocean. We stopped in front of a "permanent house," as such houses are called to distinguish them from "local" houses, which have a life span of about five years, unless it gets windy. This would be our house. Painted lime green, it looked like one of those single-story structures one might see in rural Oklahoma with car parts in the front yard, the sort of house that would be considered a step up, just, from a trailer. On Tarawa, though, this was one of the better homes on the island, a B-class house according to the government, which owned the majority of permanent houses on the island and classified them on a scale of A to F. It had a tin roof that allowed rain water to pour into gutters and then down into two large cement water tanks that stood like mute, massive sentries in front of the house. A water pump, bolted into a cement block, brought the water through the pipes. Instead of glass windows there were plastic horizontal louvers, plus security wire. Someone had once taken the trouble to plant flowers and maintain a garden, but this had long gone untended, and so there was a pleasant lushness to the front yard as the bush crept in and leaves were left unswept. There were tall coconut palm trees, stately casuarina trees, and slender papaya trees and also ferns and a squat tree-bush that looked to produce dimpled potatoes. Inside the house, the floor was gray linoleum and there was simple cane furniture, but what was most striking was the view out back. Our backyard was the Pacific Ocean, which is regarded by many as a very large ocean and believed by many more to be misnamed, and I found its presence in our backyard intimidating. We were just a foot or so above sea level, and it wasn't even high tide. From the house, the reef extended about a hundred yards, where it met the deep water, the swells that had traveled thousands of miles so that they could rise up into steep vertical masses and blast into our fragile little atoll. These were breakers, as apt and succinct a description as can be. A steady roar came into the house, as did a fine salt mist from the fracturing waves. In each room, the walls were ringed with spittles of rust sent hurtling by corroding ceiling fans.

Kate had left several bottles of boiled water and a few cans of lemonade for us and as I satisfied my thirst I regretted every bad thought I'd had of her. She told us that we should boil our drinking water for twenty minutes on account of the rats in the gutter and god-knows-what parasites in the water tanks. There was a shower, but it had only cold water, and while normally I would find the lack of hot water immensely distressing, climatic circumstances were such that I was not troubled in the least. More worrisome was Kate's claim that it hadn't rained at all during the year she had lived on Tarawa and that, therefore, there was not likely to be much water in the tanks and that we should consider carefully every drop we might use.

She also suggested we continue to employ her "housegirl." I had a vision of a lithe, undulating young woman, possibly wearing a grass skirt, swaying about the house casting come-hither glances my way, and I became amenable to the idea for a few fleeting seconds until the absurdity of the prospect set in. We were in our mid-twenties, barely solvent, here to do good deeds, or at least one of us was here to do good deeds, and having a housegirl would only stoke our inner guilt. I smoothly expressed our reservations.

"Bah," I said. "We don't need servants."

Kate went straight for the jugular. "All right then. I hope you don't have a problem spending your days washing Sylvia's clothes, by hand, and mopping the dust and sea spray that coats this house each day. Sylvia certainly won't have any time."

Sylvia looked as if she was not entirely displeased by this possibility. "Make sure you separate the colors from the whites," she grinned.

Kate, thankfully, went on. "And I'm sure you won't mind if yet another girl is pulled out of school because her mother can no longer afford the school fees."

Who was I to deny a child's education? "So will she be coming once or twice a week?" I asked, silently noting that as the mother of schoolchildren, the housegirl was unlikely to be young and lithe, and she probably wouldn't undulate either.

Sylvia and Kate departed for the FSP office and I was left alone to ponder the immensity of the ocean and the giant sharks that were undoubtedly lingering behind the house waiting for some stupid foreigner to go for a swim. Probably tiger sharks. And black and white–tipped reef sharks, of course. Maybe hammerheads and blue sharks and bull sharks too, though it's really the tiger sharks one needs to worry about. I wondered if sharks would swim over the reef. I scanned the water closely. I began to imagine things. Terrible things.

But that water looked outrageously appealing. It was, to reiterate, to stress, to accentuate the point, to leave no doubt, hot. Staggeringly hot. The heat blasted from a contemptible sun; it came unbidden from the white coral sand; it floated in on humid waves. A faint breeze brought nothing but the stench of decomposition and the slight, acrid smell of burning leaves somewhere not too distant. As I stepped outside, little moved save for the flies that gathered around my legs, my sopping shirt, my face, seeking to feed off the salt I was steadily expelling. I yearned for Canada. I imagined tundra. I thought of boyhood winter days when I would return from excavations in the snow, hands so frozen that only with deft elbow movements could I turn the faucet and reclaim feeling in my fingers with cold streaming water. But it was pointless. The powers of the mind could not overcome the reality of the equatorial sun. A choice, therefore, had to be made. I could either melt into an oozing puddle, drop by drop—a slow, torturous death, for certain—or I could ease my suffering with a swim in the world's largest backyard pool, thereby risking life and limb to the schools of sharks that were, and I sensed this strongly, circling at reef's edge, awaiting a meal featuring the other-other white meat.

I chose to go for a swim. Death, if it came, would be swift, with the added benefit of it being preceded by relief from the heat. I stripped to my shorts and approached the water. Sweet Moses, it was hot under the sun. I could feel my back swiftly turning into one enormous crackling blister. I put my T-shirt back on and decided that from here on, I would simply cultivate the world's greatest farmer's tan.

The reef near the shore had three water-carved steps, and at the base of each crabs scurried in the froth of small collapsing waves. The water was sun-warmed, uncomfortably hot in the shallows, but pleasant, if not refreshing, farther out. Waves, some cresting, some not, the remnants of breakers, rolled in as the tide began to draw water back toward the reef's edge. I swam farther out, half propelled by the tide's pull. I felt like I was inside a rainbow. Ahead, the ocean was tinted the blue of great depth, reflected as a metallic sheen by singular cotton-ball clouds. Around me, the blue was sun-dappled like a sharp, morning sky. Near shore, it turned turquoise and a limpid, pale green. A mass of coconut palm trees followed the serpentine curves of the atoll. Green-bottomed clouds drifted over the lagoon. I realized that this was the genuine blue, the pure green, the essential yellow, and until this moment I had never seen anything but dull approximations of color.

At the reef's edge, the water boiled into swirling liquid chaos. The breakers seemed colossal, looming well above me, and in their precipitous faces they reflected protruding ridges of coral and the translucent shadows of fish. There was an agitated roar, and as each swell rose and gathered height, becoming an incontestable force, there followed a crash like thunder and torrents of broken water.

Where I was, twenty yards from the break zone, I could feel the tide and the suction created by breaking waves compelling me ever closer to the edge and the mile-deep abyss. The water was chest-deep and shallowing and I leaned back and began pushing with my feet as if I were walking backward into a heavy gale.

Between the crests of approaching waves I watched an old man resting in his canoe. It was a small canoe, about nine feet long, and it had a single outrigger. As he rose with the swell he seemed to be a part of the sky. When he found a set of waves to his liking, he paddled hard, caught the crest of a six-foot wave and surfed it in for a long moment. Just as the wave began to hollow and sputter, he eased back into the trough, and then he paddled with furious dexterity through the breakwater. The canoe leapt forward. Behind him, another wave rolled in like a shadow, a heaving mound of water. It rose into a steep wall of water, crested, and broke. White water rushed forward, and this sun-baked man, shirtless with sinuous muscles, wearing a ridiculous hat that looked not unlike a fibrous, conical wizard's cap, shot ahead, riding the white water as it again gathered form and became a rolling wave propelling his canoe to shore.

I followed him in, trudging through the torrent, bodysurfing when I could. As I neared the beach, where white sand and hard, gray coral intermingled, I could see him unloading his day's catch of fish. He passed the fish to the children that gathered in the shallows. And then he lifted his canoe, balanced it on his shoulder, and disappeared through a narrow trail that cleaved the bush tangle alongside our house.

Now this was the South Pacific of my dreams. Stunning natural beauty. Challenges to test my mettle as a manly man. Sharks! Extreme heat! The pounding surf! Noble natives going about their daily lives with a quiet heroism. I would thrive here, I felt.

And then I saw what confronted me. It rested directly between myself and shore. It was massive. I had never seen anything like it. I sensed its power. I became very, very frightened.

It was an enormous brown bottom.

The possessor, a giant of a man, was squatting in the shallows, holding on to a ledge of coral rock. He emitted. He emitted some more. He was like a stricken oil tanker, oozing brown sludge. When he was done, he wiped himself with sticks. Not leaves. Sticks. Small branches. Twigs.

And they were coming my way. Riding the ebbing tide, the sticks homed in on me. I became the North Star for shit-encrusted sticks. Whichever way I moved, and I was moving very quickly, these sticks seemed to follow. They were closing in. I began to curse. In Dutch. This only happens when something primal is stirred.

"*Podverdomme!*"

I ran parallel to the shore. Swimming would have been quicker, but I dared not dive in. Not here. Not with an outgoing tide. When I thought I had moved a sufficient distance from the shit floating my way, I waded back toward the beach. Two small boys squatted directly between me and land. I calculated angles, the exact direction and speed of the tide, the location of the moon, whether it was waxing or waning. I plotted a course and walked in, diagonal to the shore, between the two streams, making no eye contact with those going potty.

There was a lesson here, I felt. I had no idea what that lesson might be, but clearly, adjustments would have to be made. Expectations would have to be altered. Perceptions changed. We were not in Washington anymore. There is bullshit in Washington, but no shit. Not so on Tarawa. It could be that Kate was right in her critique. Perhaps Tarawa was a disaster. But it felt like Paradise too. It was one or the other, sublime or wretched, never neither. Survival on Tarawa, I decided, would depend on one's reaction to the absurd, and so I resolved to ignore the shit. Just pretend it's not there, and focus on the poetic, the humorous, on the Technicolor sunsets and the like. Because the shit on Tarawa could drive you mad. Really.

CHAPTER 5

In which the Author suspends the Space-Time Continuum and just moves on, vaguely Theme-Like, beginning with an Unauthoritative Account of the Island's Beginnings.

A long time ago, Tarawa was brought forth by Nareau the Creator. Nareau the Creator was a spider and he looked upon his work and saw that it was good. Perhaps because he was a spider. Nareau the Creator then flung grains of Tarawa to the wind and from these grains other islands were born and together these islands were called Tungaru. He created demigods and people and they procreated but the demigod gene seems to have died out, and so very soon there were just people. He created distant lands and sent Nareau the Wise to tend to the land of white-skinned spirits, the *I-Matang* world, and Nareau the Cunning to oversee the land of black-skinned spirits. Their intermingling was not advised.

I sometimes wished that Nareau had been a little more expansive in his ambitions. As the primordial source of life, Tarawa is a bit modest. Which grain was it that led to the Eurasian landmass? Why couldn't we have kept that one, I wondered. How about the Bora Bora grain? Couldn't Nareau at least have left a grain or two that could have morphed into hills, mountains even, something to break the monotony of a low island? As I cycled up and down the atoll on a thirdhand mountain bike that would never see a mountain, or a hill, or even a rise requiring a gear change, I realized that Nareau, unlike the great majority of deities, was a humble god, prone to thrift and frugality, and while I believe this should be encouraged among deities everywhere, I did periodically yearn for a god who kept a grander residence. Not that Tarawa is without its moments of grandeur—it is, after all, a tropical island—it's just that it's very, very small.

The total landmass of Tarawa is twelve square miles, roughly the size of some driveways in Illinois. This figure is illusory, however, for it creates the impression of a block of land, and this Tarawa is decidedly not. Its twelve square miles of coral are divided into elongated slivers, narrow islets crowned with the tufts of palm trees, prevented from becoming a unified whole by a myriad of channels linking the ocean with the lagoon, and stretched out over a reef extending nearly forty miles. The reef itself is shaped like a tottering inverted L, with the western side open to the ocean. We lived near the nook of the atoll, in the village of Bikenibeu, and this I liked because lagoonside it was possible to see land across the way, and this comforted me because I spent my formative years on continents and grew accustomed to its presence. Elsewhere on Tarawa, however, one could see only the ocean, the lagoon, and the land below one's feet, which never seemed like enough, and I gave thanks every day that neither tsunamis nor cyclones were prevalent here, though I cast a wary eye on distant swells and ominous clouds because you never know, do you?

Soon I began to wonder about the original inhabitants of Tarawa. Settling down on a coral atoll is not quite like settling down in California, which had the advantage of fertile soil, a temperate climate, and freeways for convenient exploration. Tarawa is a difficult place. The soil, a porous limestone sediment, is lamentable, unsuitable for anything but the hardiest plants. The coconut palm trees that today dominate the island were all planted, and it is likely that the first settlers could only rely upon the humble pandanus tree, which is certainly a useful tree to have around, but its dull, starchy fruit doesn't quite tickle the palate. Mangoes they are not. The only mammal endemic to Kiribati is the Polynesian rat. A horse was once brought to Butaritari, in the northern Gilbert Islands, but it soon died of starvation. Droughts can last for years. The freshwater lens, which is typically just five to ten feet deep, is often brackish. And did I mention that it's hot?

There is little research on the first settlers to reach Kiribati. The islands form the nexus of Oceania, but unlike most nexus-type places, to be in the middle of anything in the Pacific is to be in the middle of nowhere. Kiribati lies roughly halfway between Australia and Canada, and Russia and Chile. Looking southward from Tarawa, as we did from our house, there was nothing between us and Antarctica, except, of course, half a planet's worth of ocean. Far to the southwest lie the black islands of Melanesia—the Solomons, Vanuatu, Fiji, New Caledonia, New Guinea. The heartland of Micronesia, such as it is, is found to the north and northwest—the Marshalls, the Carolines, Nauru, Palau, Guam. Its nearest neighbor is Tuvalu, a Polynesian country. Farther to the southeast are the Polynesian islands of Tonga, Samoa, and Tahiti.

The few *I-Matang* scholars who have delved into the ethnography of Kiribati tend to believe that the very first people to arrive here some four thousand years ago were Melanesians, probably from the Solomon Islands or the northern islands of Vanuatu. Why they believe this remains unclear to me. There is certainly no archeological evidence suggesting that four thousand years ago Kiribati was occupied by Melanesians. Nor is there any compelling linguistic proof. In appearance, the I-Kiribati differ markedly from Melanesians. Unsurprisingly, given the vastly different environmental realities of atolls and the lush, hilly, and (relatively) large islands that comprise most of Melanesia, there are also no lingering manifestations of Melanesian culture in contemporary Kiribati. When four fishermen from Papua New Guinea washed up on Tarawa, having drifted for several months in an open boat, they were not regarded as kin. After church groups nursed the unfortunate fishermen back to health, the I-Kiribati would stop and point at *te black man* whenever they ventured out. As one who elicited gapes and stares myself, I felt I had more in common with the few Melanesians who periodically appeared on Tarawa.

It is likely that we will never know for certain where the original I-Kiribati came from, which has led to some speculation among New Agers that they came from outer space. I find this improbable. One need only consider Air Kiribati. Those who have spent months marooned on an outer island waiting for the *wanikiba* (flying canoe) to be fixed will find it inconceivable that the same people responsible for Air Kiribati were once masters of intergalactic travel. But a dearth of evidence requires conjecture. Outside of a few Polynesian islands, where stone structures from distant eras still stand, and the enigmatic Lapita pottery, which has been found in both Melanesia and Polynesia, there is little archeological evidence to be found on the islands of the Pacific, particularly on the atolls, where nearly everything is built from wood and thatch, which rarely survives ten years in a hot, humid climate, much less four thousand years. Add to this the absence of writing until the arrival of missionaries in the late nineteenth century and the story of Kiribati can only be found in tales passed orally from generation to generation. This is too bad, of course. Myths and legends are mutable, varying in tone, meaning, even in substance, to reflect the bias of the storyteller or to accommodate changing times. I have always preferred the shard of pottery, the bronze coin, the blackened hearth, the ancient bill of receipt, and evocative statues of fertility goddesses for what they say of the past. For the I-Kiribati, however, their entire history resides in the stories told by a few old men. Fortunately, someone recorded those stories.

In 1914, the British Colonial Office sent a remarkable young cadet to its outpost in Kiribati. One would think that at the dawn of the Great War there would be numerous applicants for a position in the empire's most remote colony, but in fact there was only one. His name was Arthur Grimble, and in a boon for students of Kiribati history—both of them—the Colonial Office in London ignored his subsequent entreaties to be sent to the Somme, and he remained in the islands, rising eventually to the position of resident commissioner, which is colonial-speak for God. Grimble became very fond of the I-Kiribati and today there are hundreds of islanders who can trace their lineage to him. When not dispensing justice and promoting civilization, a burden he afflicted primarily upon frothing missionaries and perfidious traders, Grimble set about recording genealogies and the nuances of island mythology, recognizing that the unwritten story inevitably becomes the forgotten story.

Kiribati mythology points strongly toward Samoa. Grimble's research suggests that sometime around A.D. 1250, a fierce Polynesian tribe found themselves expelled from Samoa, whereupon they set forth for the islands of Kiribati. These were the same Polynesians who colonized Tahiti and New Zealand, and when they reached the islands of Arorae, Nikunau, Beru, Tabiteuea, Nonouti, Butaritari, and Tarawa, they did what they usually did upon arriving someplace new. They ate the men they found there.

The Polynesians worshipped the god Rongo, and what Rongo liked was human flesh. The sails of their war canoes were creatively decorated with the likeness of a human head, called *te bou-uoua*. There was another crest called *tim-tim-te-rara*. This translates as drip-drip-the-blood, a reference to the heads driven on stakes that Rongo liked to see scattered around like knickknacks. So, picture lolling about on the beach, idly scanning the horizon, when suddenly you see hundreds of warriors approach in canoes bedecked with the image of a severed head. It's not going to be a good day.

But who were the people they found there? One evening, I went to ask Bwenawa, an *unimane*, or old man, who oversaw the demonstration garden at FSP, a job akin to that of an alchemist on Tarawa. In Kiribati, the *unimane* and *unaine* (old women) are considered the guardians of the culture, a state of affairs that sets it apart from the United States, where the final arbiter for all things cultural is the adolescent male, which explains the otherwise inexplicable popularity of the World Wrestling Federation, gangsta rap, and Pamela Anderson. Bwenawa, a dark, stocky man with bad teeth and a forest of ear hair whose appearance was not entirely displeasing on account of his gentle face and luxurious Elvis hair, was, like most I-Kiribati, deeply incurious about the outside world. There were no distinctions between Australians, Germans, and Russians, or the languages they spoke. They were simply *I-Matang*. But when it came to the minutiae of island life, there was not a more informed, enthusiastic student and teacher than Bwenawa. He became luminous upon hearing of the medicinal uses of a shrub found on Beru. He marveled at the strength of locally made coconut fiber rope. When he danced the up-tempo traditional dances, he was full of mirth. When he sang the sad songs, he trembled on the brink of despair. He was about as agreeable a conduit to all things Kiribati as could be. And so when I met with Bwenawa in a local meetinghouse, a *maneaba*, made of coconut timber with a thatched roof that descended nearly to the ground, he seemed very pleased to answer my questions about Tarawa's beginnings.

"It is a very interesting story," he began. His eyes lit up and he seemed to go into a trance, and then he lost me completely in his efforts to translate the story of creation into English. There was Nareau the Creator and Nareau the Elder and Nareau the Younger and Nareau the Cunning and Nareau the Wise, and Grumpy Nareau, Sneezy Nareau, Dopey Nareau, and Sleepy Nareau. There was, it seems, much slumbering going on in the beginning until Nareau the Elder, or the Younger, or possibly Dopey, awoke the spirit of the land, which had been entombed (where? you want to ask, but I didn't), and united it with the spirit of the air, which was drifting aimlessly, as air is often wont to do. There was the North Wind and the South Wind and the East Wind and the West Wind and they blew, from the North, South, East, and West, respectively. There were eels and bats and rays and they all came to bad ends. Ditto an octopus.

"You see, it was like the movement of a turtle," said Bwenawa. No, I didn't quite see. I picked up the severing of limbs, the tossing of flesh, and the general sense that the world's creation was largely due to the boredom of the gods, but the poetry of creation—the movement of a turtle—escaped me, and I was too incurious of mythology to find out more. I'll take just the facts, if you please. What I did find interesting, though, was the implied permanence of the ocean. Before all else there was that great blue mass of water. That the I-Kiribati could not conceive of a world or a state of existence that precluded the immutability, the constancy of the ocean, was not surprising. To view life from the perspective of an atoll, where land and all that resides upon it seems acutely impermanent, is to view the ocean as other, more tethered, cultures perceive the universe. The ocean does seem infinite when seen from an atoll, by day merging with the blue sky, by night extending toward the stars, seamlessly. Just as many westerners cannot conceive of God without placing him within something—the black void of space, a puffy white cloud, the throne room at a Renaissance fair—the I-Kiribati could not conceive of life without it being immersed within the context of the ocean. But someone had to have crossed that ocean to be the first to set foot on the islands of Kiribati. I pressed Bwenawa.

"Some educated people think that the I-Kiribati came from someplace else. But most believe that we have always been here, as descendants from the spirits."

We were sitting on mats. A kerosene lantern offered a dim light.

Shadows flitted across the rafters of the *maneaba*. The ocean offered its usual white noise. It was easy to believe that what is always was. But the great Pacific migrations that brought people from Asia into the Pacific were all about change and movement. Beginning several thousand years ago, many of the remote islands of Oceania were reached by people whose feats in seamanship and navigation have never been equaled, not by Columbus, not by Magellan, not even by Cook. That these peoples took to the seas at a time when Europeans were still exploring the utility of femur bones is staggering, and one can only wonder about what would have caused these people to take sail, for these were no mere voyages of exploration, but of colonization.

But where did these people come from? And who were the first to arrive in Kiribati?

Bwenawa seemed amused by my efforts to discern a beginning that did not involve a divine spider. He was much more inclined to tell me more of the Nareau family.

". . . and then Nareau killed his father and he cut out his father's eye and threw it to the sky and it became the sun."

"Do you believe that, Bwenawa?"

"We are all Christians now. . . . And then Nareau cut out the other eye and threw it to the sky and it became the moon . . ."

I asked him about any legends that refered to islands other than Samoa.

"There are legends that speak of high islands to the west. They are there to protect us from the westerly wind." The westerlies are the storm winds.

And then he whispered, as if revealing secret, ancient knowledge. "Some think that the first I-Kiribati came from the west."

I looked pleased. Bwenawa looked pleased.

"From where in the west, Bwenawa?"

"They say Sumatra."

This was interesting.

"They came with the coconut palm tree and the breadfruit tree and the pig," he said, listing trees that are not indigenous to Kiribati, but native to Southeast Asia. "And then, maybe a thousand years ago, men came from Tonga and they killed all the men in Kiribati, but not the women. And then, maybe seven hundred years ago, men came from Samoa and on some of the islands they killed all the men again, but not the women. And so you see," he smiled beatifically, "that is why all I-Kiribati look different from one another."

It was a heartwarming story. And possibly true. Grimble noted the similarities between the I-Kiribati sailing canoes and those found in the Moluccas Islands in Indonesia. The I-Kiribati language, like all the languages of Oceania (except those found in parts of New Guinea), falls in the Central–Eastern Malayo–Polynesian subfamily of the Austronesian language family, which originates in Taiwan. And though it is indeed a great distance from Indonesia to Kiribati, as the drifting fishermen from Papua New Guinea demonstrated, there is a strong west to east current in this part of the Pacific. While the predominant winds in Kiribati are the trade winds from the east, a strong westerly wind usually blows from November through February. Long-distance downwind sailing would certainly be possible in the large outrigger sailing canoes ostensibly used by the ancient seafarers.

More likely, however, is that people from Southeast Asia first settled in nearby Melanesian islands, possibly interbred, and then subsequently moved farther into the Pacific, perhaps to Kiribati. It is also likely that Bwenawa's recounting of the Tongans' friendly arrival in Kiribati is true. Tonga has lately been recognized as a possible "founding colony," a place from which subsequent expansion and exploration in the Pacific occurred.

But, alas, we don't really know much about the ancient I-Kiribati. Any evidence of pre-Samoan horde settlements dissipated long ago. We can speculate, look for links between island groups, even do DNA analysis, but in the end it will tell us very little. Bwenawa is correct. There is remarkable variation in the appearance of the I-Kiribati, not in skin color (brown) or hair type (straight and black), but in facial features. One can see the sharpness of Asia, the roundness of Polynesia, even the eye coloring of Europe, as if every intrusion of the outside world has been marked indelibly on the faces of the I-Kiribati. When outsiders arrived upon the islands of Kiribati, they inevitably adapted to the demands of place. The Samoans may have feasted upon the flesh of the I-Kiribati, but very soon they became I-Kiribati themselves, altering hardly at all the culture they found on the islands. This is because one cannot conquer an atoll. The atoll trumps all.

CHAPTER 6

In which the Author, in case Anyone was Wondering what exactly he was Doing on Tarawa while his Girlfriend Toiled, discusses his Plan for making Productive Use of his Time on an atoll.

Each morning, Sylvia would rumble to work in a pickup truck, confident that through her endeavors the lives of the I-Kiribati would soon be a little brighter, a little healthier, and a little longer. After Kate left, Sylvia was the only *I-Matang* at FSP. She had a staff of ten, all of whom were older than her, and together they managed programs that sought to improve child and maternal health, alleviate vitamin A deficiency, raise environmental aware-ness, and advance the cause of sanitation, which included building composting toilets, or Atollettes, because, as mentioned earlier, something really needed to be done about the shit on Tarawa, and Sylvia was the woman to do it. "It's really cool," she said, uncharac-teristically. "We're going to use it as fertilizer in the demonstration garden." Great, I thought. One more potential source of dysentery to worry about. But use the poop she did, and every few months the most malodorous stench imaginable would waft over the island as Bwenawa mixed the compost with fish guts and pig manure and spread it around the garden, teasing the tomatoes and cabbage to life. Sylvia was happy. She was in her element.

I too was very busy. Thinking. I had decided to write a novel. It would be a big book, Tolstoyan in scale, Joycean in its ambition, Shakespearean in its lyricism. Twenty years hence, the book would be the subject of graduate seminars and doctoral dissertations. The book would join the Canon of Literature. Students would speak reverentially of the text, my text, in hushed, wondrous tones. Magazine profiles would begin with *The reclusive literary giant J. Maarten Troost* . . . I had already decided to be enigmatic, a mystery. People would speak of Salinger, Pynchon, and Troost. I wondered if I could arrange my citizenship so that I would win both the Booker and the Pulitzer for the same book.

To get in the right state of mind, I read big books—*Midnight's Children* by Salman Rushdie, *Infinite Jest* by David Foster Wallace, *Ulysses* by James Joyce (okay, I skimmed parts of that one). I read *King Lear*. Inexplicably, Sylvia thought I was procrastinating.

And so one day, I plugged in my laptop. I opened a new document. The cursor blinked. I looked out the window. I watched ocean swells. Were those dolphins? Tuna, maybe. I gazed at a few passing clouds—a horse, a battleship, my aunt's nose, breasts. I boiled a pot of water. What's that floating stuff? It's probably dead. It's okay then. I turned back toward my computer. The cursor was still blinking. And then . . . nothing. Writer's block.

I was not worried. I read somewhere that it took Gabriel García Márquez months to come up with his first sentence, and then all followed, the sweet pouring forth of a writer's vision. Sylvia suggested I write an outline. Outlines are for the creatively impaired, I explained. Did Kerouac use an outline? Not likely. The important thing was to attain a certain state of being, a transcendental awareness of life, and then the words, the magical words, would simply appear and the writer simply had to transcribe those words. Sylvia noted that Kerouac was a drug-addled drunk and quite dead as a result. Well, writing is pretty edgy, I said.

I went back to my first sentence. The hours passed. The days, too. Also the weeks. And then finally . . . a sentence. I read it. I read it again. I altered it. I erased it.

The cursor blinked.

CHAPTER 7

In which the Author settles into the theme of Absence, in particular the paucity of food options, and offers an account of the Great Beer Crisis, when the island's shipment of Ale was, inexcusably, misdirected to Kiritimati Island, far, far away from those who needed it most.

I t is entirely possible that somewhere on planet Earth there exists a cuisine more unpalatable than that found in Kiribati. I accept this possibility like I accept the possibility of intelligent life elsewhere in the universe. I have never encountered it. I cannot imagine it. I simply accept that there is a statistical probability of its existence. An eensie-weensie tiny little probability.

How can this be, you wonder, when Kiribati is really nothing more than a vast habitat for fish. Good fish. Delicious fish. Dip a line with six baited hooks off reef's edge (about 150 yards of line), tug for a minute or two, and you will pull up six large, succulent red snappers. Got a hankering for octopus? Just wander over the reef shelf during a neap tide and look under the rocks. Are you thinking mantis prawns? Search the lagoon flats at low tide for the telltale burrows, insert a sliver of eel, and pluck the creature out. Shark fin soup? Cut open a few flying fish, toss liberally around your boat, bait your hook with the liver of a ray, shake a rattle in the water, watch your arm now, await inevitable arrival of frenzied shark, hook it, tie line to boat, enjoy sleigh ride as shark tires itself out. Cut fin. Want a turtle? Well, you shouldn't.

Elsewhere in the world, people are willing to pay good money for the fish found in Kiribati. And they do. Every now and then a decaying Chinese vessel limps toward Kiribati to gather the hundreds of shark fins culled by fishermen in the outer islands. The Chinese also take on live lagoon fish—the more luminous, the better—which are then transported to Hong Kong, where a meal isn't a meal unless something endangered is served. Octopi and bêche-de-mer, turdlike creatures that function as reef cleaners, are rounded up for the Japanese, perhaps the most fastidiously hygienic people on the planet, who are clearly unaware of what exactly a reef cleaner in Kiribati cleans.

The real prize, however, is tuna and Kiribati has the world's richest tuna fishing grounds. Dozens of industrial fishing boats from Japan, Taiwan, South Korea, Spain, and the United States ply across the more than two million square miles of ocean that comprise Kiribati's exclusive economic zone. Quite likely, these floating colonies of trawlers and mother ships—Death Stars to the fish community—that receive and process the catch, are the very same ships that have emptied the North Atlantic and the South China Sea of life. Add to this an unknown number of illegal fishing boats—Chinese, Taiwanese, Korean, Russian—and you begin to understand that industrial fishing is something very different than the fishing rhapsodized about in the tomes churned out with alarming regularity by big city writers who summer in Montana. Rich countries are good at offering sweet words, little odes to environmental sensitivity, the homage to sustainable harvesting, haiku for nature—but appetites are not to be denied.

In an average year, nearly $2 billion worth of tuna is *legally* caught in the Pacific. This is a lot of money, particularly for nations where flipflops are regarded as evidence of conspicuous consumption. Yet, Pacific island nations typically only receive around $60 million annually in fees from fishing licenses. Kiribati, no surprise, receives a disproportionately small share. This is because—how to put this politely?—in the Pacific your average minister of fisheries is a) an idiot, or b) corrupt, and c) usually both. It does not help that license fees are tied directly to foreign aid. Japan, for instance, balks at paying more than 4 or 5 percent of the catch value in fees, arguing that it more than compensates in aid. But consider the aid. In Kiribati, this consists of the Fisheries Training Center, where young I-Kiribati men are groomed to work Japanese fishing boats for wages no Japanese would accept, and the construction of a new port to service, yes, Japanese fishing boats. Neat, huh?

Of course, it is not just rapacious foreigners doing the fishing in Kiribati. The country survives at a subsistence level, and subsistence is maintained almost solely by the consumption of fish. Consider this: Annual per capita fish consumption in Kiribati is over four hundred pounds. Pause for a moment and absorb this startling fact. The average man, woman, or child in Kiribati eats more than four hundred pounds of fish every year. That's fish for breakfast, fish for lunch, fish for dinner. And in Kiribati, there are really only two ways to eat fish, raw or boiled. This, of course, was a dispiriting discovery. Raw fish has a place in my culinary world, but raw fish consumed before an intermediary stop in a refrigerator is, I can attest, a very effective way of eliciting weight loss. And boiled fish, well, I think it's safe to say that we can blame the English for that. Not for the first time, I wished Kiribati had been colonized by the French, particularly after I asked Bwenawa if there were any local spices on the island.

"Spices?" he said.

"Yes. You know, like salt, pepper, saffron, that sort of thing."

"Ah yes . . . like the salt fish."

"Salt fish?"

Bwenawa brought my attention to two wooden planks raised about four feet above the ground. On the ledges were lagoon fish sliced open and lying in the sun, the carcasses just visible through an enveloping blizzard of flies. "You see," said Bwenawa. "The water dries in the sun, leaving the salt. It's *kang-kang* [tasty]. We call it salt fish."

"Ah," I said. "In my country we call it rotten fish."

Since I had, as Sylvia liked to point out, "more time," it was left to me to gather the daily fish for our evening meal. In the late afternoon, after a hard day of thinking, I usually went biking. Sometimes I turned left and went down the atoll, sometimes I turned right and went up the atoll, but mostly I wished I had somewhere else to bike to, because frankly, biking up and down an atoll every day for two years does little to alleviate island fever. The quest for something edible gave my journeys up and down the atoll a welcome purpose.

As I soon discovered, finding food on Tarawa that is tasty, nutritious, and available is no easy task. After biking the entire length of Tarawa, I realized that the island is, in fact, two distinct places. Where the island's lone road unfolds along the southern axis of the atoll is called South Tarawa; where a narrow bush trail links the village of Buota with the wind- and sea-blasted end of the atoll at Na'a is known as North Tarawa, and the differences between the two are vivid. North Tarawa, officially classified as an outer island, is beguiling. It is isolated from any hint of modernity. There is no electricity, no running water, no towns, not even a road. With the light and the water and the snow-white fairy terns fluttering in the casuarina trees, it feels very much like paradise ought to feel, except, of course, it is too hot. We were drawn there most weekends, enticed by long swaths of golden beaches, where we tramped like beachcombers, sifting through the tide's curiosities, eyes straining along the reef, searching for turtles. To reach North Tarawa, we crossed the channel separating Tanaea from Buota—at high tide with a villager poling his canoe through the current—and walked along a footpath through a grove of coconut palm trees until we reached the aptly named Broken Bridge, a slab of cement that functions as a seesaw over a fish-laden channel. Across the bridge lies the islet of Abatao, the first of twenty-nine such islets in North Tarawa, perpetually chiseled by an ocean rushing and running twice daily, and the farther one walks the more elemental the islets seem. There is always the sea, the blinding light, but the wind begins to feel strangely potent, and soon you understand why the three thousand inhabitants of North Tarawa rarely go to Na'a, the northernmost tip of the atoll. Na'a is haunted. To stand in this desolate place, where drought has rendered most trees into lifeless stumps, where the ocean runs high, where enormous waves pound the reef with majestic indifference, is to feel an unshakable eeriness, until you turn around and march quickly back, past the graves of the last ten Japanese soldiers to die on Tarawa—suicides—until you reach the village of Buariki, overlooking the friendly lagoon and some friendly mangroves, where you sit in the *maneaba*, gratefully slurping a proffered coconut, and inquire of the resident *unimane* the correct I-Kiribati word for spooky.

Fishing here is not a job, or a way of life. It is, like water, an essential precursor to life, and befitting something elemental, it is accompanied by magic and governed by taboos. On North Tarawa, like on the other islands in Kiribati, each family provides for its own needs, and the mechanics of fishing—places and methods—are deeply held secrets, no less guarded despite the replacement of bone hooks by metal, and coconut fiber by industrial-grade line and mesh. Between tides, fish traps are built with stone, tidal pools are scoured, rocks are lifted, and food is secured for another day. Water is procured from shallow wells. *Babai*, or swamp taro, is grown in pits. Homes are made of wood and thatch. Alcohol is forbidden. Disputes are settled in the *maneaba*.

South Tarawa is a different place. In the velvet light of early evening, with the tide in and the men high in the trees cutting toddy and singing epics about either a woman or a fish that got away, it is possible to believe that all is well, that here on distant South Tarawa, far away from the hubris of continental life, the good life has prevailed. It *was* awfully pretty at sunset, and with such an ostentatious sky, the sweet finality of each and every day, illusions and delusions were tolerated. But in the glare of midday, with the tide out and revealing the desolate emptiness of the reef shelf; with the lagoon retreated, its water replaced by desert; with the aesthetic imbalance of sunsets and high water corrected, South Tarawa is exposed as a wretched island, often indistinguishable from a forgotten refugee camp. From Bonriki through Bikenibeu, past the great *maneaba* in Eita, across the causeways to Ambo and Bairiki and finally Betio, Tarawa's lone road unravels from idyllic to raw to a Malthusian hell.

There are, simply, too many people on South Tarawa, particularly on the islet of Betio, which has the world's highest population density, greater even than Hong Kong. Unlike Hong Kong, a city in the sky, there is not a building above two stories on Betio. Some eighteen thousand people, nearly a quarter of the country's population, live on this shattered islet, one square mile of blight linked to the rest of Tarawa by a mile-long causeway. The tangible squalor of their lives shocked us initially, before we became numb. Housing was most often a strange fusion of coconut wood, thatch, corrugated tin, plywood, and rice bags, and it took time before we could distinguish the dwellings of humans from those of pigs. The beaches on Betio, both facing the lagoon and the ocean, were a minefield of fecal droppings. The odor at low tide, as waste both human and otherwise sizzled in the sun, was repellent, like eighteen thousand stink bombs going off at once. To be on the beach at low tide is to feel your body absorb the stench, internalize the repulsive, until you too feel the need to emit something somehow. Clean water was impossible to find. Most people relied on well water. They did not have to dig deep. The water lens is only about five feet below the surface, which would be convenient if coral wasn't so porous, allowing everything dropped or spilled, such as piss and diesel, to quickly be absorbed by the groundwater, which soon becomes the happy abode of interesting parasites. Boiling water was essential, but few had stoves or the money to pay for gas canisters. There were still palm trees on Betio, which provided coconuts and toddy, but there wasn't any shrub left for firewood, which is a poor emitter of heat anyway. Everyone had worms. Every child had hepatitis A. Tuberculosis was rampant. There were lepers. Cholera was inevitable: It had struck once before. It would strike again. Betio still functioned as a village, but it was no longer a village. It was a slum. The rest of South Tarawa trailed behind.

In this environment, the odd mixture of Robinson Crusoe–like isolation combined with the favelas of Rio, good eating was hard to find. On South Tarawa, anything caught inshore—lagoon fish, octopus, mantis prawns, sea worms—was guaranteed to induce gastric explosions in the unfortunate diner. More distressing, ciguatera poisoning was common. This occurs when untreated wastewater, which is the technical term for shit, leads to toxic algae, which is then eaten by fish, which are in turn consumed by humans, who soon feel a tingly, numbing sensation in their mouth, the first sign of the impending collapse of the body. The hands and feet become paralyzed. The skin feels like it is carrying an electric current. Bones creak. And if you are old or very young or if your immune system is weak, you may very well die. The most sensible advice we received from a volunteer teacher on the outer islands, who had became ill with ciguatera poisoning from a contaminated red snapper at a first birthday celebration, a feast that ultimately claimed the lives of three children and one old man, was to stick your finger down your throat at the first tingle and keep puking until you can puke no more. Even then, it might be too late.

We would have been happy to avoid reef and lagoon fish altogether, but dining options were few. Little grows on Tarawa. A drought combined with nutrient-deficient coral does not do wonders for the cultivation of fruits and vegetables. The I-Kiribati are quite possibly the only people on Earth without a tradition of gardening. As a result, FSP had a demonstration garden where people were taught how to cultivate something besides coconut trees. The garden was Bwenawa's pride and joy, though it looked very much like an overgrown dump yard. Tin cans were strewn about and buried to boost the iron content of the soil. Fish guts and pig manure were regularly shoveled into the trenches. And the compost that was the happy result of Sylvia's Atollette was placed around the banana trees, where, at the staff's insistence, it would not touch anything edible. Every day, the garden was calibrated just so, but the yield was nonetheless meager for the effort. Tomatoes were no bigger than pinballs. Eggplant could not be coaxed to grow larger than crayons. A head of Chinese cabbage would not feed a rabbit. Bananas refused to bud without rain.

Despairing at the utter meagerness of the island's culinary world, I too decided to start a garden. Like many writers, I believed that clearing brush under the equatorial sun was preferable to actually writing, and so with machete in hand I carved what would become our garden. It was more like recovering a garden, since years earlier the shady plot conveniently located to take advantage of any leaks in the water tanks, was, by all accounts, a particularly fertile garden, quite likely because years earlier there was rain. I had high hopes that one day soon we would be dining on light and refreshing salads and snacking on tasty fruit. I asked Bwenawa about compost and shade and water and all sorts of other highly technical gardening questions, but he dismissed my inquiries and told me that the most important thing about gardening on Tarawa was a sturdy fence. "Dogs, pigs, chickens, and crabs," he said. "They must be stopped." Fortunately, I had the remnants of the old fence and I set about constructing what Bwenawa called a "local" fence. This consisted of sticks tightly knotted together with coconut fiber rope. The effect was to enclose the garden inside something like a mock colonial fort. I say *mock* because deep down I knew that if a pig so much as huffed and puffed on my garden fort it would blow down, but it looked good and it provided me a fleeting sense of accomplishment. Sylvia too was very impressed with my fence, though her confidence in my construction skills, and possibly even my judgment, suffered when she took a closer look at the gate.

"Where did you find that?" she asked.

"What?"

"That," she said, pointing at the thin plastic tubing I used as a latch for the gate.

"Oh that. I found it on the reef."

She stared at it. Her face contorted. She was appalled. I had, it appeared, done something wrong.

"That's a hospital IV. It's full of blood."

And so it was. It's funny how you can miss things. The hospital incinerator hadn't worked for years, and so hospital waste, like so much of the detritus that Tarawa generated, was thrown on the reef, where each day the tides took it out and redistributed it a little farther down the atoll. I unraveled the IV—how could I have missed that?—and tossed it into our burn bin. "Maybe I should wash my hands."

My adventures in gardening ended soon enough. One morning, I discovered that the fence was gone. I knew immediately what had happened. Every evening, the neighborhood kids swept through in a quest for firewood and *te non*, a foul-smelling fruit that was used for pig food and traditional medicine. They were very polite about it at first. A few boys shyly asked if they could have the *te non* that dropped uncollected and possibly gather any twigs that might be lying about. Soon though, armies of children besieged what remained of the natural world around our house. A dozen boys would climb the casuarina tree and hack at the branches with large bush knives. The *te non* would get shredded from the bush, and then the bush itself would be taken. When I saw the kids begin to chop down the one tree that provided us with any shade, I decided that the time had come for a few limits. "Hey, you kids," I found myself saying, suddenly feeling very old. "Please don't cut down the tree." The following day we found our pickup truck smeared with *te non*, the island equivalent of being TPed. In Kiribati, as elsewhere in the world, there is no more destructive force than an eleven-year-old boy. My fence, as I knew it would, had become firewood. The garden, and the mango tree I defiantly planned on cultivating, remained an unrealized dream.

AND SO WE BECAME dependent upon the ship. Every six weeks or so, a ship arrived to discard food deemed unsuitable for Australian consumption—rusty cans of vegetable matter, corned beef with a fat content guaranteed to induce a cardiac event within minutes of consumption, weevils together with rice and flour, rubber that was alleged to be meat, packaged chicken "pieces" that had been frozen and defrosted so often that each package had right angles, food products generally that had expired three to twelve months prior, and all priced beyond the range of everyone except those truly desperate to nibble on something beside a fish. Fortunately, the Australians came through with the beer, which was a good thing because South Tarawa had a prodigious appetite for beer. On a few rare occasions potatoes, oranges, and cheese could be found, but one had to be quick because certain unnamed wives of foreign men on lucrative aid contracts were unscrupulous hoarders (you know who you are). Bonriki wives we called them, after the village where most of them lived in their A-grade houses. Nonetheless, among the I-Matang on Tarawa it was gleeful pandemonium whenever a ship arrived as rumors swept the island of exciting edible goods to be found in the otherwise depleted stores.

"There's broccoli at the One-Stop!" Sylvia would inform me, calling from her office.

"Hush. Don't be saying things like that."

"*Go now!*"

And I would pedal with demonic fury only to see one of the Bonriki wives—women who referred to the I-Kiribati as "the blacks," doughy, petulant women who never ever should have been allowed to leave suburban Adelaide—inevitably marching out of the One-Stop with the entire shipment of broccoli, the last potatoes, the only oranges, and every package of Tasty Cheese that had not yet turned green. I would be left stewing in my bile, empty-handed once again. I wished them ill.

The ship—it was always The Ship—was what sustained existence on South Tarawa, if not always by what it carried, then through what it promised. Often enough there were very real shortages of the basics—rice, flour, diesel—and it was just the knowledge that, sometime in the foreseeable future, replenishments would arrive that enabled us to endure. In the meantime, I hunted for surprises at our local shop, the Angirota Store, which despite its modest cinder-block façade, represented the entirety of the I-Kiribati free enterprise system. There were five I-Matangs on Tarawa, long-term residents with I-Kiribati wives, who had started businesses of their own—the One-Stop, Betio Hardware, a used-car dealership, Yamaha Motors, and a sign-painting/electrical repair conglomerate, but the Angirota Store was the only business, the only true business, to be run by I-Kiribati. Every other shop on Tarawa was a government-run cooperative, where you were as likely to find a dead rat on the shelves as anything edible, though now and then, a startling find could be made at the Nanotasi, such as when an entire wall was devoted to the display of fabric softener, which was very interesting because there is not one dryer on Tarawa. Not one. I checked.

At the Angirota Store in contrast, one could find seven different audiotapes featuring "La Macarena," which might actually constitute an argument against capitalism, but I admired the Give the People What They Want attitude. It was subversive in Kiribati. But even at the Angirota Store, there was only so much that could be done to improve the fare on Tarawa. There was a counter behind which the available goods would be displayed—canned tuna, canned tuna with tomato sauce, canned corned beef, cans of Ma-Ling Chicken Curry, "cabin biscuits," Milo powdered sport drink, powdered milk, Sanitorium brand peanut butter. It was little different than the victuals found on an English ship, circa 1850. There was a refrigerator with a glass door that contained cans of Victoria Bitter, Longlife milk, apple-cranberry juice, and now and then wilted cabbage. In a wooden cabinet with a fly screen there were loaves of sweet white bread. In addition to the aforementioned collection of "La Macarena" tapes, one could also find *A Techno Christmas, Melanesian Love Songs, Big Band Celebration*, and what appeared to be the collected works of Wayne Newton.

The routine was almost always the same. The woman tending the store would be draped over the counter, a pose that reminded me of tedious school days when the boredom would creep in and slowly I would lean and extend myself forward and breathe the ammonium scent of my desk, dreaming, until clubbed by the chalk or eraser that a thoughtful teacher would hurtle my way. I would enter with a hearty *"Mauri"* (greetings) and with colossal willpower she would heave herself off the counter and arch her eyebrows. English was an official language of Kiribati and so I just plowed forward. "Any fruit today, apples, oranges, strawberries, something, anything?" The brow would crinkle and this would mean no. "How about bread, a rustic batard, a loaf of sourdough, Jewish Rye perhaps?" She would twitch her nose and nod toward the bread cabinet, which contained the weevil-infested loaves of what passed for bread on Tarawa. It was mere stomach filler. I would ask for the peanut butter and she would arch her eyebrows in acknowledgment. Apple-cranberry juice? And once again the eyebrows were launched. Inevitably, once I got home I would discover that the juice had expired three months before, and that the jar of peanut butter contained a colony of ants entombed in a sticky, nutty quagmire. The juice would get drunk, the ants would get scraped out, the weevils plucked from the bread, a peanut butter sandwich would be eaten, and I would be pleased with myself for finding sustenance that did not involve a fish.

It was difficult, however, to go through an entire day without resorting to the consumption of a fish. Almost always it would be a tuna, either skipjack or, preferably, yellowfin. One fish, say about two feet long, cost roughly 50 cents American, and its purchase was the culminating errand of my bike rides. At this point, because I tended to bike hard and it was always—I really want to stress this—hot, I was usually sweaty, not sweaty like northeasterners get after a brisk workout in an air-conditioned gym, but sweaty like Humphrey Bogart in *The African Queen*, drenched, and the reason I bring this up is because it is really difficult, almost impossible actually, to bike on a road congested with pigs and chickens and pedestrians and minibuses while carrying a large wet fish in a perspiring hand. The women who sold me the fish were amused by my efforts. I was a novice to fish buying at first and I spent a lot of time shuffling from cooler to cooler, prodding the fish, studying the eyes, sniffing for fishiness, and this, because they are fish people, was the source of much mirth and cackling to the vendors. That I would stand soaked from head to toe in sweat induced by exercise, which is an unfathomable concept in Kiribati, further confirmed that I was a fool and in need of mocking. When I accused them of being *tokonono* (naughty), they emitted screams of laughter.

With my fish selected and paid for, and confident that my very existence on Tarawa was amusing to so many, I eased myself back on my bike, a tuna fish dangling from one hand, the tail fins hooked between my middle fingers, and weaved precariously until I built sufficient momentum to continue in a more or less straight line, steeling myself for the gauntlet. It was always very exciting biking past several hundred hungry, emaciated, mange-ridden, angry dogs while swinging a fish past their snouts. The trick was to bike very, very slowly, sneaky-like, particularly when confronted by a pack of dogs. Under no circumstances should eye contact be made. And never let them sense your fear. This knowledge, of course, is hardly intuitive. I lost three fish to the snarling hell demons before I figured out that a pack of hungry dogs will always move faster than a cyclist gripping the handlebars with one hand while using the other to swing a fish like a club, a tactic that was remarkably unsuccessful, though it did leave bystanders doubled-over in belly-rumbling laughter. I am sure they are still talking about it today.

Once safely home with an intact fish I set about preparing it. Off went the head. Then the tail. The knife sliced open the underside of the fish. The skin was pulled off. The dark, blood meat was trimmed, worm indentations were scoured for, and if none were found and I was hungry, I had myself a snack of raw tuna. Then there was the question of what to actually do to the tuna steaks. How to dress it up, as it were, for the dinner plate? Sylvia might inquire if the mayonnaise I purchased for a tuna salad was actually safe to eat, given that it had expired six months earlier. She would sniff it and wonder,

"I can't tell if it's bad because it's turned or because it's Australian." It was a pet peeve of hers, Australian mayonnaise, but if it wasn't rancid it was eaten. If there were a couple of tomatoes available, I would make tortillas from scratch, sear the fish, and have fish tacos. When finally we succeeded in cultivating yogurt from a yogurt culture that had been passed from desperate *I-Matang* to desperate *I-Matang* as if it were some sacred life force, I pasted the yogurt on the fish and sprinkled on the curry powder we found deep in the recesses of the kitchen closet. We had stir-fried tuna, sautéed tuna, pan-fried tuna, grilled tuna, boiled tuna, raw tuna. We even had tuna carpaccio. The one question that was never asked was *What's for dinner?* Until . . .

The tuna disappeared. Just like that. I biked the entire length of South Tarawa searching for a tuna. But there was nothing. Just the dreaded salt fish and a few sharks. It was as if giant nets had suddenly appeared to enmesh every tuna in the greater Tarawa area. It was like that because that's what had actually happened. The Korean fishing fleet had gathered in Tarawa Lagoon to offload their catch onto huge mother ships. Emptied of fish, the trawlers immediately set forth to empty the seas around Maiana and Abaiang, the fishing grounds that supplied Tarawa. I could see them from the house, giant fishing machines with industrial silhouettes that I had last seen in New Jersey, and I could only imagine the effect of their wakes on inshore canoes. That the government of Kiribati allowed this was deplorable. There are two million square miles of ocean in Kiribati's exclusive economic zone in which the trawlers can fish, and yet they were permitted to work the twenty square miles of water upon which half of the nation's population depends for sustenance, betraying again the ineptitude and petty corruption of Kiribati's leaders. The fish sellers were glum. Each day they appeared with a few reef or lagoon fish, all that their husbands and brothers and fathers could catch now that the deepwater fish, the fish that could be consumed with a strong likelihood of maintaining one's stomach intact, had been netted, destined for the canneries of Korea. Usually, we could weather these periodic convergences of idiocy and bad luck, but during these same tuna-less weeks an event of cataclysmic proportions occurred, an event that tested our very will to live. The beer ran out.

This was shocking. South Tarawa was completely dependent on beer. It was completely dependent on beer because a large proportion of the male population had what those of a more judgmental disposition might call a drinking problem. On payday Fridays it was impossible to drive on Tarawa, not simply because every driver was drunk, but because a good percentage of the male population could be found sprawled on the road, resting, or as some prefer, passed out. These nights were usually very lively and I made a point of always keeping a large bush knife within easy reach. I had become much more sympathetic to Kate's experience on Tarawa. The house was riddled with gaping holes in the plywood trestle that gave the roof its slope, reminders of all the attempted break-ins she'd had to endure. Most of the window screens had been sliced open by Peeping Toms, who would quietly insert a stick and pry open the curtains. This did not happen as much now that I, a man, had moved in, but still it happened, and now and then I would quietly step outside for a cigarette only to discover some cretin snooping at the window, hungrily watching Sylvia read a book. This bothered me to no end, and with a surge of angry adrenaline, I frequently gave chase, wildly hurling rocks and epitaphs to compensate for my slow feet, encumbered by flipflops, which were no match for the callused bare feet of the detected perv. No one would dare lurk around an I-Kiribati household, but we *I-Matangs* were fair game, unprotected by family and clan. I dearly hoped to catch one of these creeps, but if I sensed they were drunk, I eased my way back into the house, bolted the doors, and grabbed the machete. When sober, I-Kiribati men are typically shy and gentle and all-around good guys, but when drunk something seems to give way—let's call it reason—and the I-Kiribati male becomes the most frightening creature in the Pacific.

Outsiders tend to believe that Samoans are the islanders to fear. Ask a Pacific islander, and he will tell you that the meanest, toughest, scariest islander is the drunk I-Kiribati. There is even a word for what happens when an I-Kiribati man loses his mind and any semblance of restraint: *koko*—a word that I think nicely captures that state of lunacy caused by drink among I-Kiribati men. On payday Fridays, I put on my best *Don't Fuck With Me* face and made sure that Sylvia's pepper spray worked. The neighborhood dogs worked hard on those nights.

Despite the excesses though, I found I quite liked the easygoing, anything goes, why-not-have-another-beer air of Tarawa. It was refreshingly different from the prissiness that characterizes life in the Northwest quadrant of Washington, D.C. Government leaders in Kiribati were of an entirely different disposition than the lifeless ogres of Washington. At one function, I asked the minister of health why cigarettes were so cheap in Kiribati. We both had a cigarette in one hand and a can of Victoria Bitter in the other. "Because otherwise the people can't afford them," he said, an answer I liked very much. At the same event, the secretary of health, a doctor by training and a politician by temperament, insisted that we take a few beers with us for the drive home. "I always like to have one for the road," he said, waving us off. Some might regard this is reprehensible, but I think this why-the-fuck-not attitude was reflective of a certain joie de vivre. The daily consumption of several cans of Victoria Bitter became an integral part of my well-being, possibly because I am of Dutch-Czech stock and thus warmly inclined toward beer, but also because it is immensely fun to quaff beers with your loved one while sitting at reef's edge watching the world's most spectacular sunsets. Plus, beer tends to be parasite-free and calorie-laden, two very useful attributes on Tarawa.

So imagine my despair when I walked into the Angirota Store to buy a six-pack only to be confronted by a glaringly empty refrigerator. "*Bia?*" I asked hopefully, using the I-Kiribati word for beer, which sounds very much like the Australian word for beer. "*Akia,*" I was told. *Akia* is the most commonly used word in the Kiribati language, which can be roughly translated as "unavailable." The words *akia te bia* are the most painful words I have heard spoken. The owner of the shop, Buorere, a large man with the grooviest sideburns this side of the dateline, was as stunned as I was. As the only local capitalist on the island, he was no doubt aware of what the absence of beer would do to his profit margins.

"What happened?" I asked him.

"Kiritimati Island," he muttered darkly. "They sent the beer to Kiritimati Island."

Kirimati Island was approximately two thousand miles east of Tarawa. It seemed unlikely that they would send the beer back. In one of those screwups that seemed to typify life in Kiribati, Tarawa's shipment of beer had been accidentally sent to an even more remote corner of the country. I abandoned my loyalty to the Angirota Store, and immediately set off to scour the island's co-op stores for beer. Surely, the government would have a reserve stock of beer, hidden and well guarded, which could immediately be brought into circulation during a time of crisis. *Akia te bia* I was told, again and again. Clearly, better planning was needed.

I turned to the Otintaii Hotel, where every Friday the island's European and Australian volunteers gathered on Cheap-Cheap Night for an evening of immoderate drinking.

Akia.

This was dire. There had to be beer somewhere on the island, I thought. Tarawa without beer was incomprehensible. Life on the island just wasn't worth it without beer.

"Have you tried the Betio Saloon?" Sylvia asked. Not much of a beer drinker before arriving on Tarawa, after a few months on the island Sylvia had adapted to local cultural mores. She now crushed beer cans on her forehead. Actually, that's not true, but she had developed a taste for ale, and while she wasn't quite as shaky about the prospect of a beerless Tarawa as I was, there was no doubt that the absence of beer represented a serious downgrading in her quality of life on the island. If anyone still had beer on Tarawa, it would be the barflies at the Betio Saloon, a one-room tin shed deep in the heart of Betio, where the island's more dissolute *I-Matangs* could usually be found.

"It's a fucking tragedy, mate," said Big John, one of the proprietors.

Akia. A fucking tragedy, I agreed.

"We're going to have to fly a few cases in," he said. Big John, who had lived on Tarawa for twenty-odd years, was a man of action. I admired this. Soon the entire island was talking about Big John, who at six foot five was easily the biggest man on Tarawa. *Big John's flying in three hundred cases from Nauru.*

We waited. Five weeks would pass until beer returned to Tarawa, via a fully laden Air Nauru. They were dark days. True, they were peaceful days, but in no way does this compensate for the ache of a beerless evening.

Sitting over a bowl of rice, Sylvia plucked the weevils out, and declared, apropos of nothing: "Avocado."

I hated when she did this, for it triggered so much. "Blueberries," I said.

"Bagels," she said.

"With lox and cream cheese."

"Apple-leek soup."

"Asparagus."

"Antipasto."

"Risotto."

"Salad. A real salad."

"Steak. Grilled medium rare."

"Beer."

"Anchor Steam."

"Harp."

"Bitburger."

"Duvel."

Sigh.

"More rice?"

CHAPTER 8

In which the Author continues with the theme of Absence, which will be a pervasive theme throughout this narrative, there really being a lot to say, but here the focus will be on water and electricity, the absence thereof.

Before I moved to Kiribati, I had never spent much time considering the topic of infrastructure. If someone had asked me where does drinking water come from, I would have said from the tap, of course. The provenance of electricity was equally mysterious. It seemed to somehow involve lightning, a kite, a key, and men in frocks who conveniently stored the power inside walls. This all changed when I noticed with some alarm that water was no longer streaming from the tap. I had hesitated to look inside the water tanks, fearing the knowledge that awaited, but one day the dry rasping of our water pump forced the reckoning. Inside the tanks, a thick layer of mud, the remnants of leaves, nettles, and insects, covered the bottom. On the sides, I saw the outlines of several geckos silhouetted in relief, their decomposition having slowly occurred in our water supply. Not knowing what to do, but feeling the need to be useful, I clambered inside one of the tanks with a shovel and bucket and began cleaning. This ranks very high on my list of exceedingly dumb things I have done in my life. It was nearly midday and the sun had transformed the tank into an oven, which cooked and basted me until I finally gasped and, with the last of my strength, I hoisted myself out of the roasting tank and began to wretch. I stammered into the shower thinking cold water would do me good. I turned it on and nothing happened, of course, except the bleak sound of air moving through the water pump and the sudden awareness that the tropics had so far not been very kind to either my body or my mind.

I caught sight of myself in the mirror. I was filthy. Not only was I pasted in a thick layer of primeval slime, no doubt the kind of tropical muck of abiding interest to those with degrees in the life sciences, but I could also see bonded to my skin the dark remains of several geckos. What on earth were so many geckos doing in our water tanks? Ah, eating, of course. And what were they eating? Bugs. And what happens when geckos eat bugs? They poop. But what would have killed all those geckos? I was stymied there. Tottering on the cusp of heat exhaustion, I could only think, again, *And we moved here why?*

There was nothing to do but go for a swim. The tide was going out, but there still remained enough water over the reef to bathe, a shallow layer that the sun had heated to a near scalding temperature. I walked out about forty yards where the water was nearly waist-deep though not much cooler and dove in, enjoying the salt water and the feeling of sweat and grime departing me. And then I turned back to shore. Two large women were walking toward the water. *Please no.* They carried sticks. *Oh, please, please, no.* They moved toward the ledge of coral rock, which I had begun to call the Ledge of Coral Rock Behind the House Where Large People with Bottoms I Have No Wish to See Go to Defecate. *Maybe they're just going to talk about that cute guy they saw in the coconut tree.* They squatted. *Nooooo.* Up went the lavalavas. *Ugh.*

When finally I returned to the house I immediately doused myself with half a bottle of antiseptic, and, to complete the catastrophe, drank our last liter of boiled water. Then I tried to think constructively about the water problem. In the short term, I would have to find water, any water at all that did not contain too much salt or too many parasites, for our hour-by-hour needs. In the medium term, I would have to find a sufficient quantity of water to fill, at least partially, one of the water tanks. And for the long term, I would have to learn the local rain dance. I contemplated sacrifices. Would the gods accept a dog? I would sacrifice a lot of island dogs for water.

I headed out with two large plastic canisters. On our little road were a few oceanside houses that were similar to ours, and across from these houses were smaller, decrepit permanent houses that appeared fatigued and burdened with the task of sheltering what seemed to be forty people per house. Surrounding each house like satellites were customary shelters of wood and thatch, raised on platforms and partly enclosed by mats. These, unlike the permanent houses and their crumbling walls, were always kept tidy and in tip-top condition. Each contained bodies in repose, mostly asleep, but a few awake, watching me, whispering to their neighbors, giggling and smiling. Two young girls, wearing lavalavas and plaited, locally made sleeveless shirts sat on a stoop in front of a house, one picking at the long cascading black hair of the other, seeking out the lice, and smiling radiantly at my passing. Everywhere there were dogs, mangy and spotted, their bones jutting against mottled, hairless skin, sleeping in freshly dug shallow pits, seeking the cooler earth below the surface that seemed to cackle and hiss in the sun.

I hesitated to ask anyone at all for water, knowing that most people relied on well water and that well water was brackish and the happy abode of numerous parasites and probably the reason why everyone was always shitting on the reef. Also, I knew that due to the drought even the wells were often nearly dry.

There is, I should note, a water system of sorts on Tarawa. Twice daily, for about twenty minutes, water is pumped from Bonriki and piped toward Betio. The water pipe was a gift from the good citizens of Australia. It was also so punctured that rare was the drop that actually reached Betio. It is technically illegal to puncture the pipe, but since there are way too many people on Tarawa and few homes actually connected to the water system, there really was no choice for people but to puncture the pipe in order to satisfy their basic water needs. This was usually done in a very orderly fashion. I had even seen policemen politely standing in line with their buckets awaiting their turn. A few *I-Matang*, confronted with their own empty water tanks, had taken it upon themselves to attach portable water pumps to the water system, ensuring that during the twenty minutes or so when water trickles down the main pipe, nearly every drop would get pumped into their tank. Like most houses, ours was not connected to the water system, so this was not a possibility for us, which was probably a good thing, because while I recognize that expropriating the island's water supply to satisfy your own needs is just wrong wrong wrong, I might have been sorely tempted.

Instead, I decided to inquire at the neighbor's house, which like ours had rainwater tanks. Most of the oceanside houses were allocated to the Ministry of Health. Our immediate neighbors were two female Chinese doctors, a psychiatrist and a gynecologist. I once attempted some friendly, neighborly banter—*looks like it will be sunny today*—but I was rebuffed. I mentioned this to Sylvia, who made her own foray. When she returned, she looked puzzled.

"They don't speak English," she said.

"Do you think they speak I-Kiribati?"

"No."

We contemplated this for a moment. The psychiatrist represented the entirety of Kiribati's mental health services. She was well known for favoring powerful tranquilizers, unlike her predecessor, who was partial to straitjackets. Her roommate was the only gynecologist in the country. "Well," said Sylvia, "it's good to know that if a schizophrenic Mandarin-speaking woman with a bad yeast infection ever shows up on Tarawa, there will be help for her."

That's the thing about Sylvia. She's always thinking positively.

I knocked on their front door. I practiced my pantomime. No answer. Next to them was the surgeon, also from China. I knocked on his door. No answer. Of course, I thought. They have jobs. Just as I turned to go, however, the door opened and a sleepy, rumpled surgeon, wearing only briefs, emerged, blinking into the brightness of day. "I'm terribly sorry to bother you, but we just live two doors down, and . . . well, we've run out of water and—"

Before I could finish, he had relieved me of my canisters. He went to the laundry basin beside the house and filled them with water. "Any time you need water, just take. No problem." The kindness of strangers is a great thing. Regrettably for the surgeon, his kindness did not go unnoticed and soon the entire neighborhood was helping themselves to his water, which may be why a few days later his water basin/laundry area was encased behind a chicken wire fence that extended from ground to ceiling. I took this as my cue to seek other water sources.

Fortunately, Sylvia had discovered that it was possible to actually buy water. The Public Utility Board sold it for $3 per cubic meter. I went to their office and bought five cubic meters of water, all that our two tanks could hold. This felt good. We now owned enough water to last us a year, no small feat on a dry atoll. The problem was transporting the water from the water tower at the airport to our water tanks. Any suggestions? I asked the clerk at the PUB. He picked up his telephone and after a few minutes he told me that, regrettably, I could not use the fire truck. It was still broken, alas.

A fire truck. This was well beyond my expectations. It was like calling a veterinarian to inquire about a cat's fleas and suddenly finding an ambulance complete with police escort to transport the kitty to the hospital. I was curious, however. "Um . . . what's wrong with the fire truck?" I inquired.

"It can't carry water."

This was an interesting problem for a fire truck on an island without anything like hydrants. Tarawa's lone fire truck was of a certain age and long past its prime. It resided at the airport, where, to satisfy regulatory need, it was trotted out to the edge of the runway to attend to each landing and takeoff. That it could do nothing in case of fire was entirely beside the point. Air Marshall and Air Nauru, the two airlines that occasionally flew to Tarawa, insisted on having a fire truck present to attend to their crashes. And so Kiribati obliges them.

The clerk made another call. I was impressed with how helpful people were. Nothing seemed to work on Tarawa, except the telephone system, which as Kate pointedly noted, was managed by *I-Matangs*, and yet everyone seemed very willing to attend to whatever troubled another, which posed a curious dilemma: If people were so helpful why was Tarawa such a mess?

The clerk asked me where I lived. There are no addresses on Tarawa. There is the one road, called the main road, and it slithers halfway up the atoll, uninterrupted by stoplights or even stop signs. I described where I lived and the clerk asked me whether it was the green house or the pink house. I said the green and he mentioned as much to whomever he was speaking with on the telephone. He hung up and told me that a truck with a water tank would pick me up and haul the water I now so happily owned. It would cost $70.

The truck was a flatbed with a blue tank, the kind often seen in rural areas, used to store fertilizers and pesticides and other things one doesn't want to mix with drinking water. The tank could hold one cubic meter of water and so we would have to make five trips. The driver grunted. "Maybe two trips today. Three another time."

I didn't care. Every morning I approached a neighbor as a supplicant, empty canisters and buckets in hand, and I knew that each drop I took from them brought them that much closer to our own situation. The dishes we used remained barely cleaned. Bathing was done with a sponge. Washing our hair seemed out of the question. The toilet was flushed with buckets of seawater. We still boiled our drinking water, but just for a minute so none was wasted through evaporation. And I was a mess. All the little insignificant cuts I had received turned septic. Sylvia too found herself with a festering mosquito bite that soon began to discharge fluid in ever deepening shades of green. It was impossible to battle the microscopic critters of Tarawa without water. We needed water.

I hopped into the cabin of the truck. We were in search of Abato, the gatekeeper of the water tower. He lived in the village of Bonriki and we found him asleep on his *kie-kie* (sleeping hut). Jobs and sleep seemed to blend easily on Tarawa. He took us to the water tower, unlocked the gate, ran a hose from the tower to the truck, and suddenly water shot through into the tank. My water. Don't spill it, I felt like hissing as the driver struggled to direct the flow into the tank. There was no lid on the tank and as we drove back to the house I dreaded each pothole, each curve, anything that would cause the precious water to slosh and dribble out the top.

"You have a water pump?" the driver asked me.

"Eh?"

"A water pump. We have to pump the water."

"You don't have a pump?" I asked, brilliantly.

"No pump."

We did have a pump, but it was bolted solidly into place and fitted for the pipes that brought the water from the tanks into the house. We contemplated it.

"Do you think . . . ?" I asked him.

"I don't think so," said the driver.

We stood there, our eyes darting back and forth between the

truck and the water tanks. So close. It took the rest of the afternoon to locate a water pump that we could borrow or rent, and when finally we found one at Tarawa's lone hardware store, it was nearly dark. And then, just as we started the portable pump and water began to flow into our tank, a shadow passed above, the sky darkened, and I felt a drop of water, then another, and soon there was a deluge of rain, a tropical downpour of the kind that the island had not seen for more than a year. I became primal man—man need water, man get water—and I scurried around the house, checking the gutters that would stream this clean, fresh rainwater into our tanks, and I became horrified when I saw that the gutter was corroded and that this precious water was flowing uselessly through a gap onto the ground. I ran into the house, grabbed a chair and a notebook, and for the eight minutes that it rained, I stood underneath the gutter, pressing the notebook up to fill the gap, conceding that when one reduces life to its essential needs, it is water that precedes all else.

When the shower passed, the driver was smiling. "Maybe tomorrow it will rain again."

But it didn't rain the next day, nor the day after that, nor did it rain in the following weeks. It didn't rain for months. Tarawa remained parched. The truck became perpetually unavailable and we never saw the other four cubic meters of water. We tracked our water as others track their money. And then, of course, the electricity failed.

At first, it wasn't so bad. For a few hours every couple of days, the ceiling fans would cease their whirling, the water pump would stand idle, and my computer remained off, which was just as well, in case inspiration hit me and I completed my novel in a month or two, and what would I do then? Best to pace myself.

But soon the electricity was off for days at a time and we became dependent for our light on kerosene lanterns, which are extremely useful and easy to use, except when you turn the lever-thing the wrong way and your filament disappears into the kerosene basin and, of course, it's dark so you can't see what you're doing, and inevitably your girlfriend is standing there beside you saying, "What, again?" and you remind her that from the beginning you were very up front about your competence as a handyman.

More troubling than lighting issues, and more irritating than slogging buckets of water from the tank to the house, was trying to sleep without a fan, which we typically had to set to hurricane force for it to become cool enough to sleep. A cinder-block house might be useful to have on the Siberian steppes, but not so on an equatorial atoll devoid of power. The heat was enraging. Rivulets of sweat streaked the body. When I turned, Sylvia would declare: "You're too close. Don't touch me." Throughout the night, no longer softened by the white noise of a whirling ceiling fan, the waves, the booming earth-quaking sound of breaking waves, would cause heart palpitations. Meanwhile, in the absence of our nightly gales, mosquitoes humored themselves with a few flybys, causing us to slap ourselves senseless, until they quietly did their feeding and, as the night progressed, an even tempo would be reached—*buzz-slap-scratch buzz-slap-scratch*.

And then the ants came marching in. Apparently, they found their living quarters in the exterior mortar of the house a little cramped and so they dug through and suddenly we were sharing the bedroom with a billion ants. On that awful dawn, I awoke with a howl to the bites of hundreds of ants clambering all over me, though curiously they left Sylvia alone, which may say something about how ripe I was then. But just as Sylvia began to feel confident that my magnetism within the bug world would save her from the visitations of night creatures, she awoke to find a beetle in her ear. Naturally enough, she wanted to share this news with me, which she did, with considerable aplomb. "There's a bug in my ear," she declared, and indeed there was. It was a coconut beetle, burrowing toward her brain, and this Sylvia wanted removed pronto. It took some work. I tried floating it out with water, but the little bugger was persistent, and so tweezers were needed and I'm pretty sure I got most of it out. Sylvia didn't think it funny when I speculated about eggs.

It wasn't all glum, however. I forged a strong friendship with Buebue, who was the chief electrician on Tarawa. In the United States, when one calls, well, just about any corporate-type organization for any reason at all, one is inevitably left seething after three attempts to navigate the automated customer-service line ("to serve you better") and eighteen hours on hold ("your call is important to us") only to finally be connected with the rude, abrasive morons that the American corporate world feels inclined to use as their link to their customers. And the experience of calling a U.S. government agency, of course, is what leads people to join the Montana militia. On Tarawa, however, a simple call to the power station to determine whether there might be any electricity forthcoming was directed straight to the man who knew all, Buebue, even on his days off, when I would be told to call him at home. He was like an oracle. If Buebue said there was to be light, then there was light. If Buebue said that all would be dark, darkness prevailed. And he didn't spin the situation either. He just told it like it was, which left me bewildered at first, when he explained that there would be no electricity this evening because they forgot to bring the diesel, or because the technicians were too drunk to be trusted around a generator, or because he had absolutely no clue why the generator wasn't working but that he was pretty confident it wasn't going to work for a while yet, or—and this really hurt—the power station in Betio caught fire, reducing Tarawa's power generation capabilities by half and spare parts weren't expected until 2012, but I soon found this brutal candor refreshing.

He was such a nice guy too, always inquiring about Sylvia's welfare and thanking me kindly for wondering about his kids, that I felt guilty as Judas the one night that I took advantage of his obliging nature. We were experiencing rolling blackouts at the time, with each corner of the island taking its turn in darkness, when we heard the exciting news that Australian friends of ours, volunteers, had received in the mail a package containing a videotape of the funeral of Princess Diana, whose death had greatly saddened Tarawa. I cannot quite overstate the importance of this vestige of our own world—what with Elton John and all that—particularly as we were then feeling acutely isolated from happenings of global import, and we immediately set upon procuring a television and VCR and organizing a gathering, complete with scones and jam and a highly prized bottle of sherry, which may strike some as morbid, but for us the videotape was like a revered talisman connecting us to our people and was cause for celebration. Of course, the power went out just as I was about to press the play button, which was highly disappointing and led me to call Buebue. I explained that the *I-Matang* community was present in our house and that they had clustered here to mourn Princess Diana, and could we please, please have some electricity, particularly since we were expecting the Australian high commissioner, which wasn't true at all, since the Australian high commissioner was an uptight nitwit who carried on as if he were assigned to London, not Tarawa, which for diplomats is, frankly, an assignment portending the end of one's career. However, I dropped his name because Australian foreign aid pretty much comprises the entirety of the government budget of Kiribati and, therefore, I thought it likely that the Public Utility Board could be browbeaten by mentioning the Australian high commissioner and his need for electricity-driven entertainment. This turned out to be true and we watched and mourned and speculated about Dodi while the rest of Tarawa remained dark. I have felt guilty ever since.

CHAPTER 9

*In which the Author seeks wisdom on the ways of Tarawa
from Tiabo.*

W hen I was a youngster, I often found myself in conversations that began with, *If you were stuck on a deserted
island, what ten . . .* And then we would spend hours listing the
absolutely essential can't-live-without-them top ten records, or
books, or, as we discovered the delusions of adolescence, girls we
needed to make our stay on a deserted island an enjoyable one. As the
years went by, the lists changed. Iron Maiden was no longer essential
listening, but The Smiths were, until they too were tossed off in favor
of Fugazi, which was soon discarded to make room for Massive
Attack. After crossing off Elizabeth and Carla and Becky, I settled on
the woman I wanted to live with on a deserted island, and so this just
left books and CDs. As I packed, I was acutely aware of the importance of bringing just the right combination to ensure that no matter
what my musical or literary desire, I would have just what I needed,
right here on my deserted island. True, Tarawa wasn't actually
deserted. In fact, it was overpopulated. But there were no bookstores
or record stores, and so I packed as if I were departing for Pluto. For
books, it was a mixture of authors we were both likely to enjoy
(Philip Roth), combined with a few books we were unlikely to ever
read unless stuck on a deserted island (*Ulysses*), as well as a couple of
compromise authors (the novelist Anne Tyler for her, the Polish

journalist Ryszard Kapuściński for me). As CDs are lighter, I packed thirty-odd discs that I felt could comprehensively meet any likely musical desire. Did I feel funky? Well, we could go to Sly Stone or the Beastie Boys. Did I want to kick back and chill? Mazzy Star was there to help me. Did I wish I was in Paris, walking on a rain-slicked cobblestone alley on a drizzling October evening? Miles Davis would take me there. Was I up for a bout of brooding? Hello Chopin's Nocturnes. Was I feeling a little romantic, a little melancholic? Cesaria Evora would tell me to pull up a chair and have a cigarette.

I was thinking about these CDs a few months later, when once again I was being driven to the brink of insanity by an ear-shattering, 120-beat-a-minute rendition of "La Macarena," the only song ever played on Tarawa. It was everywhere. If I was in a minibus, overburdened as always with twentysome people and a dozen fish, hurtling down the road at a heart-stopping speed, the driver was inevitably blasting a beat-enhanced version of "La Macarena" that looped over and over again. If I was drinking with a few of the soccer players who kindly let me demonstrate my mediocrity on the soccer field with them, our piss-up in one of the seedy dives in Betio would occur to the skull-racking jangle of "La Macarena." If I happened across some teenage boys who had gotten their hands on an old Japanese boom box, they were undoubtedly loitering to a faint and tinny "La Macarena."

What finally brought me to the brink was the recent acquisition of a boom box by the family that lived across the road. One of their members, a seaman, had just returned from two years at sea and, as is the custom, every penny he earned that was not spent on debauchery in a distant port of call was used for expensive gifts for his family. Typically this took the form of televisions, VCRs, and stereos, all unavailable in Kiribati. A few shops had begun renting pirated movies sent up from Fiji. These movies were typically recorded by a video camera in a movie theater, with the result that the actors' faces appeared strangely dull and elongated, as if the movie was filmed by El Greco. Audience members could be seen stretching and heard coughing. If renting a movie, one made sure to avoid comedies since you could hardly hear a word over the laughter and chatter of those fortunate enough to see the movie in a theater. "Could you keep it down," you find yourself telling the screen. But while you could locate copies of *Titanic* and *Forrest Gump* on Tarawa, there was little music available beyond "La Macarena." I know because I looked. I looked everywhere. I looked everywhere because I forgot our CDs in my mother's garage in Washington, thousands and thousands of miles away.

It is difficult to convey the magnitude of this catastrophe. I would have been very pleased if I had forgotten my sweaters, which were already rotting in a closet, or my shoes, which within a month had turned green with mold. Each day I stared forlornly at our stereo, which we had purchased for an outrageous sum of money from Kate, who had bought it from her predecessor. "If you don't want it," Kate said, "there are plenty of others here who do." No doubt this was true, and we forked over a large amount of bills. Every day at noon, I turned the stereo on to listen to the broadcast from Radio Australia, which Radio Kiribati carried for ten minutes, while they searched for yet another version of "La Macarena" to play for the remainder of the day. Radio Australia claimed to deliver the international news, but you wouldn't know it from listening. Presumably, the world was as tumultuous as ever, but inevitably the lead story on Radio Australia would involve a kangaroo and a dingo in Wagga Wagga, followed by a nine-minute play-by-play summary of the Australian cricket team's triumph over England. And then it was back to "La Macarena."

I had sent a fax to my mother, asking her to mail the box of CDs. *They're right beside the ski boots,* I wrote. A few days later, we received a fax from her. The CDs were in the mail, she assured us. They were sent by super-duper express mail and would arrive any day. The months ticked by.

In a fit of despair, I went to the Angirota Store and bought *Wayne Newton's Greatest Hits* and *Melanesian Love Songs*. When I put in the Wayne Newton tape, the stereo emitted a primal groan and ate the tape. It was trying to tell me something, I felt. The stereo was more amenable to *Melanesian Love Songs*. With the moon shimmering over the ocean, Sylvia and I listened to Melanesian love ballads—*You cost me two pigs, woman/ I expect you to work/ While I spend my days/ drinking kava under the banyan tree.*

With musical selections reduced to *Melanesian Love Songs* and "La Macarena," I began to yearn for power failures. When these occurred the techno thump of "La Macarena" would cease, and soon the air would be filled with the soft cadences of ancient songs sweetly delivered by honeyed voices. The I-Kiribati are a remarkably musical people. Everyone sings. There is something arresting about seeing a tough-looking teenage boy suddenly put a flower behind his ear and begin to croon. Everyone sings well too, so it was a mystery to me why their taste in recorded music was so awful.

Sadly, on many days the power remained on, sometimes for hours at a time, and I would be reduced to an imbecilic state by the endless playing of "La Macarena." It was hot. My novel—and this is a small understatement—was not going very well. My disposition was not enhanced by "La Macarena." I wondered if I could simply walk across the road and kindly ask the neighbors to shut the fucking music off.

Small matters tend to be complex matters in Kiribati. Fortunately, I had Tiabo, our housekeeper, to turn to for guidance. I had been wrong about Tiabo. While it is true she did not direct any come-hither glances my way, she did undulate. She moved with the languorous hip sway of a large woman in the tropics. Two mornings a week, she arrived to clean the house. I felt deeply uncomfortable about this at first, but after some long rationalizations, I convinced myself that there was nothing intrinsically exploitive about the arrangement. She was a single mother, without connections or education. She needed a job. We had a job for her. She was paid well. She conducted herself with dignity. I treated her with respect, and with time we became friends. On her other days, she worked at the FSP office, where Sylvia soon promoted her from cleaning lady to managing the seed distribution program. As it was considered scandalous for a woman to be in a house alone with a man, particularly an *I-Matang*, who were well known for groping their housegirls, Tiabo often arrived with her sister Reibo. It was after one little incident when it occurred to me that I needed to watch what I said in Kiribati.

"Reibo," I said. "Have you by chance seen a twenty-dollar bill lying around? I thought I had left it in the basket."

"No," she said. Reibo spoke very little English. Each month, I acquired a little more I-Kiribati, but when my language ability failed, which was often, I usually spoke in English, Reibo replied in I-Kiribati, and we understood each other perfectly. Or so I thought.

Later that afternoon, Ruiti, the FSP accountant, stopped by the house. "Tiabo and Reibo are very upset," she said. This worried me. Had I done something obscene or disrespectful? I was sure I hadn't. Nevertheless, misunderstandings do occur, and I began to worry about being besieged by the male members of their family demanding some particularly gruesome form of island justice. But I was certain I had done nothing wrong or untoward. I had no idea why Tiabo and Reibo might be upset.

"They say you accused Reibo of stealing twenty dollars. They are crying. They are very ashamed."

Oh, dear.

Stealing, I was told, was a major offense in I-Kiribati culture. I could see why. There is absolutely no good reason for stealing in

Kiribati. This is because of the *bubuti* system. In the *bubuti* system, someone can walk up to you and say *I bubuti you for your flipflops*, and without a peep of complaint you are obliged to hand over your flipflops. The following day, you can go up to the guy who is now wearing your flipflops, and say *I bubuti you for your fishing net*, and suddenly you have a new fishing net. In such a way, Kiribati remains profoundly egalitarian.

I-Matangs can choose to play along. I know one volunteer, determined to go native as they say, who lost her shoes, her bicycle, her hat, most of her clothing, and a good deal of her monthly stipend to the *bubuti*. She was a little dim, however, and it never occurred to her to *bubuti* others, and so she spent her days walking barefoot, with a sunburned scalp, dressed in rags, wondering how on earth she was going to afford her daily fish.

One day, a man, a complete stranger to me, walked up to the door and politely said: "I *bubuti* you for bus fare." Warily, still attuned to big-city panhandlers, I gave it to him. As the *bubutis* rolled in, however, I felt no obligation to comply. Pocket change, sure. The FSP pickup truck, no. It was my ability, or rather the *I-Matang*'s ability to say no to a *bubuti*, that made foreigners useful on Tarawa. Because of the *bubuti* system, the I-Kiribati tend to avoid seeking positions of power. This was made clear to me when I met Airan, a young Australian-educated employee of the Bank of Kiribati. He was one of a dozen or so Young Turks on Tarawa, benefactors of Australian scholarships and groomed by the Western aid industry to be a future leader. He was, however, miserable. He had just been promoted to assistant manager.

"This is very bad," he said.

"Why?" I asked. "That's excellent news."

"No. People will come to me with *bubuti*. They will *bubuti* me for money. They will *bubuti* me for jobs. It is very difficult."

Jobs are fleeting. Cultural demands are not. Airan begged not to be promoted, and so the management of the Bank of Kiribati remained in *I-Matang* hands. The *bubuti* system was why FSP always had an *I-Matang* director. Sylvia's presence ensured that the organization would not crumble under the demands of the *bubuti* system, which is exactly what occurred when the only other international nongovernmental organization to work in Kiribati decided to localize. Its project funds were soon gobbled up in a flurry of *bubutis* and the organization dissolved. Within the *bubuti* system, outright stealing is regarded as a perfidious offense, though this didn't stop someone from stealing my running shoes.

Tiabo and Reibo arrived again in the evening. They were still sobbing.

"Reibo said she did not steal twenty dollars," Tiabo explained. "But if you think she did, you must fire us."

"No, no, no," I said. "Really, I was just wondering where it was. I found it later in my pocket."

Tiabo explained this to Reibo, who began to beam. I did not actually ever find the errant twenty dollars, but I crumble when confronted by tears.

As I continued to be flailed by "La Macarena," I took small comfort in the fact that at least no one on Tarawa had ever seen the video, and I was therefore spared the sight of an entire nation spending their days line dancing. Still, the song grated, and I asked Tiabo if she thought it was permissible for me to ask the neighbors to turn the music down. I did not care if I was polite or not, but I did want to avoid antagonizing the household's youth. They were not in school. They did not work. The traditional rigors of subsistence living did not fully occupy them on Tarawa. And like elsewhere in the world, idle youth have a way of being immensely irritating.

"In Kiribati, we don't do that," Tiabo said.

"Why not?" I asked. "I would think that loud noise would bother people."

"This is true. But we don't ask people to be quiet."

I found this perplexing. Kiribati is a fairly complex society with all sorts of unspoken rules that seek to minimize any potential sources of conflict. Who has the right to harvest a particular coconut tree, for instance, involves an elaborate scheme in which the oldest son has that right for the first year, and then relinquishes it to the next eldest, and so on, until it loops around again, and then it's the turn of the first son of the eldest brother, and on and on, with the result that no one feels slighted or deprived. Then it occurred to me that the repeated playing of a dreadful song like "La Macarena" at provocatively loud levels is an entirely new problem for Kiribati. In the United States, we have more than seventy years of experience in dealing with noisy neighbors. After much experimentation, we now resort to a friendly, *Turn it down, asshole*. This is greeted with a polite *Fuck you*, which is followed by a call to the police, who arrive to issue a citation, and once again peace and tranquility are restored. Noise pollution in Kiribati, however, hasn't been around long enough for the I-Kiribati to develop such a sophisticated form of conflict resolution. It was like many of the problems on Tarawa. The problems were new and imported, yet the culture remained old and unvarying.

This thought occurred to me again when I began to notice with no small amount of disgust the sudden appearance of a large number of soiled diapers scattered around the house. They had been thoughtfully deposited there by dogs, who had picked them up from the reef, and happily emptied them of their contents. I will not hear another word about the alleged intelligence of dogs. A soiled diaper is like catnip for dogs. They are ravenous for them, and what the dogs didn't ingest, they left in disturbing little piles around the house.

Disposable diapers should have been banned on Tarawa, as they are on a number of other islands in the Pacific. Their availability on the island was a new and disagreeable development. Tarawa lacked a waste management system. There was no need for one until a few years ago, when goods began to arrive packaged in luminous and indestructible material. Before, bags were made of pandanus leaves, food was encased in fish scales, and a drink was held inside a coconut. When you were done, you simply dropped its remains where you stood, and nature took care of the rest. Now, however, bags were increasingly made of plastic, food was found in tins, drinks sloshed inside cans, and sadly, poop resided in diapers, but, unlike the continental world, there is no place to put the resulting trash. There is no room on an atoll for a landfill, and even if one did bury mounds of garbage, it would soon pollute the groundwater, which on Tarawa was already contaminated by interesting forms of life. Waste disposal on an overcrowded island like Tarawa was an enormous problem, and while governments elsewhere in the world could be expected to do something about it, the government of Kiribati carried on as it always did, blithely passing the time in between drinking binges.

Actually, that's not fair. They did do something about it. Once upon a time there was a can recycling program. Kids gathered all the beer cans that were strewn about the island, and there were many, and carried them to a privately owned recycling center, which had a can crusher that molded the cans into exportable cubes. The kids were paid. The beer cans were recycled in Australia. Excellent program, one would think. Income was generated. Trash was disposed of in a pleasantly green sort of manner. But then the government, displaying the brain power of a learning-impaired anemone, decided to institute an export tax. Never mind that the product being exported was the rubbish that was fouling the island, the government, as a minister explained to me, "deserved its cut." He sounded like a Staten Island capo. The tax put the can recycling program out of business. The island remains awash in beer cans.

Beer cans, however, are merely unsightly, whereas soiled diapers are repulsive, particularly for those who are unrelated to the soiler. I grabbed a stick and collected the diapers, placing them in the rusty oil drum we used as a burn bin. Without other alternatives for waste disposal, we burned everything—plastic, Styrofoam, paper, even the expired medicine we found in the cabinet, a tangible catalogue of the ailments that bedeviled Sylvia's predecessors. In case anyone was wondering what they should do with an old asthma inhaler, I can state with some authority that throwing it into a fire is not a good idea, unless you are prepared to spend the rest of the day deaf and bewildered from the subsequent explosion. As I doused the diapers with a generous amount of kerosene, Tiabo came by to see what I was up to.

"You are going to burn the nappies?" she asked.

"Yes," I said.

"You cannot do that."

"I am fairly certain that I can burn the nappies."

"You must not burn the nappies."

"Why?"

"Because you will burn the baby's bum."

This gave me pause. As I stood with match in hand, I did a quick mental inventory to see if I missed something. I checked the tattered remains of the diapers a little more thoroughly. There were, as far as I could see, no babies in the diapers. I pointed this out to Tiabo.

"It does not matter," she said. "If you burn the diapers you will burn the baby's bum."

Tiabo scooped out the diapers and returned them to the reef. I was baffled. I am very fond of babies, and under no circumstances would I ever wish for any harm to come to a baby's bottom, but I was mystified here. Somewhere between cause and effect I was lost.

"Tiabo," I said. "I don't understand how burning diapers will lead to a scorched baby bum."

"In Kiribati," Tiabo explained, "we believe that if you burn someone's . . . um, how do you say it?"

"Shit," I offered.

"Yes," she giggled. "If you burn someone's shit, it is like burning a person's bum."

To readers, I wish to apologize for the frequent references to all things scatological, but such is life on Tarawa. I tried resorting to cold, heartless, Western logic.

"Tiabo," I said. "I can prove to you that burning diapers will not harm the babies. We can do an experiment. I will burn the diapers, and you listen for the wail of babies."

Tiabo was aghast. "No!"

"I swear. No babies will be harmed."

"Yes they will. You are a bad *I-Matang*."

I did not want to be a bad *I-Matang*. I thought of myself as a good *I-Matang*, a good *I-Matang* who happened to be at wit's end. "But, Tiabo, something has to be done. It's not healthy to live surrounded by dirty diapers."

She pondered this for a moment. Then she came up with an idea. "I will make a sign," she said.

On a piece of cardboard, she wrote something in I-Kiribati. The only words I understood were *tabu* and *I-Matang*. "What does it say?" I asked.

"It is forbidden to throw diapers on the reef here. All diapers found will be burned by the *I-Matang*."

"That's good. Will it work?"

"I think so."

We posted the sign on a coconut tree near the reef. The real test came on a Sunday. Due to their expense, diapers are used sparingly, and it was only on Sundays when mothers resorted to their use. The churches in Kiribati are, without exception, shamelessly coercive. It mattered not whether it was the Catholic Church or the Protestant

Church or the Mormon Church or the Church of God, or any other of the innumerable churches to have set up shop on Tarawa; if a family found itself unable to pay their monthly tithe to their church, which typically took 30 percent of their meager income, they were called up to the front of the church by their pastors and loudly castigated for their failure to pay God His due. And woe to the mother who decides to skip the four-hour service to stay home and tend to a newborn.

On a Sunday afternoon, after the churches had released their flocks, I was pleasantly surprised to see a woman approach the reef with her child's morning output, pause for moment to read the sign, and turn around, no doubt searching for someplace where she could be assured that her baby's poop would be spared the flame. That's right, lady. Not In My Backyard.

I GREW MORE appreciative of Tiabo. She was helping me along, conscious of the realities of Kiribati and the foolishness of the *I-Matang*, and it was not long before I began to feel at ease on Tarawa. I felt I understood its rhythms and peculiarities. I was adapting. Sylvia and I were temporary residents on the island, visitors really, and as much as we could we adjusted to island life. Here and there, we drew certain lines—the outrageous *bubuti*, the diapers in the backyard—but mostly we shrugged our shoulders and accepted that that's just the way it goes here. It's their island. Sylvia, of course, spent her days encouraging the I-Kiribati to manage their islands a little more thoughtfully, and were it not for the enthusiasm and good sense of her staff, she would have been brought to the brink of despair, but there is only so much a foreigner can do on Tarawa. It's their island.

And so when a man walked by the window and gave me a friendly *mauri* as I stared miserably at my computer screen, I turned to Tiabo and said: "You know, Tiabo, I think I have adapted to Kiribati."

She gave me a quizzical look.

"You see," I said, "in my country if a very large man wearing only a tiny lavalava were to walk through my backyard while carrying an enormous machete, I would be worried. I would probably call the police. But here, I just give a friendly wave."

Tiabo looked upon me as if I was irredeemably stupid. She sighed.

"He is only walking here because you are an *I-Matang*. He does not respect you."

"Oh."

"He would not walk on this land if I-Kiribati people lived here."

"Oh."

I had noticed that when people visited one another, they would first yell out from the road, announcing their presence. I had assumed it was because of the dogs.

"I see," I said. "What would happen if that man had walked by and I-Kiribati people lived here?"

"They would kill him."

Well. That seemed a mite severe. I thought of the hundreds of I-Kiribati I could have killed. Lucky for everyone that I was blissfully ignorant. I was vigilant when it came to nighttime prowlers, but I was unaware that those who walked by during the day were also slighting me. But no more. Now that I knew that my manhood was being dissed, I resolved to do something about it. I did not think I was capable of murder, but I felt that I could at least look like I was capable of murder. The next time a man walked near the house I fixed him with an ice-cold stare, every muscle coiled with barely contained violence, and I felt pretty confident that my body language expressed contempt and agitation, and if this trespasser did not leave now he would meet his end, and it would be swift and merciless. The trespasser, for that is now how I thought of him, rather than as a friendly villager, met my gaze and quickly his smile turned into an expression of savage hostility, and that's when I noticed that he was an extremely muscular man and that he was carrying a machete, and that he did, in fact, look like he was capable of murder.

"*Mauri*," I said, with a friendly wave. My smile wrapped around my head. I wondered if he might like a glass of water.

Tiabo shook her head sadly. She turned to the man and began to yell at him, chasing him off.

Clearly, Tiabo was not much impressed with my manliness. It did not help when several weeks later I returned from a short snorkeling expedition beyond the reef. The tide had been exceptionally high and for a half hour or so, when the tide was no longer surging, but not yet receding, the breakers had been reduced to flat water. I was curious about the coral and fish life beyond the house, and so I donned my mask and flippers and swam out. By now, I was no longer worried about sharks. I often saw a man swim out with a long spear. Inevitably, he returned a short while later with a half-dozen fish tied around his waist. This could only mean that he possessed an astonishingly small brain, or that this particular slice of reef was devoid of sharks.

Past the break zone, the reef wall descended about forty feet, where it plateaued. Fifty yards farther, the reef plummeted into a blue-black void. As I snorkeled, I hugged the initial drop, periodically emerging to see what the waves were doing. I was pleasantly surprised to see live coral. It was nothing to rave about, a clump here, a branch there, some brain coral, a few splashes of color on an abused reef. Elsewhere the color was provided by those with advanced degrees in marketing and package engineering. There was rubbish everywhere, cans and rags and diapers listlessly swaying in the current. Swimming through and around this garbage were parrotfish and Great Trevallies and longnose emperors, some quite big. It was disheartening seeing what was being done to their habitat. Above an outburst of brain coral I saw a lionfish, a magnificent and exceedingly poisonous fish. I dived to get a closer look, and as I did so I nearly blew out my sphincter. I had dived directly on top of a shark.

In my panic, I filled my lungs with water. Then I began to flail and kick and otherwise behave like weak and injured shark fodder. I was out of sorts. Jittery adrenaline bursts are not helpful when you happen to be in deep water with lungs full of seawater. I had no idea what the shark was doing. I was too busy drowning. For all I knew, it was having a cup of tea, merrily watching me die, which saved him the trouble of having to kill me before he set to work dismembering me limb by limb. Then I heard that little voice that has saved me so often in the past—*relax, get a grip, swim up, clear your lungs, breathe, and get the hell out of the water, you twit.*

There is nothing quite so disconcerting as having your head above water as the rest of your body dangles below the surface, knowing that there is a shark near, a shark with which you have had an interaction, and not knowing exactly how the shark feels about the interaction. Did I make him mad? Did I make him hungry?

Apparently I had frightened the shark. And it is no wonder. I was twice as big as he was. With my mask back on I could see it swimming rapidly away. It was only about three feet long, a young reef shark. Nevertheless, as I swam back to shore I kept glancing back. Did he rush off to tell his parents? Was papa shark looking for me?

I was breathless by the time I entered the house. My heart was still going thump-thump-thump. Between gasps, I shared my adventure with Tiabo.

"There was a shark . . . *pant, pant* . . . boy oh boy . . . never seen a shark before . . . *pant, pant* . . ."

"You are scared of *te* shark?" Tiabo asked with raised eyebrows.

"Yes, of course, I am scared of *te* shark."

"Ha, ha," Tiabo laughed. "The *I-Matang* is scared of *te* shark. I-Kiribati people are not scared of *te* shark."

"That's because I-Kiribati people are crazy people."

She laughed mirthfully. She had another story for the *maneaba*.

AS THE MONTHS went by and "La Macarena" was etched deeper and deeper into my consciousness, I became increasingly despondent that our package of CDs would never arrive. With each incoming flight I biked to the airport, hoping desperately that our package was on board. The arrival of the Air Nauru plane, the last plane to fly to Tarawa, after Air Marshall finally canceled their service, had become an erratic occurrence. Often weeks passed between flights.

Nauru, a one-island nation of eight thousand people, once had six Boeing 737s. They did not need six planes, of course. But flush with the cash generated by the mining of their phosphate deposits, Nauru set about looking for creative outlets to squander their money. This included financing Broadway shows, supporting the lifestyles of every con man between Taiwan and Costa Rica, buying the world's most overvalued properties, and maintaining a fleet of six Boeing 737s. No one on Nauru actually worked. The mining of their island was done by I-Kiribati laborers under Australian management. Instead, Nauruans spent their time becoming grotesquely fat. In this they were successful. They are officially the fattest people on the planet. Their planes, when not requisitioned by the wives of ministers who needed them for their global shopping sprees, were often used to ferry Nauruans to Australia, where they obtained the treatment they needed for adult-onset diabetes.

The good times, however, came to a crashing end. The phosphate deposits are nearly gone. The island has been thoroughly

ruined. It is nothing more than a desolate moonscape. And the Nauruans have nothing to show for it. They have destroyed their country and wasted its wealth. The planes have been sold off, leaving just
the one leased 737. The Broadway shows have closed. The property
they own around the world has been allowed to rot. A half-dozen
cities are littered with abandoned buildings owned by Nauru. A new
government takes power approximately every four months, and
during their short terms they do their best to gobble up what
remains of Nauru's cash. Today, the country exists as an international pariah. Nauru has become the global epicenter for money
laundering. One would think that by opening up its country to the
Russian mafia, Colombian drug lords, African warlords, and Middle
Eastern terrorists, Nauru would at least be getting a tidy cut of the
loot. But this is not so. Nauru receives no more than a few thousand
dollars in shell-company registration fees and mere pennies for
washing the money through its system. Clearly, the fat has settled on
their brains. Nauru is the most pathetic country on Earth. Try as I
might to feel sorry for them, I cannot manage anything better than
contempt. The tragedy of this, of course, was that I was dependent
on Nauru to bring me relief from "La Macarena."

Seven long months passed. Once or twice a month, depending on
whether Air Nauru had arrived, I biked to the airport, where I
searched among the delivered packages for our precious music. The
trip was inevitably dispiriting. Not only were the CDs nowhere to be
seen, there were often boxes sent from Australia covered in bright red
signs: URGENT MEDICINE INSIDE KEEP REFRIGERATED DELIVER
IMMEDIATELY TO HOSPITAL. Three weeks later the boxes would still be
there, in the suffocating heat. It was tragically typical. A Western
donor sends urgently needed medicine, but the government cannot
manage to pick it up. I offered to deliver it myself, but the clerks
would not release the medicine to me. And so it went to waste.

Then, one day the stars aligned, the gods smiled, and as I rummaged among the packages I saw with indescribable happiness my mother's distinctive handwriting. Oh, the sweet joy of it. I claimed the package, stuffed it my backpack, and biked like the wind.

"Tiabo," I said, full of glee. "You must help me."

She eyed me suspiciously as I plundered through our box of CDs.

"You must tell me which song, in your opinion, do you find to be the most offensive."

"What?" she asked wearily.

"I want you to tell me which song is so terrible that the I-Kiribati will cover their ears and beg me to turn it off."

"You are a strange *I-Matang.*"

I popped in the Beastie Boys' *Check Your Head.* I forwarded it to the song "Gratitude," which is an abrasive and highly aggressive song.

"What do think?" I yelled.

"I like it."

Damn.

I moved on to Nirvana's *Lithium.* I was sure that grunge-metal-punk would not find a happy audience on an equatorial atoll.

"It's very good," Tiabo said.

Now I was stumped. I tried a different tack. I inserted Rach-maninoff.

"I don't like this," Tiabo said.

Now we were getting somewhere.

"Okay, Tiabo. How about this?"

We listened to a few minutes of *La Bohème.* Even I felt a little dis-combobulated listening to an opera on Tarawa.

"That's very bad," Tiabo said.

"Why?"

"I-Kiribati people like fast music. This is too slow and the singing is very bad."

"Good, good. How about this?"

I played *Kind of Blue* by Miles Davis.

"That's terrible. Ugh . . . stop it."

Tiabo covered her ears.

Bingo.

I moved the speakers to the open door.

"What are you doing?" Tiabo asked.

I turned up the volume. For ten glorious minutes Tarawa was bathed in the melancholic sounds of Miles Davis. Tiabo stood shocked. Her eyes were closed. Her fingers plugged her ears. I had high hopes that the entire neighborhood was doing likewise.

Finally, I turned it off. I listened to the breakers. I heard the rustling of the palm fronds. A pig squealed. But I did not hear "La Macarena."

Victory.

"Thank you, Tiabo. That was wonderful."

"You are a very strange *I-Matang.*"

CHAPTER 10

In which the Author recounts the arrival of the I-Matang, who introduced fair Trade (say, one bead for three women), the Wonders of Civilization (tobacco, alcohol, cannons), the Maxims of Christianity (Thou shalt wear thy Mother Hubbard, never mind the heat), and Modern Administration (Queen Victoria knows what's best for you), which has resulted in a Colonial Legacy, as evidenced by the continued use of the fathom as a unit of measurement.

The first westerners to stumble across the islands of Kiribati were Spanish mutineers. They murdered their captain, Hernando de Grijalva, in 1537 after months of desultory sailing across the vast, seemingly boundless Pacific Ocean. Theirs had been a voyage of exploration, and just like Magellan in 1521, de Grijalva and his crew had pretty much missed every island in the Pacific, except for two, which they called the Unfortunate Islands. One can only imagine their disappointment, having rounded the Horn, endured mountainous seas and the searing doldrums, only to discover *nada* except for two islands so pitiful that their very existence was deemed regrettable.

De Grijalva then decided to head toward California. Sadly for him, the winds drove him back, and when he refused the crew's pleas to run with the wind to the Moluccas, they killed him. While following the equator, the mutinous crew was racked with scurvy and mad with hunger, and yet they did not stop at the two islands they encountered, which they called Acea and Isla de los Pescadores (Island of the Fishermen). It is probable that Acea was Christmas Island, then uninhabited and awaiting a visit from Captain Cook two centuries later, and that Isla de los Pescadores was Nonouti, four islands south of Tarawa in the Gilbert group. No doubt worries about finding a safe anchorage dissuaded the crew from attempting to land anywhere near an uncharted coral atoll, but still, as someone with an affection for the islands, I can't help but feel a little miffed by this. Surely, some trade could have been attempted with the I-Kiribati fishermen they saw. Coconuts are useful for treating scurvy. Maybe they could have pretended to be gods, though as Captain Cook learned, this could lead to problems. Instead, the crew kept sailing, dying one by one from their deprivations, until finally the seven remaining survivors arrived in New Guinea, where the natives promptly sold them into slavery. The mutineers could be heard muttering: "Hey, Pepe . . . Isla de los Pescadores . . . what was wrong with it again?"

Nor did the next Spaniard to sail this way bother stopping. This would be Pedro Fernandez de Quiros on Spain's final great voyage of exploration in the Pacific. He spotted Butaritari, in the northern Gilberts, and called it Buen Viaje, but apparently the *viaje* wasn't *buen* enough to risk losing his ship on the reefs. And that was pretty much the end of contact between the *I-Matang* and the I-Kiribati for the next two hundred years.

In the two and a half centuries that passed after Magellan's crossing, only five expeditions cruised the Central Pacific, discovering a mere six islands and it is a wonder that it wasn't fewer. One can see the prominent hills of Samoa and Hawaii from many miles away, but to see one of the low-lying atolls of the equatorial Pacific one has to be very close. Ships that had the misfortune of stumbling upon an atoll at night found themselves desperately tacking away from the ominous sounds of a reef-breaking surf.

One gets the sense that after a few months of sailing the great emptiness of the Central Pacific, where no land exists save the occasional boat-chomping atoll, captains simply gave up looking for anything interesting. *After much Traversing of the Equatorial Pacific,* one can imagine a captain writing in his journal, *in which we were often Tormented by Heat and frequently Becalmed, I have decided in the interest of Scientific Curiosity to Examine more Thoroughly the Peculiar Mating Rituals of native women in Tahiti.*

Without recourse to the Global Satellite Positioning system, or—at least until well into the nineteenth century—an accurate chronometer to determine their longitude, it behooved captains to stay close to the known routes across the Pacific. As early as the sixteenth century, Spanish galleons laden with gold made frequent crossings between Mexico and the Philippines. By the late eighteenth century, there was a bustling fur trade between China and the Northwest United States. But this movement of ships occurred far to the north of Kiribati, which bestrides the equator where maddening doldrums sap the spirits of even the most well-provisioned ships. Sailors learned to fear the heat and windless stagnation of the equatorial Pacific as much as the towering seas of the Roaring Forties in the Southern Ocean. Commodore John Bryon, known as "Foul-Weather Jack"—a name which suggests that he was not easily disturbed by weather—wrote that when he was off the coast of Nikunau in the southern Gilberts, the heat of the doldrums had caused his crew to be "seized by the flux." I could relate. I too often felt seized by the flux.

It was the settlement of Port Jackson in 1788 that finally brought a few ships to Kiribati. Port Jackson, which was to become Sydney, was where England sent its unlucky people. I am not exactly sure why they did this. It seems to me a lot of bother to ship thousands of petty criminals from one side of the planet to the other. And it's not as if they were just dropped off there and told to fend for themselves. No, they were placed in dank, wretched prisons that were similar to the dank, wretched prisons back in merry old England. What was the point? Plus, as the medal tallies at subsequent Olympics suggest, England managed to ship out its entire gene pool of athletes.

Nonetheless, it was this movement of convicts that initiated the first real contact between the *I-Matang* and the I-Kiribati. Once ships had divested themselves of the English convicts who would one day become the hale, hearty Australians who regularly whup English arse on the playing fields, a few headed toward China on what became known as the Outer Passage. The more direct route between Australia and China was fraught with reefs and islands, whereas the Outer Passage contained uncharted reefs and islands, which made sailing on a wooden boat particularly interesting.

In 1788, after delivering the very first convicts to Sydney Cove, Capt. Thomas Gilbert of the *Charlotte* and Capt. John Marshall of the *Scarborough* were chartered by the East India Company to ferry tea from China to England. On the way, they passed Aranuka, Kuria, Abaiang, Tarawa, and Butaritari. Gilbert and Marshall decided to call these islands the Gilbert Islands. They did this because they could. The next island group they encountered to the north was called the Marshall Islands. Why not, they figured. In the 1820s, the name *Gilbert Islands* was validated by the Russian cartographer Adam von Krusenstern, and so to this very day, the islands retain the name of Gilbert, which I think is a great shame. When it comes to naming things, vanity and flattery are dull motivations best suited for deciding on a child's middle name. Much more interesting are the descriptive names that suggest a story or happening of interest. Captain Cook was pretty good about this. From him, we have Cape

Good Success, Cape Deceit, Cape Desolation, Adventure Cove, Devil's Basin, Great Black Rock, and Little Black Rock, all in Tierra del Fuego, names that suggest that rounding Cape Horn in the late eighteenth century was probably a fairly up and down experience. So too was getting stuck within the Great Barrier Reef—Cape Tribulation, Thirsty Sound, Isle of Direction, Wednesday Island, Thursday Island, and finally, Providential Channel. In New Zealand, Captain Cook was good enough to leave us with Hen and Chicken Island, Cape Kidnappers, Poverty Bay, Murderer's Bay, Cannibal Cove, Cape Runaway (clearly, this was an eventful trip), and, my favorite, Young Nick's Head. In 1777, Cook found himself spending Christmas on an uninhabited atoll, and so it was inevitable that he would call it Christmas Island, the only island he visited that would one day become part of Kiribati. The crew caught fish and turtles, but Cook was not much impressed with Christmas Island. "A few Cocoa nut trees were seen in two or three places, but in general the land had a very barren appearance." No doubt, early Pacific explorers came to the same conclusion, which is why Christmas Island would remain uninhabited until well into the modern era.

Gilbert and Marshall were a little more taken by what they saw, particularly the I-Kiribati sailing canoes, which Marshall called "lively, ingenious and expert." Still, they could not persuade the I-Kiribati to come aboard, nor did they think it wise to seek an anchorage. With no reason to tarry, they sailed on to China, which they called Gilbertland. In 1799, the explorer George Bass, traveling aboard the *Nautilus*, reached Tabiteuea and Abemama. He described the I-Kiribati as "a brown, handsome and courteous people." James Cary, captain of the American ship *Rose*, wrote of his encounter with the I-Kiribati off Tamana in 1804: "By their behavior, we suppose they never saw foreigners before. They were inoffensive and knew not the use of firearms and seemed pleased with the reception they met with from us."

By 1826, when the American whaler *John Palmer* alighted upon Beru and Onotoa, all of the Gilbert Islands had encountered, in one manner or another, the world of the *I-Matang*. These first encounters were almost always benign, though they no doubt left the I-Kiribati perplexed. In the book *Kiribati—Aspects of History*, which is the only book on Kiribati written by I-Kiribati, Ahling Onorio recounts the arrival of the *I-Matang* on Makin:

> It is said on Makin that the coming of the I-Matang was foretold many days before the actual voyage by old men who could interpret signs in the rafters of the maneaba, which was then under construction. When the strange sailing ship approached the island, the people were frightened and called upon Tabuariki (the god of thunder) to cause a great storm to blow the ship away. It is said that Tabuariki succeeded two times in preventing the ship from approaching Makin, but the third time the ship arrived safely and anchored off the island.
>
> The people of Makin were both frightened and astounded at what they saw. They had their weapons ready, but were mostly curious about the strange object. Because of its U-shape, they called the boat "te ruarua" (babai *pit*), and when several boats were lowered into the sea they exclaimed "te ruarua *has given birth*." When several oars came out from the sides of the boats, the bewildered people shouted, "Look, its fingers are falling off." They hid when the boats landed and the men inside came ashore.
>
> According to the story, the people were even more astounded at what they then saw. The gleaming white beings with strange color hair began to rub their bodies with something that, when mixed with water, made white foam like the waves breaking on the shore. Then they wrapped their bodies in clothes—very strange to the Gilbertese since they were used to going naked. When the strangers put on their shoes the people later compared them to hermit crabs—they hid their feet inside things which looked like shells.

Curiosity finally overcame the Gilbertese. They came out of their hiding places to investigate more closely these new beings and the strange things which they had brought with them. As the story goes, they were especially interested in the slippery, fragrant substance which formed white foam when wet. It is said that several people started biting bits off and soon several became sick. Thus, this first contact with the Europeans had a dramatic ending—the soap victims became the patients of these strange beings.

What this story illustrates, of course, is how really sick and tired people were of eating fish. Nothing else could explain the peculiar urge to eat a bar of soap that had just been used to wash the critter-ridden body funk of a pale and hairy sailor. But as first contacts go, these early encounters between *I-Matang* and I-Kiribati were remarkably untroubled, particularly when compared to elsewhere in the Pacific, where often enough it was cannon shot that marked the beginning of a new era for the islands. This would not last, of course. The islands of Kiribati, as became apparent after even the most cursory exploration, had almost nothing of value to the early-nineteenth-century *I-Matang*. They lacked fresh food, potable water, gold, silver, spices, fur, fabrics, sandalwood, just about everything that drove trade and exploration during that era. What Kiribati did have, however, was women.

By the 1830s, whalers had begun cruising the waters of the southern Gilberts. They were after sperm whales, and after months of hunting sperm whales, the whalers got to thinking and they drifted over Kiribati-way. I-Kiribati women soon became renowned for their beauty, and fortunately for the whalers, some of the islands had a class of women called *nikiranroro*, fallen women who were not quite married and not quite virginal, and these were made available to the whalers. The cost for their services was typically one stick of tobacco, and it was not long before the I-Kiribati became mad for the weed. Soon, whenever a ship was spotted nearby, the I-Kiribati would yell *te baakee, te baakee!* They gorged themselves on any tobacco that made it to the islands, smoking it, chewing it, even swallowing it, and here things began to go wrong. The whalers soon discovered that there weren't that many women of the *nikiranroro* class and that the licentious reputation of Tahiti was well deserved, and like apparently every other male who rounded Cape Horn in the eighteenth and nineteenth centuries, the whalers too began seeking most of their entertainment in Polynesia.

This was good for Kiribati, which was not nearly as afflicted by the epidemic of venereal diseases that racked Tahiti. But, as I can attest, nicotine withdrawal can make one decidedly grumpy. This is why the crew of the *Columbia* found themselves taken hostage one day by nic-fitting I-Kiribati, who refused to release them until they received one hundred pounds of tobacco. Soon the I-Kiribati developed a reputation as devious marauders, a reputation that was no doubt enhanced by the local custom of considering anything and anybody to wash ashore, ships included, as fair game. In addition to the assault on the *Columbia* in 1846, raids were conducted on the *Triton* (1848), the *Flying Fox* (1850), and the *Charles W. Morgan* (1851), among others, and whalers soon began to avoid particular islands all together, including Tarawa, no matter how great their lust or hunger. A number of these attacks, however, could probably be attributed to simple misunderstandings. Stealing or borrowing? There can be a gray area. The I-Kiribati perceived property differently than the Americans and the English, two societies whose very foundations were based on property. And being surrounded by canoes does not necessarily mean one needs to blast them with cannon shot, which is what the captain of the *Charles W. Morgan* ordered when he found himself becalmed off Nonouti.

Nonetheless, the I-Kiribati reputation for forging cunning attacks on visiting ships proved to be well deserved. It wasn't the ships themselves they wanted, but their tobacco and their parts. If taken, the vessel was stripped of iron and nails, weapons and wood, tools and sails, and what was considered useless was allowed to rot on the reef. It was a good thing, however, that the I-Kiribati gained practice and confidence in assaulting ships. By the 1840s, the blackbirders had arrived. These were slavers contracted to obtain labor for the plantations in Fiji, Hawaii, New Caledonia, and Peru. The slavers used both force and deceit to fill their holds. On the friendlier islands, they invited villagers aboard, where they were promptly given rum until the entire village lay passed out on the deck, at which point the crew would quietly sail off with them. At other times, blackbirders raided a village, hunting in particular for women. Said one blackbirder: "They fetch in the Fiji Islands twenty pounds a head, and are much more profitable to the slavers than the men." According to one account of a raid on Arorae, "thirty-eight young women were all made fast by the hair of their head and led into the boat." Most never saw their home islands again.

By the 1850s, however, resistance from the I-Kiribati and changing European attitudes toward slavery convinced the plantation owners that they had a bit of a marketing problem. From here on they would no longer engage in slavery but in the "Pacific labor trade." Instead of armed slavers, there were now recruiters visiting the islands. Instead of being sold as slaves, the I-Kiribati were contracted as laborers. Possibly, contracted laborers might even return home one day. It says much about the hardship of life on an equatorial atoll that over the following seventy years, thousands of I-Kiribati left their islands to work the sugar, cotton, and coconut plantations of Fiji, Tahiti, Samoa, Peru, Central America, and nearly everywhere else where Europeans needed labor. One often reads of the masses of Indian and Chinese indentured laborers in the nineteenth century, but when one looks at the labor trade as a percentage of a country's population there is probably no nation that exported more of its people than the I-Kiribati. Between 1840 and 1900, nearly a third of all I-Kiribati were laboring abroad. Half never made it back. Still, during this era most of the I-Kiribati recruited to work abroad went willingly. Drought and starvation were the most compelling reasons. No place on Earth is more unforgiving than an atoll during a drought. For generations, starvation and infanticide kept populations in check, but the labor trade offered another way. The laborer's life was a harsh life, but it was life.

Curiously, upon returning to their islands the laborers were quickly reabsorbed into the village community, where they followed the same beliefs and traditions as those who had never left the islands. It was as if the intervening years abroad counted for little more than a source of colorful anecdotes to be shared in the *mane-aba*. There was no challenge to religion, no usurpation of local hier-archies, no defiance of custom. That you could take one-third of a country's population and scatter them around the world, where they would toil in strange environments, eat peculiar foods, and be exposed to a life profoundly different than what they knew, and then return some of them to their islands without social consequences, suggests that the I-Kiribati are a fairly stubborn people, utterly con-tent with the culture they have developed to survive on an atoll. It would take a little doing to mess with the culture here. Enter the beachcomber.

Consider the situation of an illiterate, low-class English seaman in the mid-nineteenth century. The pay was low, floggings common, death at sea highly likely, possibilities for advancement negligible, and when he returned to England he would be cast adrift into a country that was well on its way to becoming the industrial hell vividly described by Charles Dickens. Life on a tropical island where polygamy was the norm might not seem like such a bad option. Some jumped ship and hoped search parties would decline to search very hard. Atolls are very small and hiding places few, particularly when the I-Kiribati were offered a tobacco bounty for the seaman's return. Occasionally, escaped convicts from Australia were deposited by obliging whalers. Most often though, it was a seaman who had made such a nuisance of himself aboard the ship that the captain felt either compelled to maroon him or accede to his wish to be marooned.

The first beachcomber known to have set ashore in the Gilbert Islands was one Robert Wood, who arrived on Butaritari in 1835, where he quickly taught the locals how to brew sour toddy, an ill-tasting alcoholic concoction for which a certain *I-Matang* was nonetheless thankful for more than 150 years later, when he was experiencing acute beer withdrawal. By 1860, there were around fifty *I-Matangs* living in the Gilbert Islands. I think it is fair to say that the early beachcombers in Kiribati were Question Authority kind of people. Most were itinerant, spending a year or two on an island before seeking a working passage elsewhere on an obliging ship, but a number settled for the remainder of their lifetimes, where they happily acquired wives, leaving enough offspring to ensure that within a couple of generations every I-Kiribati carried a dollop of the beachcomber. It is a small country. Of the beachcombers, Richard Randall, originally from England, lately of Australia, became the most renowned. He asked to be set ashore on Butaritari in 1846. His ship's captain obliged him and within a short while Randall had four wives and was living the beachcomber's dream. Soon enough, four wives led to forty children and Randall began thinking about getting a job. He became a resident trader.

Early trade in Kiribati consisted of bêche-de-mer and turtle shells, which were exchanged primarily for tobacco. Randall was thinking bigger. Coconut oil was used in the manufacture of soap and candles and its trade had long been a sideline for the whalers. Randall muscled in and within a decade he was by far the most important player in the coconut oil trade in the Gilbert Islands. Producing coconut oil did not alter the I-Kiribati lifestyle. They used it themselves, primarily as a skin lotion. The coconut oil trade, however, did lead to change. According to one local historian writing of Randall: "For [coconut oil] he traded such things as rifles and ammunition, food, cannons, whiskey, gin and rum. There was, thereafter, much drunkenness and fighting and many people were killed. The cannons, some of which were quite big, were used for making a noise and frightening people."

Clearly, in the latter half of the nineteenth century there was a lot of sinning going on in the Gilbert Islands. And if there's sinning, there will be missionaries. The first appearance of missionaries in the Gilbert Islands occurred in 1852 when the American Board of Commissioners for Foreign Missions sent three missionary families to the Marshall Islands. The missionaries called on Butaritari and, I must confess, I really wish I had been there. With Richard Randall acting as the interpreter, the missionaries offered Bibles and a letter of introduction from King Kamehameha IV of Hawaii to the high chief of Butaritari. The high chief of Butaritari, Na Kaiea, was fourteen years old. Like most fourteen-year-old boys, Na Kaiea was a little preoccupied and so he had but one question for the missionaries. Does Christianity permit polygamy? When he heard that Christianity forbids polygamy, Na Kaiea decided to hold out for the Mormons. One can imagine Richard Randall escorting the missionaries back to their ship. "Well, it's been fun. What's that? Do you mean those four naked women? No, no, we're just friends. Off you go now. Bye-bye."

It would take a lot of doing before Christianity supplanted traditional I-Kiribati beliefs. Indeed, it wasn't until well into the twentieth century that most islanders proclaimed themselves Christian. It is a wonder that it did not take longer. Think of the I-Kiribati male of the nineteenth century—he's smoking, he's drinking sour toddy, he's naked, he's dancing, and he's got options, fornication-wise.

These are significant lifestyle issues for the missionaries to overcome. The first to try was Hiram Bingham, a frail Yale-educated American, who arrived on Abaiang in 1857 accompanied by his wife, as mandated by the Missionary Board, lest he be tempted by a dusky savage. Bingham immediately saw that he had a lot of work to do.

> The sight of naked men, boys, girls and more than half naked women, their observance of their extreme poverty, their worship of false gods, their extremely immodest manners and customs, their great licentiousness, their unbounded lying, their covetousness, theft, warlike spirit and bloody warfare, a realizing sense of their ignorance of a final judgment of heaven of hell of Jesus Christ, have made me long to preach to them.

To do so Bingham set about learning "the heathen jargon which noisy savages were shouting about my ears." Bingham was successful in mastering the heathen jargon. He essentially created the written I-Kiribati language, though one senses he failed to offer every letter of the alphabet out of spite. By 1890, he had translated the Bible into I-Kiribati. There his success as a missionary more or less ends. His services were poorly attended, and Bingham found that those who did attend were "very slow to learn propriety in the house of God. Many of them, caring little if anything for the truth, habitually sprawl themselves out to sleep; not a few often laugh, talk, move about." His first two converts soon reconverted to heathenism, while Abaiang was beset by a long period of drunkenness and clan warfare.

Bingham's work was largely carried on by Hawaiian missionaries, who were increasingly sent to the Gilbert Islands because the Missionary Board deemed the islands too savage for the white man. By the 1870s there were Hawaiian missionaries on seven islands and they had managed to convert 112 I-Kiribati, though only seventy-eight were church members in "good standing." A number of missionaries were a little lackadaisical in their work, preferring instead to concentrate on trading opportunities, but here and there Hawaiian missionaries conducted their work with the zealotry of the newly converted. This was particularly true on Tabiteuea, which had the misfortune of finding its mission led by Kapu, a Hawaiian missionary entrusted by Bingham to spread the good word. Tabiteuea means "kings are forbidden," and it seems likely that Kapu took this as a challenge. Evoking the hellfire and damnation that would surely befall those who clung to the old beliefs, Kapu managed to convert much of North Tabiteuea. He became known as Kapu the Lawgiver, and soon he drew his zeal toward South Tabiteuea, where the inhabitants remained stubbornly opposed to him. Kapu decided that this would not do and he organized an army of the converted to descend on the south. Until then, warfare had been unheard of on Tabiteuea, where disputes were traditionally settled mano a mano. Unlike a number of other islands in Kiribati, Tabiteuea had no experience with a chiefly system and the wars that chiefs initiate to keep themselves busy. Instead, on Tabiteuea every family had land, every man was a king, and governance, what there was of it, was conducted in the *maneaba* by the village *unimane*. Kapu's effect on Tabiteuea was like Napoleon's on Europe—revolutionary and immensely destructive. With his army of Christians, Kapu descended on the south of the island. Armed with shark-teeth swords and spears fitted with the lethal barbs of the stingray, Kapu's army swarmed around the pagans, who had gathered around an old cannon salvaged from a wrecked ship. The cannon was fired once until rain extinguished any hope of fighting the onslaught. Within hours, nearly a thousand southerners lay dead. Most had been decapitated. And thus Tabiteuea became Christian.

As the years went by, the zealotry of the early Protestant missionaries lessened, primarily because on most islands it got them nowhere, but also due to competition from Catholic missionaries, who were amenable to smoking and drinking and dancing, which gave them a powerful competitive edge in the pursuit of I-Kiribati souls. Indeed, by the early twentieth century, the northern Gilbert Islands, long the domain of the American Board of Missionaries, had become predominantly Catholic, while the southern Gilberts, which had come under the sway of the more lenient Samoan missionaries sent there by the London Missionary Society, had become largely Protestant, a division that continues to this day. The Catholics, however, drew the line at polygamy and nakedness and gradually, island by island, the tradition of having multiple wives withered into memory, and the I-Kiribati began to cover themselves up in cloth, which allowed them to experience the same skin infections that bedeviled the *I-Matangs*.

Into this atmosphere of agitated missionaries, unscrupulous traders, and chiefly wars fueled by drink, guns, and delusions, the arrival of the British Empire was not entirely unwelcomed by the I-Kiribati. In 1892, Capt. E. H. M. Davis of the *Royalist* arrived on Abemama to plant the Union Jack and declare that henceforth the Gilbert Islands would exist as a protectorate of Victoria, by the Grace of God, Queen of the United Kingdom of Great Britain and Ireland, Defender of the Faith, and Empress of India. He then moved on to every other major island in the group and said likewise. The I-Kiribati said okeydokey, possibly because Davis immediately banned trade in guns and alcohol, and soon went so far as to banish the more obstreperous missionaries, including Kapu the Lawgiver, two moves that in a very short while returned to the islands a peaceful languidness that they had not seen since the advent of the whalers. The chiefly wars that had riddled life in the northern Gilbert Islands gave way to Land Commissions and local magistrates. A few of the more murderous *I-Matangs* who had long stirred trouble on the islands were tried and either expelled or shot. The activities of traders were regulated, and as a result of there now being actual rules, many traders left. The Protestant missionaries were told to lighten up when it came to dancing. The power of the chiefs, which had been artificially enhanced by guns and traders, devolved to the *unimane*. In short, within a remarkably brief period of time, Pax Britannica descended on the islands. That this occurred I think is less a tribute to the peripatetic colonial officers, who were ordered to administer both the Gilbert and Ellice Islands without the Colonial Office actually providing them with a boat, but more to the desire of the I-Kiribati to reclaim their world from the rancorous influence of the *I-Matang* reprobates who had settled on the islands. The British certainly didn't invest much in Kiribati. In fact, they didn't even want it. The islands were claimed solely as a check on German and American aspirations in the region. But the power of empire resonates, and for a few happy years, the British colonial model of benign paternalism brought to the islands a stability and order that many had thought lost. The British colonial habit of training locals to handle most administrative tasks is quite likely what introduced something approaching a national identity among the I-Kiribati, whose collective identity was focused almost exclusively on their home islands.

The British experience in Kiribati, such as it was, considering that at no time did the British have more than a dozen colonial officers stationed there, might have remained essentially benign were it not for the discovery that on one of the islands there existed an actual, honest-to-goodness, extremely valuable natural resource. Since this is Kiribati, it is not surprising that this resource was based on shit, specifically old bird shit, which is also called phosphate, probably because it is considered impolite to discuss bird poop, whereas discussing phosphate seems sophisticated and manly, if also boring. This treasure trove of bird shit was discovered on Banaba, long called Ocean Island by *I-Matangs,* an island that lies by itself, roughly three hundred miles southeast of Tarawa. Unlike the other islands in Kiribati, Banaba is a raised island, shaped like an upturned canoe, with a peak that rises to a lofty one hundred feet above sea level. The island is only about four square miles in size, but it had twenty million tonnes of phosphate deposits. For these twenty million tonnes of phosphate, in 1900, the Pacific Islands Company signed an agreement with someone they presumed to be the chief of Banaba. This agreement gave the Pacific Islands Company, which was to become the British Phosphate Commission, the right to mine all phosphate deposits on Banaba in exchange for an annual payment of fifty pounds sterling, "or trade to that value." The agreement would be in force for 999 years. Someone listed as King of Ocean Island signed with an X mark. Of course, there was no need for such a lengthy contract. The phosphate deposits were thoroughly extracted by 1979, the year of independence for Kiribati. But with the phosphate, so too went the soil, the pandanus trees, the coconut trees, and pretty much everything else necessary to sustain life on an island. Today, only about thirty people live on the blasted remains of Banaba. The rest of the Banabans were removed to Rabi, an island in Fiji, in the 1950s, when the British realized that phosphate mining had rendered Banaba uninhabitable.

Obliterating islands in the Pacific, of course, was the prerogative of superpowers, both rising and diminishing, and in the 1960s the British decided to drop a few nukes on Christmas Island, just to see what would happen. I am always stunned by the presumption of nuclear testing in the Pacific. What if some Pacific Islander decided to blow up an A-bomb in Yorkshire, or a hydrogen bomb in Minnesota, or a nuclear bomb in Provence, just to see what would happen. There would be a fuss, I'm sure. Just imagine the letters to the editor. The British say that their testing on Christmas Island, a renowned bird colony, led to no long-term ill effects. The Fijian soldiers stationed there, however, might think otherwise. They were subsequently bedeviled by cancer. Their wives miscarried and the children that were born often had birth defects.

One would think that the I-Kiribati would at least have some very mixed feelings regarding their historical experience with the *I-Matang* world, but this turns out not to be the case. When I asked Bwenawa what he thought of about it, he said: "It was very good. They civilized us. Before, we were very savage. And now we are all Christian." You never knew for certain whether Bwenawa was just messing with your head, or whether he meant to casually dismiss the entire narrative of colonialism and exploitation that fills Western college textbooks. Christianity was certainly very important for Bwenawa. He has, at various times in his life, been a Catholic, a Jehovah's Witness, a Seventh Day Adventist, a Mormon, and even a Baha'i. Today, he is an elder in the Kiribati Protestant Church. "It is all the same. We must love God and we must love one another." To this end, Bwenawa was seeking to unify the Kiribati Protestant Church with its archrival, the Catholic Church—just a heads-up for the guys in Rome.

And the I-Kiribati are positively effusive when it comes to the British colonial era. This was brought home to me one night when we were invited to attend a reception for the visiting British high commissioner. Typically, the diplomatic cocktail circuit on Tarawa, such as it is, is characterized by a highly immoderate consumption of beer, the occasional fight, and a general atmosphere of keg-party debauchery. The reception for the British high commissioner, however, had ambition. I knew this because on the invitation it mentioned that men would be required to wear "trousers." The English, of course, are well known for fancying a peculiar sense of decorum over things like climate. They are, remember, the nation responsible for kneesocks. The half-dozen lawyers in Kiribati still do their business in horsehair wigs and black robes that billow above their flipflops. But never before had an invitation on Tarawa stipulated that men had to wear "trousers." I could understand shirts, and possibly shoes, but pants on Tarawa seemed pretentious. Only Mormon missionaries wore them.

Nevertheless, on the appointed evening I donned a pair of trousers, and like everyone else at the beachside reception, began to sweat profusely. I envied Sylvia.

"I'd kill to wear a skirt," I said.

"I think you'd look very fetching," she replied.

Sylvia was unfazed by my sartorial preference. Every culture that has developed along the equator has very sensibly included skirtlike garb for men. Like most men in Kiribati, I generally wore a lavalava. Shorts were for formal wear. Pants were an imposition by an alien culture.

My mood lifted, however, when I saw the British high commissioner. He was an enormous man, freakishly tall with a beefy heft, and he lived in Fiji with his diminutive mother, which struck me as a very English arrangement. The British no longer have an embassy on Tarawa. They have, in fact, been doing everything possible to disentangle themselves from the Pacific. Their semiofficial representative in Kiribati was the wife of a Scottish aid worker, and so, once a year, air travel permitting, the British high commissioner of Fiji made an appearance. This year he had been taken to Buariki on North Tarawa, where Captain Davis had first planted the flag on Tarawa. It takes about two hours to cross the lagoon in a Kiribati-8 canoe powered by an outboard engine. It took a little longer for the high commissioner when it was discovered midway on the return trip that they had run out of fuel. In the long hours of paddling that followed, the high commissioner developed what must have been an excruciating sunburn, and so when he finally appeared at the reception, in khakis and a blue shirt that would have looked perfectly respectable were they not stained dark throughout with sweat, he looked like the world's largest, ripest tomato. He was good enough to inform us, however, that he had recently spoken to the queen and that she was thinking of her subjects in Kiribati, a Commonwealth country. More likely, the queen was busy considering the implications of leaked tapes and licked toes, but this is why high commissioners get paid the big bucks. The president of Kiribati, looking uncomfortable in pants and sandals more commonly found in Bulgarian flea markets, circa 1974, rose and spoke about how grateful the I-Kiribati were to the British for their wise rule during the colonial era. "You civilized us," he said. The high commissioner nodded magnanimously. And then we tinked our beer cans and toasted the queen.

Feeling very silly, I looked around and watched the gathered ministers, who were all as sodden through as I was in their ill-fitting pants. "Hear, hear," they enthused. "To the queen." As one, we guzzled our beer. If it were not for the beer, and the heat, and the bad clothes, the scene would not have been out of place in the House of Lords. They wish the queen well in Kiribati. They really do.

CHAPTER 11

In which the Author tells the Strange Tale of the Poet Laureate of Kiribati, who, in fact, was not a Poet, nor was he from Kiribati, but he was the Poet Laureate, sort of, though more than anything, despite considerable gumption, he was a Cretin.

Shortly after we arrived on Tarawa, there appeared in the back pages of newspapers around the world a small item regarding Kiribati. The instigator of this tiny tempest in the human-interest media was the English magazine *Punch*, which published a story about a twenty-one-year-old man from Northampton, UK, named Dan Wilson, who in a cheeky display of tactless ambition, sent a letter addressed to "The Government, Kiribati," offering himself for the job of poet laureate. In his letter, Wilson stressed his range—"I can write poems about anything you want; happy poems, sad poems, songs, anything"—and noted that for a remuneration package he wished for nothing more than a hut overlooking a lagoon. Also enclosed was a sample poem, a three-stanza ditty that began: "I'd like to live in Kiribati/ I feel it's the country for me/ writing poems for all the people/ under a coconut tree."

The letter, as one would hope, was delivered to the head of government, President Teburoro Tito, who was sufficiently moved to extend an invitation to Wilson to live the simple, literary life in Kiribati, hut included. That Kiribati is pronounced *Kir-ee-bas*, which undermines the rhythmic structure of the poem, mattered not, since even in Kiribati it is understood that poems no longer have to rhyme. Wilson, however, perhaps unaware of the aching sincerity of the I-Kiribati, decided to pass on his sample poem and a letter from the president's personal secretary to *Punch*, a satirical rag moving ever further from its illustrious past, and this was followed by a media paroxysm that lasted for a full one-day news cycle. Newspapers from Europe to Asia to Australia carried stories. Even CNN bit. And each story was more or less the same. The tiny Pacific paradise of Kiribati had made a twenty-one-year-old student from the UK its poet laureate, based on the following poem (here followed the poem). The tone was always one of sweet condescension—look at these simpleminded islanders, beguiled by a young prankster from Northampton.

This, of course, was unfair. Let some snarky "LifeStyle" journalist try to forge a living from a canoe and a coconut tree. The I-Kiribati, however, are utterly irony deficient, a liability in the modern era. And the government wasn't exactly savvy to the ways of the global media. Most governments would have shuddered in embarrassment and hired legions of media-relations specialists to advance some form of plausible denial. But George Stephanopoulos had no counterpart in Kiribati. Instead, the president was left wondering what all the fuss was about. A very nice young man from England was kind enough to think of Kiribati, write a touching poem, and inquire about the possibility of spending some time on the islands to write verse about the lovely people here. How could one say no?

And so President Tito had another letter sent to Dan Wilson. Was the poet sincere? Did he really want to come to Kiribati? Did he wish to live in a hut overlooking a lagoon? Wilson, stunned to receive another letter from the president's office, wrote back immediately and apologized for creating such a stir, observing that the media is an uncontrollable beast, and that he was, indeed, interested in writing poems in a hut overlooking a lagoon.

The mail to and from Kiribati often operates at a steamship pace. Eighteen months passed until Wilson received a reply. Soothed by the poet's good intentions, the president's personal secretary reassured Wilson that he was indeed still welcome. "Now to the question of His Excellency's hut," the letter continued, "rest assured that this generous offer still stands and furthermore, the hut is conveniently located on one of the outer islands."

This letter eventually found Wilson working on a Christmas tree plantation on the German-Polish border. It was November. Let's reiterate: German-Polish border. November. And so it came to be that one day, Dan Wilson, the first poet laureate of Kiribati, sort of, arrived on Tarawa, ready to assume the wreath. Greeted at Bonriki International Airport by a presidential aide, Wilson was taken for a brief tour of the island—the brevity having more to do with the meager size of the atoll than with any shirking on the sights—and deposited at the president's private home, a spartan gray cinder-block house located on a narrow spit of land between the lagoon and the Mormon high school, which is where I found him one morning, utterly inebriated.

It appeared that the president's family had discovered kava, a narcotic mud water ritually drunk in much of Polynesia and Melanesia. I put aside my bicycle and entered a room barren of all furnishing or ornament, save for mats, where a dozen men reclined in a satisfied stupor around a kava bowl. Kava is derived from the roots of *Piper methysticum*, a pepper plant requiring water and rich soil and hillsides and occasional cool weather and all sorts of other conditions not found in Kiribati. The I-Kiribati have a great appetite for intoxicating substances, and since the country lacked anything like a Food and Drug Administration, it was probably in the spirit of public service that the president had enlisted his family, at least the male members, to imbibe the mud water, presumably for research. Bowl after bowl was consumed without fuss or ceremony. Women brooded on the fringes. Punctuating the strange, stoned silence was Wilson, who sat around the kava bowl plucking a guitar. *Twang.* Snort. *Twang.* Giggle.

I politely declined a bowl. I am very firm when it comes to the consumption of intoxicating substances. Not before 10 A.M., I say. It's a slippery slope. I was eager to speak to Wilson. Our only knowledge of the poet laureate saga came from a couple of faxes sent to us by friends, which simply left us befuddled, and we forgot all about it until we heard, through the coconut wireless, that the poet laureate had indeed arrived on Tarawa. Wilson, who in person looks much like a diminutive Liam Gallagher, the loutish front man of the one-time supergroup Oasis, agreed to join me outside, where we sat in the shade offered by the presidential lean-to, and where I asked him about his first impressions of Tarawa.

Snort, he began. "I's fookin small, i's wha ie is."

Pardon?

"I's fookin small, i's wha I sed. N i's fookin hot too."

Yes, quite. The poet laureate, it appeared, did not speak the Queen's English.

"Y gut a fag?"

Pardon?

"I sed y gut a fookin fag? A ciggy?"

I gave him a cigarette. With trembling hands he drew the smoke in. "Ugghhh." *Snort.* "Hrrmgghh." *Snort.*

As a skilled journalist, I knew how important it was to establish a connection with one's subject and find a common language. I asked him, "So what the fuck were you thinking, fucking poet laureate and shit?"

"I's a feelinn out a jub application to deliver fookin newspapers 't fookin four o'clock n the mornin, n I thut to meself ther ass to be somethin better n this, u know wha I meen? N wha cuud be better n bein e fookin national poet, sittin round writin fookin poems all day."

Indeed. But not in England.

"Problem wi fookin England is A, u'v got to be fookin good, and B, the fookin job's taken."

These inconvenient facts would dissuade many, but not Dan Wilson. He consulted an atlas. "I's lukin fur someplace remute. I luked at the fookin Pacific, luked at the fookin middle, n found Kiribati." *Snort.* "Y gut another fag?"

I gave him another cigarette. "Y mine if I take two?" He lit one and placed the other behind his ear. "Hrrmmph. Hak-hak. Chhhhhhh-thwoooo."

Wilson was not quite the semiliterate wreck of a being that he appeared to be. His answers, despite the *fookins*, were practiced, smoothed over after dozens of interviews in the UK. His correspondence with the government of Kiribati was arranged chronologically in a neat folder. His round-trip air ticket was paid for by a film production company, which had provided him with a camera to record a video diary. But now that he had arrived on Tarawa, far away from the media glare, what on earth was he going to do here? I asked him how he had been spending his time.

"I'm jus swimmin, sleepin, chillin out, partyin. U know, doin what the fookin I-Kiribati do." Not quite, but never mind. Did he plan on writing verse? ("Have you written any fucking poems yet?" I asked.)

"I aven't written a fookin thing. I'm waitin until me fookin hut is ready and then I'm just gonna write and see wha fookin comes out. I don't really write serious poetry, just comic verse." Who would have thunk. "So I'm jus chillin til I get to Tabiteuea North."

Tab North? The Island of Knives?

In Kiribati, whenever one hears of a murder, one's reaction is, *Really?* And then, inevitably, one hears that the murderer is from Tabiteuea North, and the reaction is, *Ah, yes, of course, that explains it.* They are very sensitive on Tabiteuea, and very quick to resort to the blade. Was Wilson aware of the island's well-earned moniker? I wasn't sure, but I decided not to tell him. I was, frankly, very curious to see how he would get along on Tab North. Perhaps the president was more devious than I thought. *Honest, embarrassing me in front of the world is no problem at all. Now here is your hut on Tabiteuea. Feel free to sleep with the women.*

But I don't think Wilson would have been perturbed. The palm fronds swayed. The lagoon shimmered. He had a good kava buzz going. An attractive young woman walked past—the president's niece? "Y know," said Wilson, who seemed very content, in a glazed sort of way, "I's temptin to fookin disappear here, to jus cut copra and make fookin babies."

A highly original thought, little explored in verse. I wondered what would become of him, carried so far by a little jest. Kiribati certainly had no need for him. Robert Louis Stevenson once wrote of a chief on Butaritari: "His description of one of his own songs, which he sang to me himself, as 'about sweethearts, and trees, and the sea— and no true, all the same lie,' seems about as compendious a definition of lyric poetry as a man could ask." Perhaps then it was Wilson's job to introduce the limerick to Kiribati.

But this would not happen either. In the weeks that followed, Wilson disappeared into the belly of Betio, the seaman's bars where it is considered bad form to demonstrate an ability to walk upright. The expatriate grapevine was rife with tales of drunkenness and lechery and, unusual for Tarawa, where expatriate drunkenness and lechery are the norm, the stories carried the faint whiff of disapprobation. It was often noted that he had no money, and that he was living off the generosity of the I-Kiribati. He had discovered the *bubuti*.

He manipulated custom. He brought women to the president's house. The president's wife was livid.

I encountered Wilson once more in the bar of the Otintaii Hotel, a modest cinder block hotel donated by Japan, where *I-Matangs* and government workers gathered on Cheap-Cheap Fridays. Wilson was shit-faced, and deliriously, rapturously happy. He was getting married. The lucky bride was a Chinese woman who had arrived in Kiribati to buy a passport, and Wilson kindly offered himself as a husband to improve her chances of escaping China. He liked Asian women, he explained. And island women too. They knew their place. A man could be a man and a woman a woman. None of this gender equality nonsense. Sylvia said: "It must be very difficult being so short."

Snort, said Wilson, and then he retreated into the night, two more cigarettes dangling behind his ears, continuing on his dissipated journey, shortly to end with a ticket back to the UK and the resumption of the (brideless) life of an English lout.

CHAPTER 12

In which the Author discovers, while rolling in a swell, Sunburned and Stinging with Sea Lice, and circled by a very large Thresher Shark, which, contrary to his nature, he was trying to catch, that the Pacific Ocean is a Very Great Thing Indeed.

There is a moment, shortly after you accept the imminence of your demise, when it occurs to you that you could be elsewhere, that if you had simply left the house a little later or lingered over a coconut, you would not be here right now confronting your own mortality. This thought occurred to me just as I encountered a very large wave, a rare wave, a surprising wave, a wave that really had no business being where it was, pitching and howling, leaving me with a fraction of a second to make a decision. The options were not good.

Ahead, I could see Mike paddling his surfboard furiously up the face of the wave. Mike had lived on Tarawa for seventeen years. Mike was not a normal guy. He had arrived all those years ago with his wife, Robin, a renowned artist from New Zealand who was seeking both a new motif for her work and the opportunity to bring a few I-Kiribati souls into the Baha'i faith. And so, like me, Mike found himself living on Tarawa more or less as an accessory to his wife. He had taught in every school on Tarawa and was currently working as an administrative aide at the New Zealand High Commission, but his world revolved around surfing and books. If a book arrived on Tarawa it would soon be in Mike's hands, and this made him very valuable as a source for reading material. We often had deep and lively discussions about the books we read.

"What did you think of *Midnight's Children*?" he would ask.

"I thought it was pretty good."

"It was baroque drivel," he would inform me. "What about *Infinite Jest*?"

"I really liked it."

"It was the most profoundly disappointing book I have ever read."

I decided that under no circumstances would I ever let him read a word I had written. Unfortunately, just days after the *Washington Post* published an article of mine, an article that I dearly wished would never be read in Kiribati, because it was a fusion of two separate articles which had been conjoined by the editor so that it became, in his words, "a Frankenstein-like monster sent lumbering into the world," Mike stormed into the house with a copy. It had been faxed to the high commission by the New Zealand Embassy in Washington. "What kind of hack work is this?" he demanded.

Sigh.

As a source for books, Mike always tried to be helpful. "I think you should read this," he proposed, handing me Frederick Exley's *A Fan's Notes*. This particular book is about a guy who really wants to be a novelist, but instead of becoming a novelist he becomes a loser alcoholic living a sad, sad life.

"Thanks, Mike," I told him afterward. "I really enjoyed that one."

"I thought you would," he said with a sly grin.

It was Mike who introduced to me to the world of surfing. In the late afternoon, I often saw him riding the waves behind the house. He lived a few doors down, and so one day I asked him if he would teach me how to surf.

"What should I do now?" I yelled, once I'd finally managed to bring both myself and a surfboard through the break zone, something that took me the better part of an hour to do, of which a good forty-five minutes were spent underwater in various states of distress.

"Look for a wave shaped like an *A*."

An *A*. Hmm. I saw *Z*s and *W*s and *V*s. I saw the Hindi alphabet and the Thai alphabet. I saw Arabic script. I saw no *A*s. Finally I gave up, and chose the next wave that would have me, which turned out to be a poor move. The demon wave picked me up, and after that I have only a very vague recollection of spinning limbs, a weaponized surfboard, chaotic white water, all kind of churning together over a reef. I decided this was not for me.

"That really sucked," I declared.

"You picked the wrong wave," Mike said, after surfing the same distance in a state of such languid repose that he seemed to be mocking my anarchic tumble through the water. "Maybe you should try body boarding first."

And so it came to be that I became a body boarder, a very good, very serious body boarder. I recognize that in the world of water sports body boarding does not rank very high, being regarded about as manly as synchronized swimming, but I spit on such opinions. Body boarding offers one the opportunity to become extremely intimate with a reef-breaking wave. You are in its bosom, sharing its fate, and when the wave is large and glassy smooth, and you are riding it just where you should be riding it—ahead of the break—and the wave doesn't do anything really nasty like suddenly collapse above a boulder encrusted with sea urchins, well then, you find that you are really, really stoked. I don't want to get all purple about it, but body boarding the waves just offshore a tropical island on the equator is about as sublime an experience as one can find on this planet.

Unfortunately, on Tarawa waves are rarely like those pictured in the glossy surf rags, the ones with the perfect barrels heading inexorably toward sandy beaches populated exclusively by buxom girls in string bikinis. The waves on Tarawa are, in fact, mean. They are breakers and dumpers and entirely unpredictable. They will lift you up high, as in twelve feet high, above a rapidly dwindling layer of water covering a very sharp reef shelf, and then just as you think you are going to race diagonally down and across its face, it will suddenly disintegrate, and you will feel yourself free-falling, and then there is an impact that leaves you winded, which is highly unfortunate because the wave, or rather the remains of the wave, still has forward momentum, and you will find yourself hurtling forward somewhere in the midst of tons of very angry, chaotic white water that is both lifting you and pounding you. Under no circumstances do you let go of your body board, because it will always float and you will not, and this is important, because you can hardly breathe from being winded, until finally you are spat out. You spend a few moments putting yourself together, and then you go back, certain that you have acquired just a little more knowledge, enough to ensure that next time you are going to let waves like that just roll on by.

Generally, I no longer engage in adrenaline rush–type activities that carry with them a strong likelihood of lifestyle-altering injury. I have been to a war zone. I have seen a mortar explode in alarming proximity to my being. I have fallen over a cliff. I have driven my mother's car at speeds well in excess of 100 mph. In the rain. I have, on one night in particular, consumed prodigious amounts of alcohol, magic mushrooms, and marijuana, all more or less at the same time, just to see what it would feel like. I have engaged in . . . um, reckless personal behavior. After enough incidents and experiences, there came a moment when I realized that mortality is nothing to be trifled with. I suppose this is called aging. And yet, there is something about being on top of a wave, just at that moment when it catches you and you prepare to hurtle down its face, that brief moment when you are now *committed*, and even though you are now perched very high, and from this perch you can see with remarkable clarity the jagged coral reef below, with its body-sucking crevices and toxic spines, you are at this moment—and really, I am trying to find a better word, but can't—*pumped*.

Whenever conditions looked particularly promising, Mike and I put our gear in the back of a pickup truck and searched the island for the best breaks. The smoothest waves were about a half mile off the Nippon Causeway. The biggest waves were off Temaiku, the southeast point of Tarawa, and to reach it we drove down the airport runway. The first time I drove down the runway, I wondered at the wisdom of doing so, but Mike accurately pointed out that Air Kiribati was down, Air Marshall had stopped its service, and the Air Nauru plane was impounded in Manila, so there was no need to worry about air traffic, just mind the pigs.

As the months went by and time drifted from one year to the next, I found that I had become completely enraptured by the water, possibly because from the water Tarawa always looked good. All evidence of squalor was pleasantly concealed, and the island seemed idyllic with its masses of coconut trees rising from sun-streaked water colored every shade of blue and green.

If there was wind I went windsurfing. I had been windsurfing ever since I was a small child, when my grandmother purchased for my cousins and me a windsurfer with a glorious red sail. She had declared herself bored with the white sails of sailboats that typically populated the lake in Holland upon which my family has a summer cottage and sought to enliven the view. I had grown accustomed to windsurfing in frigid water underneath slate-gray skies, and so when Wieland, a German agronomist who had spent his career flitting from one Pacific Island country to another, declared that his beginner skills were no match for the custom-made board he had brought from Fiji, I eagerly purchased it from him, and in a very short while I was skimming across the lagoon in the presence of dolphins. I knew then that it was unlikely that I would ever again even raise a sail on the icy waters of a Dutch lake.

I happened to be traversing the lagoon, just minding my own business, when I saw four fins slicing through the water, approaching me with intent, and my first thought, of course, was that I was about to meet my end and that it would be a gruesome, horrific end, the kind of end that becomes Pacific lore—*Did you hear about that guy windsurfing across Tarawa Lagoon? Four Tiger Sharks. Nothing left but a scrap of sail.* My heart rate approached five hundred beats a minute. But then the creatures began to leap alongside me and I saw that they were not man-eating sharks but playful, curious dolphins, and I suddenly felt very happy to be alive here in the middle of Tarawa Lagoon, windsurfing in the company of dolphins. For a long while they stayed with me, darting underneath my board, swimming alongside, and then they went on their way, and as they left I sincerely hoped that they knew what they were doing, because dolphins trapped in the shallows of the lagoon were unlikely to avoid the dinner plate.

On other days, I saw flying fish that vaulted a hundred yards and more, and huge silky rays that glided below like shadows, and long sea pikes that leapt urgently above the waves, and schools of silver fish capering off the bow of the board. I saw a green turtle. Even when there wasn't much wind, I sometimes went out just to glide across the lagoon in the late afternoon, when the island was flushed with color. Sailing canoes drifted by, and we waved the wave of lazy contentment, a flick of the hand reciprocated.

The more time I spent breathing in the currents of sea life, the more I wanted to be on the ocean proper. I had windsurfed, just a few times, on the waves breaking on the reef behind our house, but when I faltered and went down and saw my board and my one sail being ravaged by the surf, I decided that I had had just about enough of that. Crashing here, when the waves had already sent my gear rushing toward shore, also left me in the unhappy situation of having to swim back through the break zone—*panic, dive, swim; panic, dive, swim*—and this was something I never wanted to do again without big, floppy, speed-enhancing flippers. But of course the ocean, the real Pacific, lay beyond the reef. For a while I thought about asking around to see if I could join some of the fishermen who worked the waters off North Tarawa, Abaiang, and Maiana. I have no doubt I would have been taken aboard; the I-Kiribati are the most obliging people on the planet. But I was dissuaded by the knowledge that I-Kiribati fishermen are crazy.

I would go anywhere in a traditional sailing canoe, perhaps not happily, but at least with some confidence that with sufficient sunblock, a bit of rain, a few yards of fishing line and a hook, we would reach our intended destination, and possibly be alive too. Not so on an I-Kiribati–operated vessel of more modern design. There are only a couple of state-owned cargo vessels, rusting hulks kindly referred to as floating *maneabas*, and within a short span of time, one was impounded in Hawaii, where it was deemed unseaworthy, and released only after assurances were made that it would never ever enter American waters again, while the other spent nearly three weeks floating aimlessly in the great emptiness between Tarawa and Kiritimati, victim of an electrical problem. That it was overloaded with schoolchildren should have made this an international incident, but it is not the I-Kiribati way to proclaim Mayday. This is not due to excess pride, but to an unnerving combination of self-reliance and fatalism, a cultural attribute not to be confused with stupidity, which, frankly, is a mistake I sometimes made. How else to explain the monthly tally of fishermen lost at sea?

The numbers, truly, were astonishing. There is one radio station in Kiribati and most weeks it dutifully reported the number of boats that had failed to return. These are all open boats, typically about fifteen feet long, made of wood, and powered by a single outboard engine. They do not carry sails, or oars, or life preservers, or radios, or flares, or spare parts for the engine. They do not even carry fishing rods, just fishing line, some hooks, and some bait. The rest is done by sheer muscle. Imagine trying to pull in a fifty-pound tuna, a fish that clearly does not want to go where you are taking it, with a slippery line just a few millimeters in diameter. And now imagine that you are out of sight of land. And the engine dies. Imagine that awful silence, the only sound the Pacific Ocean, an ocean that with each passing hour is taking you far, far away from land. If you are a normal person, you panic and die. If you are an I-Kiribati, you say, *Oh well, shit happens*, and then you set about doing what needs to be done to survive.

And here is the really astonishing thing. Very often, they do survive. I do not have the figures on who has the record for spending the longest time adrift in an open boat, but I would bet that the top ten positions are all held by I-Kiribati, which bespeaks of both the lunacy of I-Kiribati fishermen and their jaw-dropping capacity for survival. One day Radio Kiribati reports that three men failed to return from fishing, and you think, well, they're done for, and then nine months later Radio Kiribati will announce that the fishermen have been found drifting off the coast of Panama, which is approximately four thousand miles away, and that they are reported to be in good condition. Good condition! If it were me, there would have been nothing left except the powdered remains of my bones.

Of course, not everyone lives and so you would think that when family members hear that one of their loved ones has gone missing at sea there would be worry, there would be vigils, there would be gnashing of teeth, but this is not so. When Abarao, a health education officer for the government who often worked with Sylvia in a collegial, professional kind of manner, which made him a rarity among government workers—not the collegial part, but the professional part—failed to return from Maiana, where he was sent to gather the family's pigs for a celebratory feast, there was a notable lack of consternation among his family and colleagues. When I asked one of his cousins why this appeared to be so, he said; "In Kiribati, we don't worry for the first two weeks."

And after two weeks?

"Then we worry a little bit, but we keep it to ourselves."

Two weeks passed and still no Abarao. Kiribati's lone patrol boat, another gift from the good people of Australia, was dispatched to look for him. It returned to Tarawa several days later, listing strongly and belching long plumes of black smoke. They had not found Abarao. They had, however, encountered some excellent fishing off Nonouti, which was a considerable distance from where Abaroa was likely to have drifted, and in their enthusiasm for the excellent fishing, they had hit a reef, nearly sinking the boat.

And then, a week later, Radio Kiribati announced that a Korean fishing trawler had found Abarao off Nauru. He was reported to be in good condition. I wanted to hear how, exactly, does one remain in good condition after spending three weeks adrift in an open boat under the glare of the equatorial sun.

"Pig's blood," he said, when I met with him a short while later. I suppose desperation can lead one to think creatively about the uses of a pig, but I'm not sure it would have occurred to me. I see a pig and I see bacon, pork chops, pork tenderloin, ham, but not water.

Abarao was in his thirties, and though he was quick to laugh about his experience, he had a haunted air about him, as if the weeks drifting with the ocean current and all its attendant terror and tedium had led him to develop a knowledge of death that he did not wish to have. To find relief from the sun, he had spent much of his time in the water, hanging from the stern of the boat.

"What about sharks?" I asked. It is one thing to encounter a shark on a reef, where there are so many other tasty nibbles to choose from, but it is another thing altogether to meet a shark in the open water, where you are more likely to be treated as an unexpected meal.

"Yes, I saw sharks, but I couldn't catch them."

The I-Kiribati are different from you and me. They take their position on top of the food chain very seriously. Abarao's answer reminded me of a story that John, an English volunteer, once told me. He was snorkeling in the lagoon when he noticed that he was being circled by a large shark. He popped up and spoke to his companions on a boat a short distance away. "There's a shark here. Would you be so kind as to bring the boat over?" But it was too late. At the first mention of shark, his two I-Kiribati friends had leapt into the water to go shark hunting. Like I said, the I-Kiribati are different from you and me.

The cause of Abarao's adventure on the high seas was the simple fact that halfway between Maiana and Tarawa he'd run out of gas. "I forgot the petrol," he said sheepishly. This is probably the primary cause of adriftedness in Kiribati, but it wasn't the most painfully dumb reason I'd ever heard for getting oneself lost at sea. This would belong to Epi and Joseph, two Catholic missionaries from Samoa and Tonga, respectively, who one day took the boat belonging to the Catholic high school out for a day of fishing. They got lost.

"We followed the birds," Joseph told me when I spoke to him a few months later. "We thought that's where the fish were, but then the birds flew away. We followed the birds again, but still we couldn't find any fish. And then we noticed that we couldn't see land anymore."

"So what did you do?"

"We shut off the engine."

It occurred to me that I would now trust Samoan and Tongan fishermen even less than I did I-Kiribati fishermen. They were not more than a couple of miles from Tarawa. A simple reading of the clouds would have told them what direction to go. Clouds reflect the color of the lagoon, and so when they drift over the atoll they take on a pale green hue, which means that while you cannot actually see the atoll you know where it is. But the missionaries were unaware of this basic island navigational technique, and so they began to drift.

"On the first night, there was suddenly a loud noise and the boat nearly turned over," Joseph told me. "It was a whale and it had come up right beside us. I could see its eye."

He was nearly quaking at the recollection. For a Catholic missionary adrift at sea, the appearance of a whale must be a fairly evocative thing.

"But that was the last fish we saw," he continued. "We didn't catch a thing. And then, one day, a bird landed on the boat and I was able to grab it."

I asked him about water.

"It rained once, and we gathered about three liters."

"And so that's it?" I asked it. "One bird and three liters of water."

"That's it."

The hapless missionaries were adrift for three weeks. They turned on the engine periodically when the sea ran high threatening to overturn the boat, but mostly they drifted silently across the largest ocean in the world. They prayed. A lot. Apparently someone was listening: They too were found by a Korean fishing boat, which took them to Papua New Guinea. Eventually, they made it back to Tarawa, where they have been feeling guilty ever since. Not only had the Catholic high school been forced to pay the exorbitant costs of their air travel from Papua New Guinea—there is not a more expensive corner of the world to travel in than the Pacific—but it had also lost its boat.

STILL, DESPITE MY very great fear of drifting aimlessly across the ocean, I thought that I should at least gather some ocean-oriented experience. I was on an atoll in the very middle of the world's largest ocean, an ocean whose sounds were omnipresent, whose very sight was unavoidable, and because the atoll is a very small place to be, the ocean is the only option for expanding one's world. I made arrangements with Bitaki, a teammate on the soccer team I played with, to go fishing with his brothers, who typically worked the waters off Maiana, the nearest island south of Tarawa. When I mentioned to Sylvia that I was going, she said: "No, you're not."

"And what do you mean by 'No, you're not'?"

I determined right then that I would go out fishing every week. No, every day. I would become a professional fisherman. I would become sun-browned and sea-weathered. I would smell like fish. I would be a Salty Dog.

"I mean," Sylvia said, "that when the engine dies and you start drifting, which will happen, because things like that do seem to happen to you, you will not survive two days. Your skin will fry, you will collapse from dehydration, and because you will be the most useless person on the boat, you will be regarded by the others as a potential food source."

I didn't like the imagery here.

"And," she continued, "if you're off drifting on the ocean, who will do the shopping? And what about the nights when it's your turn to cook?"

Can you feel the love?

Nevertheless, I proceeded with my plans because a line had been drawn and lines must be crossed. I would, however, bring extra sunscreen and lots of water. I tried to think of ways to be useful on a boat adrift in the Pacific, but I could not come up with anything except shark bait.

The following day Sylvia came home and said that she had spoken with Temawa, Bitaki's sister. Temawa worked at FSP as an environmental education officer. It often seemed as if the FSP staff alone were related to the entire country.

"She said Farouk had gone fishing with her brothers."

"And . . . what did he say?"

"You should ask him."

I sensed a trap.

Farouk was Temawa's husband. He was, like nearly every other foreigner in Kiribati, a missionary. What made him a little different was that he was a Muslim missionary from Ghana. If you were an I-Kiribati woman looking for a way to subvert traditional mainstream island society, you could not do better than to marry a Muslim missionary from Africa. This streak of good-hearted independence is what drew Sylvia to hire Temawa when she was eight months pregnant with their second child. Temawa held a graduate degree in environmental studies from a university in Canada ("It was so cold," she said), and rather than seek lifetime employment with the government, she genuinely wanted to do something which would allow her to "make a difference." You believed her too.

Her husband Farouk was a gentle man with a sly sense of humor. "A man walks into a bar and says 'Allah Akbar.' What should you do?"

"What?"

"Duck."

Farouk had yet to convert a single I-Kiribati to Islam. Not even Temawa would make that kind of leap, but he remained in buoyantly good spirits, working primarily as a minibus driver to help out with the family's expenses. When I asked him about his experiences fishing, he broke out into a wide grin and declared: "I have never been so scared in my life."

Did I mention that Farouk had fought the Russians in Afghanistan? No? Well, he did. Farouk was one of those fearless souls whose life had become one long adventure. He was deeply at ease with himself, exuding an air of preternatural calmness, and so when he remarked that he had been shit-scared while fishing with his brothers-in-law, I paid attention.

"I just wanted to lie down in the middle of the boat, close my eyes, and pretend that I was somewhere else. The waves were so big, and the boat goes up and down, up and down, and I became very sick," he said. "But I couldn't lie down."

"Why not?"

"Because I was busy bailing. It is a very leaky boat. For twelve hours I did nothing but get sick and bail."

Score one for Sylvia.

Fortunately, sweet necessity soon reared its head. We had planned to fly to Maiana with Bwenawa and Atenati, who also worked in the FSP garden, in order to conduct nutrition and gardening workshops in each of the island's villages, but Air Kiribati was once again grounded, awaiting spare parts from the other side of the globe. An efficient airline Air Kiribati is not, and a sea journey was thus happily needed. One would think that given the troubles of its airline, inter-island shipping would be a high priority for the government, but this is not so. There is but one creaking, rusting hulk of a vessel that periodically sails to the outer islands to deliver supplies and gather copra, the dried coconut meat used in soaps and oils, which provides outer islanders with their only source of income. The ship's schedule is mysterious, its sightings infrequent, and most islands go four months and more between ship visits. Pleas from outer islanders requesting more shipping are duly and ceremoniously acknowledged and then ignored altogether. The more cohesive and industrious islands have taken it upon themselves to buy their own island boats. There is the Abaiang boat, and the Onotoa boat, and so on, and the man who builds them is John Thurston, a Californian who left the United States some thirty years ago.

It is one of the small pleasures of living in Kiribati that the foreigners one meets tend to live life in a vivid and eccentric sort of way, and when you listen to their tales of high adventure in the South Seas, you find that you are subsequently ruined from a conversational point of view, that you can no longer even pretend to be remotely interested in someone's trip to the mall, or their thoughts about the stock market, or their opinions about the relative merit of a football player, and soon you will be branded as aloof, simply because once, on a faraway island, you heard some good stories. John had some of the more colorful tales. He was a surfer from Anaheim who one day picked up and left for Hawaii to surf the big waves. In appearance and mannerism, he reminded me of Brian Wilson, the tormented genius behind the Beach Boys. There were demons. They were slayed. And the story of that battle manifested itself in the lines on John's face and the near-stuttering quality of his speech. He had become a Baha'i, which is something I never asked him about, because I once heard that members of the Baha'i faith are not permitted to proselytize unless someone asks them about their faith, and it says much about the graciousness of John and Mike and the other Baha'is I met that I remain as clueless about the religion now as ever.

In the early 1970s, John set out for Tarawa, where he was charged by the Baha'i powers that be to start up a youth center similar to the one he had run on Maui. Soon enough, he discovered he was broke and so he began to build boats, catamarans, and trimarans with shallow drafts to accommodate lagoons and reefs. They were made of plywood and whatever other material he could find, and John set up business as an inter-island trader. With independence in 1979, he moved on to the Marshall Islands, Tuvalu, Fiji, Samoa, and eventually to Papua New Guinea, where he lived for six years, trading food and tobacco (but no alcohol) in exchange for shells in areas where few had ever encountered a westerner. The violence and mayhem of

Papua New Guinea eventually compelled him to leave, and he returned to Kiribati with *Martha*, his yellow 36-foot homemade trimaran, which would become our home on the voyage to Maiana.

His house, an airy bungalow that took him two months to build after a fire reduced his old place to little more than flickering embers, overlooked the lagoon. It was as much a workshop as a home, and I stopped by one day to get some help repairing the sail I used for windsurfing. A tumble on the reef had created a foot-long gash. As John set about lining the tear with sail tape I set about prying stories from him. John is a modest man, friendly in that wholesome American kind of way, but hardly one to expound unbidden, but eventually he told me about the girl he'd found floating in the ocean.

"We were sailing off Abaiang when Beiataaki noticed something strange in the water," he began. "At first we thought it was a turtle, and then as we got closer we saw that it was a body, a little girl, couldn't have been more than seven or eight." His eyes widened, as if to say, *Can you believe that?* "We sailed alongside. She was just bobbing in the water. Her eyes were closed and we thought she was dead. She was about ten miles or so from land. And, I'll never forget this, swimming through her hair were all these little fish, little colorful fish, blue and red, like flowers. We were about to pull her in, when suddenly she opened her eyes. Well, that was a surprise, I can tell you. We got her aboard and gave her some water and some food. She had been drifting since the day before. We took her back to her village and arrived right in the middle of her funeral."

"My goodness," I said. John was the sort of person to whom you could say *my goodness* without feeling self-conscious. "How did she end up drifting in the ocean?"

"She saw her father and brother fishing from a sandbar in the lagoon. She tried to get to them, but the tide got her. They tried to reach her, but couldn't, and so she drifted right on out of the lagoon and into the ocean. The entire village set off in canoes looking for her, but they couldn't find her."

"You must be a popular figure in Abaiang."

"They're good people. They're all good people here." He paused for a moment. "Well, there are a few bad apples, just like everywhere."

Once, when I happened to be elsewhere, Sylvia noticed two drunks lurking around the house. It was during the day, which was unusual. Sylvia called John, who immediately rushed over. He is a big man, and he literally picked up the two men, and threw them out onto the road, loudly shaming them for their behavior. "And don't you ever come back!" And they didn't.

John had decided to move to Abaiang. He had leased a plot of land that stretched from lagoon to ocean, where he planned to build a house, a few more boats, and live out his remaining years. "Too many people on Tarawa," he said. "And the smell is beginning to bother me." It was true. Where he lived, the fetid stench of sizzling shit at low tide was breathtakingly foul. He had no plans to return to the United States. Only once in the past thirty years had he set foot on American soil, and he understood that the U.S. was no place to be for a sixty-year-old man with just fifty dollars to his name. He would have been fine were it the nineteenth century, but millennial America no longer had room for his form of self-reliance. He joked about pushing shopping carts.

Sylvia chartered *Martha*, to take Bwenawa, Atenati, and ourselves to Maiana. John, however, would not be sailing her. Our captain would be Beiataaki, John's longtime crew member. He brought Tekaii, a young Baha'i convert, to help out on board. Beiataaki had sailed the boat the length of the lagoon the day before, and we boarded *Martha* in Betio, where if conditions were favorable it would take us a day to reach Maiana. John was there to see us off and I mentioned how much I liked *Martha*'s toilet. It extended off the stern of the boat like a whimsical throne. It was exactly what Salvador Dalí would have done.

"Yeah . . . when it gets rough it's like that French thing."

"A bidet?"

"Yeah, a bidet."

The weather was faultless. A steady breeze brought lazy white-caps to the lagoon. A few scattered clouds drifted above, their colors evolving from green to a translucent blue as they passed the lagoon. Blighted Betio began to recede as we sailed toward the channel. Waves broke on the long shoal that extends north of Betio and already we could see the green islets of North Tarawa. A sailing canoe appeared and as it neared I saw that it had an unusual black sail. Peering closely, I noticed that the sail was in fact an ingeniously cut garbage bag. "Look," I said to Sylvia. "A floating metaphor."

As we cleared the channel, Bwenawa let out a long fishing line baited with a plastic squid. He knotted the line at the stern of the boat and every now and then he tugged at it.

"Maybe we'll catch something here, but I think when we are near Maiana we will catch many fish," he said.

"I want a shark," said Atenati. "A big shark."

Atenati was the scourge of Bwenawa's existence. Her last name was O'Connor, and she exhibited the devilish twinkle of her beachcomber ancestor. Atenati and Bwenawa feuded like an old couple that had been married much too long. For years, they had worked side by side in the FSP garden. Each had firm opinions about what constituted ideal growing conditions for tomatoes and eggplants, and both were stubborn. I joked with Bwenawa about the dangers of provoking Atenati. She was not above using magic.

"That's right, Bwenawa. You listen to the *I-Matang* or I will put a spell on you," she said.

"Ha-ha. You're *tokonono*, Atenati."

I could tell Bwenawa was wary of her magic. Like all I-Kiribati, at heart he believed in taboo areas, spirits, and magic. Christianity simmered at the surface—Mike called it tribalism, the need to belong to a group competing against another group—but in most ways the spiritual life of the I-Kiribati remained uncorrupted by a century of missionaries. This is why even on crowded South Tarawa there still remained swaths of land devoid of homes and people. Spirits lived in these places, and spirits were not to be trifled with.

As Tarawa receded I marveled that we had made this dust speck of an island our home. The utter isolation of it. Its starkness. Its fragility. Its beauty. Its sordidness. Its people, so engaging, so violent. That it was beginning to feel very much like home was a realization that sometimes frightened me. Most *I-Matangs* sent to Kiribati lasted only a few months before sickness and the oppressive claustrophobia of island fever drove them elsewhere. The couples that arrived generally dissolved. Everything was permitted on Tarawa. There were no rules. There were also no secrets. That was too much for many.

I, however, could not think of any place I would rather be than on a homemade wooden trimaran plying the sun-dappled water between Tarawa and Maiana. Beiataaki had caught a ray and it was drying on the mesh that laced the hulls at the bow of the boat. Sylvia was happy. It was impossible not to be. Traversing this patch of sea tinted the lush blue of the great depths in a trimaran painted a fading carnival yellow with blue trim under an equatorial sun between two tropical green isles is to have an experience in color that I did not know was possible without the aid of pharmaceuticals. At the boat's stern, Bwenawa continued to jig his fishing line, coaxing a bite. Atenati provided commentary: "Have you caught my shark yet?"

By mid-afternoon Maiana became visible and I realized that this was how atolls ought to be approached. From the sea, there is first the luminous clouds drifting over the lagoon, and then a glimmer of green that enlarges and continues to lengthen, the slender ridge of a sea mountain cresting low above the ocean, and then the water begins to change, its blue revealing the sand and coral below, and everything seems somehow both untamed and serene. Bwenawa was getting excited now.

"Aiyah, aiyah. Birds!"

Beiataaki maneuvered the boat toward where the seabirds were hovering.

"*Aiyah!*"

Something had bit. Bwenawa strained to pull the fish in. His hands clasped the line. He heaved himself back until he was lying nearly parallel to the deck.

"Aiyah, aiyah!"

"Yah, Bwenawa!" Atenati rooted.

Bwenawa began drawing the fish in. It was clearly a big fish. Bwenawa's muscles were pulled taut. He was sweating heavily. I had never seen him happier.

"Aiyah, aiyah!"

He pulled the fish in, each handful of line a small victory. The fish began to lose its fight. As Bwenawa drew the line in, one hand over the other, I recognized the motion from a traditional dance that I-Kiribati men perform. Finally, gleaming in silver light below the surface was a yellowfin tuna. Beiataaki hauled it in. The fish must have weighed a good twenty-five pounds; it would have been worth several hundred dollars in Japan. On deck, the tuna continued to leap spasmodically until Beiataaki took a club to its head. Crimson blood splattered all over the boat, and by the time the fish succumbed, the deck looked like some horrific crime scene. This surprised me. I had never associated fishing with blood.

Bwenawa retrieved the hook and the plastic pink squid and tossed the line back into the water. Below the surface, we could see outcroppings of coral and a sandy bottom and this made the water take on ever more permutations of blue. Visibility must have been at least a hundred feet. Within minutes, Bwenawa landed another fish. It fought even more ferociously than the tuna.

"Aiyah, Aiyah!"

I worried that Bwenawa might have a heart attack. He was ecstatic. Again he hauled with all his might. Watching him was like watching a heavyweight tug-of-war. He heaved. He worked the fish. He released a hard-fought yard of line and then pulled it back in. As the fish neared, I could see that it was long and slender. "What do you think, Beiataaki? A sea pike?"

"No," he said. "That's a barracuda."

A great barracuda. It was nearly four feet long. It was a primordial fish. It looked like it belonged in another era, when the size of one's teeth was the most important thing in determining whether you survived or not. It too was clubbed, more thoroughly than the tuna. Even so, Bwenawa could not bring himself to retrieve the hook. "I don't like those teeth," he said. Beiataaki gingerly unclasped the hook from Jaws and again the line was drawn out behind the boat.

"Let's see the *I-Matang* fish," Atenati taunted.

"I may need some magic," I replied.

I took the line, but not before applying some more sunscreen. After a day sailing the equatorial Pacific, I could feel my freckles mutating into something interesting and tumorous. I tugged the line and just like that I had a fish; and just like that I realized that applying sunscreen a moment before grasping a wispy fishing line that was connected to a fish, and I believed it was a mighty fish, was not a particularly clever thing to do. I don't think Hemingway would have made the same mistake. Then again, Hemingway had a fishing rod, which as I struggled with this behemoth from the depths, struck me as an eminently useful tool for fishing. I held on to the line with one hand, while trying to wipe the grease from the other on my shorts. I was dangling precariously over the edge of the boat. My arm felt like it would soon spring from its socket. I believed I had hooked a tiger shark.

"Hey, *I-Matang*!" Atenati yelled. "In Kiribati we fish with two hands."

Atenati was always helpful. Just as I was finally able to maintain a firm grip on the line, I began to notice a stinging sensation on my hands, which as I battled with my sea beast, began to rapidly spread to my arms and chest. It was a burning, itchy feeling, the kind that soon leaves its sufferer in a state of frothy madness. "I itch!" I cried. "Something stings!"

"It's only sea lice," Beiataaki informed me.

What the fuck were sea lice? So typical, I thought. Even the ocean in Kiribati has lice.

Atenati began to cackle. I wondered if she had anything to do with it. I gave her the evil eye.

I struggled with my monster. I heaved and hauled. My muscles ached. I put my legs into it. I was engaged in an epic confrontation between man and beast and I was determined to win. I would demonstrate my prowess as a hunter. I would serve notice to the fish world that there was a new master in town. This shark was mine.

Only it wasn't a shark. Nor was it a great barracuda. Or a tuna. No, it was an itsy-bitsy trevally, a little more than a foot long, and as I finally hoisted it out of the water, I was struck by its dainty color, a shimmering blue-green. No one clubbed my fish.

"Aiyah, Aiyah," Bwenawa said, with a decided lack of oomph.

I continued to itch.

"I feel sorry for the fish," Sylvia said. "Look, its colors are fading."

We stared at the fish. *Flop, flop. Pant, pant.* And then it was no more. I felt like my dominance over the fish world had not yet been conclusively demonstrated. And then Atenati yelled: "*Look!*"

We all turned.

Oh-oh.

The sea monsters depicted by early explorers in the Pacific no longer seemed so fanciful. Not far off the bow was an immense *creature*. We watched its dark silhouette displace water like an indolent torpedo. It could only be here, at reef's edge, for one reason. It was hungry.

"Is it a whale?" asked Bwenawa. "A pilot whale?"

"It's huge," Sylvia noted

"Jesus," I said.

Beiataaki stared long and hard. "Thresher shark," he declared.

I suddenly noticed how small our boat was. I remembered that it was made of plywood. Thin plywood. Thin and old plywood. Thin and old and rotting plywood. Thin and old and rotting and easily breached plywood. Imperceptibly, I moved to the middle of the boat. What were we thinking, washing fish blood off the deck in shark-infested waters? A patch of water where sharks can be confused with whales.

About forty yards distant, we watched a tail fin, a tail fin that rose four feet out of the water, of which it followed that another four feet were under water, suggesting a tail fin of eight feet—an eight-foot tail fin!—and it was coming our way.

"There's my shark!" Atenati declared. "Bwenawa! Catch me that shark!"

Bwenawa was already rummaging around for a stronger line and a bigger hook. Beiataaki was slicing up his ray. The shark was nearing. *Swish-swish* went its eight-foot tail fin.

Fuck.

These people were insane. I looked at Sylvia. She had a look of glee about her. You too, woman?

Beiataaki began to toss chunks of ray overboard. Bwenawa was fiddling with gear. Atenati was beside herself. "There's my shark. This way. This way."

The shark listened. It neared. And then it submerged. And then it became a shadow. An enormous shadow. This was exactly what Steven Spielberg would have the shark do. I could hear the music. *Do-do-do-do do-do-do-do*. The shark passed underneath the boat. It was at least twenty feet long. I braced myself for that moment of impact, when this mass of muscle and teeth would shoot up and shatter the boat, tossing us into the water, and oh, the horror of it then.

Beiataaki moved to the other side of the boat as the shark glided underneath. He was throwing big chunks of ray into the water. I did not encourage this. It was as if we were at some duck pond in a park, merrily feeding the quackers. But this was not a duck. This was a twenty-foot shark.

"They're crazy," I offered.

"Yes," Sylvia said. We stood watching, agape. Two forces, both irrational and armed, were about to collide.

But the shark was having none of it, bless him. He was a smart shark. A good shark. He just kept on swimming, leaving a turbulent wake with his eight-foot tail fin. *Swish, swish.* I began to like the shark. I liked the shark for swimming away. Swim, shark, swim. Off you go. Leave these fools behind you.

"Bwenawa!" Atenati screeched. "You didn't catch my shark!"

"Ha-ha." Bwenawa seemed energized. A yellowfin tuna, a great barracuda, and, if they had just been a little better prepared, a twenty-foot thresher shark. He was in good spirits.

THE DAY WAS FADING. We drew in the fishing line in and began to search for the channel into Maiana Lagoon. John had installed a Global Positioning Satellite receiver on board, but its accuracy was not fine enough to navigate a crooked thirty-foot-wide channel that meandered through a boat-chomping reef. The channel was marked by wooden stakes, and as we approached, lowering our sail, two frigate birds took to the air, flying in tandem, their angular wings extended, seeking an updraft to carry them elsewhere. Beiataaki climbed the mast and guided Tekaii through the reef. Here was a plump display of brain coral. There a luminous coral garden. Here a jagged finger. All of it just a yard or two distant from our hulls. The ocean seemed to trip as it encountered the reef, sending forth rolling plumes of white water. I wondered how Maiana managed to get any supplies at all. Everything would have to be offloaded in the deep water, and transported through the reef and across another four miles of lagoon by a smaller vessel.

Beiataaki gestured from his perch in the mast. Left, now right, hard right, *hard right*. Tekaii's eyes were focused solely on Beiataaki as he manipulated the rudder. Even a simple scrape against the bristling reef could sink us. We were still a long distance from land, too far to swim. Twenty long minutes passed. No one except Beiataaki and Tekaii exchanged a word. There was tension on the boat, the giddiness had dissipated. And then we were through and into the relative safety of the lagoon. Beiataaki clambered down from the mast, shaking his head. "I don't like this channel. It's the worst in Kiribati."

Ahead we could see a green palisade of trees that soon sharpened into the minaret stems of coconut trees and the great tumbling canopies of breadfruit trees. We motored across the lagoon toward the middle of Maiana, where just as on every other island in Kiribati, the government maintains a station, called Government Station, which struck me as very Conradian. This was where the island's guesthouse was located, as well as a first-aid clinic, a secondary school, and a fisheries office. A few *maneabas* were visible and then entire villages of thatch and stilts.

"The wind is changing," Beiataaki noted. "A westerly."

The wind vane began to flutter and twirl. Suddenly it hit us, a few gusts that threatened to take our hats, followed by a sustained gale that quickly turned a placid lagoon into white-streaked chop. I had never seen wind turn and strengthen so quickly, not even in Holland, where, typically, one can expect the wind to strengthen the moment you get on a bicycle and to turn as you do, so that no matter which direction you bike you will always be biking into a gale-force headwind. This was different. On a languid, sunny day the wind direction had changed by 180 degrees and hardened into a forty-five-knot gale within two minutes. This did not threaten the boat; the sail was down, the lagoon was shallow, and waves splattered harmlessly against the hull. Still, I had grown accustomed to the torporous monotony of equatorial weather, and now deeply regretted not bringing my windsurfer.

Beiataaki anchored *Martha* in shallow water just off the beach near Government Station. We gathered our gear and waded in. The coconut trees were bent by the wind, their canopies folded in like collapsed umbrellas. I could hear the dull thuds of coconuts loosened by the wind. Children on the beach ran with outstretched lavalavas like gangly birds at takeoff. Our accommodations were on the ocean side of the atoll and we walked along a path that crossed the breadth of Maiana, about a hundred yards, taking care to avoid the trajectories of falling coconuts. The guesthouse was a gray cinder-block house with a dirt floor. It had a living area with a hammock. The sleeping quarters were arranged like horse stalls with hard bunks and mosquito nets. A well and a bucket supplied our water needs.

On this side of the island we remained in the wind's shadow, and, despite the gale, we were able to get a fire going and grill Bwenawa's barracuda. The tuna was left with Beiataaki and Tekaii, who had quickly turned *Martha* around and were racing across the lagoon to navigate the channel before sunset. They planned to sail through the night back to Tarawa and return a week later to pick us up. As the day diminished into an opaque dusk, we could see the ocean churning in the graying light, deep chasms were carved as the wind sent waves rushing and hissing across the horizon. Rain began to pelt the guesthouse. Leaks appeared in the roof. Pools of water turned the floor into mud.

"I think it is raining on Tarawa too," Bwenawa said. We hoped it was. We hoped this storm marked the end of the drought.

"Just think of it," I said to Sylvia. "Full water tanks."

"Provided that the water actually gets into the tanks," she said dryly.

Sylvia still had little faith in my fixing abilities. But I was confident. I had spent hours clearing the roof and gutters of leaves and nettles. I had, very ingeniously I thought, used the materials at hand to plug the holes in the gutter—plastic lids and an extremely valuable roll of electrical tape.

"Don't worry," I said. "I'm a Dutchman. And Dutchmen know how to channel water."

"You're only half Dutch," Sylvia noted. "And you left Holland when you were six."

"It's an innate knowledge. We're water people. Soon, you'll be able to wash your hair guilt-free."

"Twice a week?"

"Twice a week. I promise."

We paused to listen. It was an angry storm.

"I am glad we're not on the boat now," Atenati said. We all pondered for a moment what it must be like for Beiataaki and Tekaii, sailing *Martha* through the black darkness of a starless night, the ocean a violent maelstrom, rogue waves unseen. And then we went to sleep.

CHAPTER 13

In which the Author discusses how unfuckingbelievably scary the South Seas can be.

The next day, in the dim blue light of a tempestuous dawn, we were surprised to see *Martha* anchored in the lagoon, the boat battened down like a fortress.

"Too rough," Beiataaki said when we encountered him on the beach. He had sailed the Gilbert Islands for thirty years. His skin was blotched from sun damage. His face was creased from wind. That he had declared the conditions too rough for sailing, particularly when he did not have any queasy landlubbers on board, suggested some intense roughness indeed. "We got through the channel, but then the waves were too big to keep sailing," he said. "We'll try again later."

But they did not try again later. As the days passed, the storm did not. Each day saw Maiana swept with wind and rain. Papaya trees were felled. *Maneabas* lost their roofs. The island was bathed in a dismal gray. Villages were sodden. Women shivered as Atenati conducted cooking demonstrations, showing how island-grown vegetables rich in vitamin A could be used in the local diet, alleviating the night blindness that stalks malnourished children in Kiribati. Bwenawa returned to the guesthouse late in the afternoons, having spent his days roaming from garden to garden, offering tutorials on the proper sun-to-shade ratio for optimal tomato growth and spreading the wonders of *chaya, bele,* and *nambere,* the only green leafy vegetables that grew on an atoll. Making the weedy leaves edible was Atenati's job.

In the *maneabas*, the *unimane* fretted about the wind and the harm it had inflicted. Each village had at least one *maneaba* with a damaged roof and the old men were concerned about the lack of young men with sufficient *maneaba*-building skills. The population on Maiana was dwindling as each year more of its young people were lured by the flickering lights of Tarawa.

Sylvia and I grew ever more intimate as we made do without a mirror.

"You have eye gunk."

"You've got a booger."

"There's something . . ."

"Where . . . here?"

"No . . . not . . ."

"Did I get it?"

"Here . . . let me."

As the storm ebbed and flowed, with rain showers followed by hard winds, Maiana seemed a gloomy, dejected island, enlivened only—from my perspective—by the unbearably pleasant feeling of coolness, a briskness to the air that meant I could now go through a day without risking dehydration, without feeling the need to douse my food with salt, without succumbing to the torpor of midday, when, typically, the entire country's energy level is reduced to just a shade above comatose. I had long wondered why the temperate world was so much more advanced than the equatorial world, but it seemed obvious to me now that the heat was the key. How productive are New York and Paris in August? Not very, and they have air-conditioning. Now imagine the perpetual August without the cool breath of a humming air conditioner. Would New Yorkers still be working eighteen-hour days, churning out lawsuits and magazines? Would anyone care if Cisco dropped by forty points? No. In the perpetual August, New Yorkers would spend their workdays draped and drooling over their desks, just like the government of Kiribati.

There was another unexpected benefit brought about by the wind. It was too rough to fish, and we had resigned ourselves to rice-intensive meals, when Kiriaata, the gracious caretaker of the guesthouse, apologized for the lack of dinner options. "I can make the chicken curry," she said, holding up a rusty can of Ma-Ling Chicken Curry, which I knew from hard experience contained only those parts of the chicken that even the Chinese would not eat—gizzards and bones. "Or we can have crayfish," Kiriaata offered, reaching for four of the largest, most delectable lobsters I had ever seen. "I am sorry. That is all we have."

Sylvia and I mewed and groaned and made all sorts of deeply primal noises.

"You want chicken curry?"

"*No!*" we barked. "*Crayfish.*"

"Really?"

"*Yes.*"

The I-Kiribati do not have a taste for lobster. I believed this was because their taste buds died when the English arrived. Not only was the I-Kiribati diet pretty grim to begin with, it was now enhanced with canned corned beef and "cabin biscuits," the staples of the nineteenth-century seaman's rations. This combination of atoll food with English food that can survive for years and years on a boat had destroyed the I-Kiribati palate. I thought it would be impolite to test this theory on Bwenawa, so I simply asked him why the I-Kiribati don't like lobster. He explained that they regarded lobster as a disgusting reef cleaner, and he looked at me knowingly, until finally I said: "Ah, yes, I see your point."

It mattered not. While I might not have eaten a lobster caught on the reef in South Tarawa, a quick risk analysis of the situation on Maiana suggested that I could eat a lobster and probably maintain my health, and even if I did get sick it certainly wouldn't be the first time I'd gotten sick eating in Kiribati, and at least I would have had the pleasure of actually eating something I liked.

"I don't suppose you have any butter or a lemon here?" I asked Kiriaata.

"*Akia*," she said.

Nevertheless, it was the tastiest meal I ever ate in Kiribati. Bwenawa and Atenati eyed us warily as we slavered over our lobster.

"Uumh . . ."

"Oooh . . ."

"Aaah . . ."

We asked, if it wasn't too much trouble, if we could have lobster every night. Each evening Bwenawa and Atenati picked at their tinned chicken gristle, while we ate our lobsters with ill-disguised obscenity. Not knowing when such an opportunity might present itself again, we took a few lobsters with us when it was time to depart Maiana.

Beiataaki and Tekaii spent the entire week riding out the storm in Maiana Lagoon. There might have been windows of opportunity for them to sail back to Tarawa, when the wind lessened to a still considerable twenty knots, but the idea of sailing across storm-tossed water only to return a day or two later to do it all over again dissuaded them. On Friday, as we gathered with our gear on the beach, so too did fifty-odd people beseeching us for a lift to Tarawa. "It's Sylvia's decision," Beiataaki informed them diplomatically. Sylvia took one look at the size of the crowd, another look at the size of the boat, and yet another look at the ominous black clouds stirring on the horizon, and said in as reasonable and polite a manner as she could muster, "No." Then she returned to gazing at the ominous black clouds stirring on the horizon.

"What do you think?" she asked me. "Should we go? You're the sailor."

Technically, this was true. I do sail. I have sailed on Lake Ontario and the Chesapeake Bay, but the vast majority of my sailing experience had been confined to a small lake in Holland, with an average depth of five feet, across which I schussed along in a Laser, a tiny little boat generally used by tiny little people learning how to sail. My only experience in blue water sailing thus far had occurred on the trip to Maiana, and though I was very favorably disposed to blue water sailing, I got the feeling that the journey back to Tarawa would be a little different.

"I think we should leave it up to Beiataaki," I said.

Beiataaki had his eyes on the sky, quietly trying to discern its intent. The wind was modest, at least by the previous week's standard, but the darkness of the sky promised nothing good.

"If we go, we have to leave now," Beiataaki said. He was considering the day's tides, which were unfavorable for us, and the fact that there were no lights on the buoys marking the channel into Tarawa Lagoon. This meant that we had to get through the channel before nightfall if we wished to avoid spending a night tacking back and forth on a heaving ocean while awaiting the light of dawn. "I think we should sail to the channel here and decide then," Beiataaki declared.

This we did. With the sail reefed and the engine droning we spent the morning hours crossing the lagoon. A week of gales had stirred the sand at the bottom of the lagoon and the swirling gray clouds gave the water a milky ice-blue tint that looked strangely surreal. As we neared the wooden pilings that marked the channel's entrance, Beiataaki put the engine in neutral and began to fret. We had arrived at precisely the low-water mark, when the channel was at its most treacherous. There would be no room for error. The boulders we had glided over on the way in could sink us on the way out. The reef that extended outward from the channel seemed to be under assault by the ocean. Ponderous waves broke with a dull thunder and dissipated into a churning froth that extended all along its contours.

Beiataaki climbed the mast and there he remained for a very long while, studying the channel and gazing at the ocean. When he clambered down, I asked him what he thought. He shrugged his shoulders like a Frenchman. It is bad either way, he seemed to suggest. And then he seemed to decide.

"I want to go home. I miss my wife."

He climbed back up the mast. Tekaai stood at the rudder waiting for instructions. Sylvia and I exchanged glances. *What the hell. Let's go sailing.* We inched forward and it was immediately clear that this channel at low tide was the nautical equivalent of a minefield. We were surrounded by great jagged bursts of coral. The channel meandered this way and that, zigzagging through jutting fingers and barely submerged boulders. The boat, as I have had occasion to ponder before, was made of plywood. There would be no chance of it surviving a collision. And then, once the passage was behind us, I wished with all my might that we would have sunk the boat in the channel, ending the misery right there and then.

The ocean raged.

Twenty-five feet. This was the height of the waves that greeted us when we emerged from the channel. *Twenty-five feet.* From cavernous trough to foaming peak. Twenty-five feet. And these were not rolling swells, gently lifting and rising. These were steep, pitching waves, tightly packed by the sudden rise of land. Nothing in my experience had prepared me for the sight of these waves.

All of us turned a ghostly white as we internalized the sheer terror of being on a plywood trimaran in twenty-five-foot seas. And then some us began to turn green. As one, Bwenawa, Atenati, and Sylvia retreated to the sheltered aft of the boat, leaned over and began to vomit, and there they remained. Beiataaki steered a course that confronted the waves diagonally, and as we crested a wave, there was a long second when it felt like we had taken flight, an airlessness that made it seem as if we were not sailing across the ocean, but above it, only to be followed by a precipitous slide over the spine of the wave, sending the left hull plowing into the next curling swell, causing torrents of white water to swamp the deck and soak those who stood upon it, stalling the forward movement of the boat until buoyancy was reclaimed, and then the boat pitched ever upward, continuing the shattering routine. The troughs were windless caverns. The mast was swallowed. The sail went limp. On the crests, momentum was regained. All eyes turned toward the waves, dreading the rogue wave, the forty-footer. We watched and judged: That wave there, the third one, the big one, when it hits us it will be a wall of water. Beitaaki would adjust the rudder to confront it head-on, and as we rose above it and the hulls went airborne, there followed the crunching slap of the boat plunging back into the sea, an ear-piercing sound that made those of us still on deck wince with worry.

"What do you think?" I asked Beiataaki. It had begun to rain. I was shivering, cold, and in a state of stupefied awe. My hands were curled around a railing. Tekaai was busy with the sail, raising it here, reefing it there, lowering it altogether, reacting to a capricious wind that gusted and howled but remained unsteady. For safety, he was hooked to the lines running the length of the boat.

"I think we can make it. Once we are away from Maiana the waves will be more round, less steep."

The waves, forged by a week of storms, continued to pound poor *Martha*. It was like being part of an endless car wreck, when you know you no longer have control over the situation, and you are just waiting for its grim conclusion. I went to check on Sylvia. There were stairs to navigate. The boat lurched and I bounced and stumbled and baby-stepped my way down. Sylvia was not well. She sat slumped on a bench, listlessly cradling her head, and muttering cryptically.

"What's that?" I asked her.

"I want to get off this fucking boat."

Hmmm . . . Sylvia is not one for cussing. There were no windows in the aft compartment. A blue tarp had been pulled down to keep the rain out. Atenati and Bwenawa sat on the bench opposite looking equally miserable. Every few minutes, one of the three would poke their head underneath the tarp and over the railing and begin to barf. Not good. Though I wasn't typically afflicted by seasickness, the pitiable sight of these three and the heaving and lurching of the boat was beginning to make me feel nauseated as well.

"Why don't you come up on deck," I said to Sylvia. "The problem here is that you can't see the waves and so your inner ear is confused. My inner ear is confused down here."

"We should have stayed in Maiana," she began to moan. "We should never have gone today. I should have said let's wait until the sea calms down. I didn't know it would be like this. Boo-hoo."

She didn't actually say *boo-hoo*, but she might as well have. I believe that if one-half of a couple becomes weepy and mopey, it is important for the other half to respond with refreshing bursts of sunnyness. This often entails lying.

"Don't worry," I said. "Beiataaki said that he has seen much worse than this. We're perfectly safe."

Actually, Beiataaki had told me that this was about the worst he had ever seen, and if the wind rose, we might have to run with the waves, dragging a sea anchor to ensure that we wouldn't flip end over end, which would add a considerable amount of time to the trip, quite likely several days.

"And because of the conditions," I continued, "we're making excellent time. This will be over before you know it."

"Really?"

"Really."

Actually, we were making terrible time. Each shattering wave stalled us and it would be a miracle if we made it through the chan-nel into Tarawa Lagoon before sunset. Beiataaki was constantly checking his watch and taking our position with the GPS. I asked him why the government didn't just put lights on the buoys that marked the passage into the lagoon. He told me they did, but that the lightbulbs were soon stolen, and so Tarawa remained unap-proachable after sunset. It was the same with the airport runway. Lights were installed, but they too quickly disappeared. Only once had I seen an aircraft land at night. A British aid worker had acci-dentally backed her truck over her young son, crushing his legs, an injury well beyond the capacity of Tarawa Hospital. An air ambu-lance loaded with doctors and medical equipment was immediately dispatched from Australia. It arrived in the middle of the night, landing under the glare of the headlights emitted by dozens of cars strategically parked along the length of the runway. The boy returned to Tarawa a few months later, unburdened by permanent injury, and fortified by the knowledge that in the years to come his mother would likely spoil him rotten.

I escorted Sylvia up to the deck. Beiataaki had been right. Away from Maiana, over the deep water, the waves had become more rounded, more swell-like, than the steep masses of water that flayed us earlier. It was still a twenty-foot trip up and down for each twenty feet we gained horizontally, but *Martha* no longer cleaved her way forward, the violence of the sea had lessened, and I was beginning to enjoy myself. The sailing was raw sailing, but it was just shy of terri-fyingly raw, and that is pretty much how I like my encounters with the natural world to be.

"See," I said to Sylvia. "Isn't this better?"

Silence.

"You know," I said. "You don't look so good."

Sylvia lurched toward the railing. She threw up. And then she eased her way back to her familiar position in the aft compartment, her head dangling over the rail, her eyes closed, muttering darkly. I felt that the moment needed recording, and I took out our camera.

"Say cheese."

This, it occurs to me now, was an unfortunate choice of words. I might as well have said *Imagine swallowing snails and warm butter*. When Sylvia was done vomiting, she turned to me, composed herself for the camera, and flipped me the bird. Click.

"Suitable for framing, I should think."

She smiled wanly, and sunk back into her misery.

The day was getting on. Beiataaki was becoming less concerned with the waves, and more concerned about the approaching darkness. There is no variation in the timing of the sunset on the equator. The sun is down at 6 P.M. each and every day of the year. As we crested the waves, Tarawa gradually came into view. The waves began to pitch and steepen once again as the deep water reacted to the approaching atoll. The sky was gray and darkening and this made the waves seem even more foreboding. We could see Tarawa clearly now, a washed-out little island. There is not a bleaker sight than an atoll in the gray twilight, hunkered down against a wet gusting rain. It was a melancholic vision.

Beiatakki knew where he was going. He had spent a lifetime sailing through the channel that opened Tarawa Lagoon to the ocean. The channel was clearly marked on the chart he used to plot our position, and using the GPS alone, he could locate the channel, give or take fifty feet. But it wasn't enough. We needed to sight the buoys before risking entry. A mistake, one that landed us on the reef, would kill us. No boat could withstand being reefed while hammered by twenty-five-foot waves.

Lights began to flicker on Tarawa. There was no majesty to the sunset. The color just seemed to drain from the sky. As we crested the blackening waves and disappeared in the troughs, so too did the buoy we sought. For a few fleeting seconds while we rose high with a wave, we scanned the water, searching for silhouettes, and as the sky darkened we worried. Only minutes remained until night utterly claimed the sky. The waves, with their height and girth, seemed ever more ominous. I realized that I could barely unclench my hand from the railing I held, it had been molded into a claw. Sylvia, Bwenawa, and Atenati now were braving the deck, lending their eyes to the search for the buoy. We wanted to go home. The mere thought of spending the night tacking back and forth in a running sea while awaiting morning light was more than most of us could bear.

"There it is!" I yelled.

It was bobbing, disappearing, visible again, a dark shadow that jerked wildly. The buoy was about four hundred yards off the left bow.

"I see it," Beiataaki said. "You have good eyes."

Sylvia gazed upon me with newfound ardor.

"You're my hero," she said. Typically, when Sylvia utters words such as those, there is—how shall I say it—a bit of a tone, and frankly, there was a bit of a tone this time too. But Sylvia was suddenly chipper again. Green, but chipper.

We made our way through the channel. It was much broader than the one in Maiana and as we entered the lagoon it was if someone had just reached for the dial and turned down the sea. It was no more than a six-foot swell that diminished into flat water as we neared the port in Betio. It was discombobulating. I had become completely used to the heaving ocean, and when I finally set foot on dry land, I experienced something very like seasickness. My eyes were adapted to a world that went up and down. I tottered with legs splayed. I was accustomed to shifting my weight from one leg to the other to maintain my balance on the boat. I had, it appeared, developed sea legs. I felt unbalanced, my sense of equilibrium disturbed by an unmoving and stable surface, and so with each step, I waited for a moment while that corner of my cranium perceived the transition from sea to land and made adjustments accordingly.

"I am so happy to be on land again," Sylvia groaned.

"I feel dizzy," I replied.

THE FOLLOWING DAY Tarawa sparkled in the sun. The island had received a long overdue cleaning. The water tanks were full. The wind had vanished. The waves remained.

"Have you seen it?" It was Mike, calling from the New Zealand High Commission.

"It's beautiful."

It was. I had forgotten that a reef-breaking wave could be something other than a wicked dumper. At low tide, I wandered out to the edge of the reef, where big, glassy waves, the kind you do see in the surf rags, rolled in with barreling perfection. They were plump and round and they broke in regular patterns.

Sylvia too was impressed. "These are real waves," she declared. Even before the recent unpleasantness on the return trip from Maiana, Sylvia had been a little less than thrilled by my growing enchantment with waves. When I had returned one day from a morning of body boarding chattering about the gnarly conditions and how stoked I was to catch a particularly awesome wave, she said: "Did you just say *gnarly*?"

"Yes."

"And did you say *stoked*?"

"Yes."

"You remind me of my ex-boyfriends."

Her ex-boyfriends went up in my estimation.

"I spent my entire youth listening to guys talk about gnarly waves and how stoked they were. This was why I left California. And now it begins again with you?"

What could I say?

"Just know this. If you ever address someone as *dude*, I'm leaving."

And go where, I thought. We're on an atoll. Besides, my English-language skills were unlikely to mutate much further. I was absorbing my surf lingo from a hyperliterate, ex-hippie New Zealander who had been living in complete isolation for much of the past two decades.

That morning, Mike suggested we go to the Betio causeway. "With this tide, four o'clock should be about right."

Technically, I was not supposed to use the FSP pickup truck to transport surfers and surfing gear from one end of the atoll to the other. The pickup truck was a perk of the job for Sylvia. When not needed to transport people and material for FSP-related business, Sylvia was allowed to use it for her own needs. She was meticulous about what constituted proper use for an FSP-owned vehicle. Everyone on Tarawa knew that this particular pickup truck belonged to FSP. People would talk if they saw a couple of *I-Matangs* barreling down the road on a workday with surfing gear jutting out of the bed of the truck. Even though I handled much of the maintenance for the truck, and I did spend an awful lot of my time ferrying FSP staff from one thing to another, Sylvia was a stickler for propriety and unlikely to be moved by a request for a favor.

"Hi," I said when I reached her on the phone at the office. "I need to get another gas canister."

"Again? I thought we got a new one last week."

"It must have been half-full. Anybody using the truck?"

"No."

"Okay. I'll be there in a few minutes."

Mike and I parked the pickup truck on the side of the causeway and gazed toward the waves. It would be a long paddle just to get there, nearly a half mile of swimming, but once there the hard work would be over. A narrow channel had been blasted through the reef. It was used by fishermen and allowed us to bypass the break zone.

"This is the best I've seen in seventeen years," Mike said.

I put my flippers on and settled on my body board, which, truth be told, wasn't much of a body board. It was more like a small paddle board used by little people learning how to swim, but it was enough. We followed the channel and spent a long time lingering beside the break zone, mesmerized by the waves. There is something hypnotic about their motion: the protuberant swell suddenly rising from the blue void, gathering a coiled height and becoming a pure force that rises into a funneling wall of water, and then a long, tense moment until it dissipates in a thunderous climax. There are times when I could spend hours just watching waves, but this wasn't one of them. We paddled ahead and lined up and for the next hour caught wave after wave, each more perfect than the last. I edged deeper into the break zone, determined to catch my waves at their maximum height and extend my rides, spending a long minute carving loopy Ss. And that's when it appeared.

The rogue wave. The wave that has swallowed several other waves. The wave that was born in some tempest in the southern ocean; the wave that grew into something monstrous and horrible during a week of gales in the central Pacific; the wave we had feared on the torturous journey home from Maiana. This wave was now approaching. We were caught inside. Waves such as these do not explode where other waves do. They do their violence farther out. Mike turned his board straight toward it. His arms were like cartoon arms, spinning and spinning like paddle wheels in overdrive. As the wave took him, he was stretched vertically on its face, and I could see that the wave was three times bigger than he. He clawed at its face, climbing this liquid mountain. He ascended, peaked, and disappeared over the frothing lip.

I was too deep. I could not follow Mike. The wave began to pitch and totter. It sucked in ever more water. I moved high up on my board, freeing my arms, and then swam faster than any man has swum before. I was headed diagonally into the face of the wave, trying to outrun the initial break. But the wave detonated. It boomed. I knew then that I would not get over in time.

And then I became stupid. I was abandoned by good sense. My survival instinct took a holiday. There was only one sensible option and that was to dive as deep as I could, but this I did not do. I did not have a leash connecting me to my board. If I dove, I would then have to swim all the way back to shore to retrieve my board, and somehow this little inconvenience caused my brain to stop working. Instead, I turned the board around, thinking, despite all evidence to the contrary, that I could catch this wave at its very peak, zip down its face, and then establish enough momentum to outrun the break. I was wrong.

I can attest now that having an eighteen-foot wave break upon your head is a remarkably unpleasant experience. There is the physical dimension, in which the wave rips off your board and your flippers, and suddenly you do not know up from down, you cannot breathe or see, but you can hear, and what this wave is telling you is that it can destroy you. There is crushing, and pounding, and hurtling. And there is pain. And there is panic. And it is terrifying. This wave is immensely more powerful than you, and it scars the psyche seeing this demonstrated in such a personal way. When I emerged, bruised and panting for air, I actually prayed, saying thank you for sparing me here, I will be very good from now on, et cetera et cetera, and then I scoured the beach for my board, found my flippers bobbing in the shallows, and I returned to the waves, to the ocean, with respect and humility.

"Did you catch that monster?" Mike asked, as I lined up alongside, my eyes on the swells and what they would become.

"No, dude," I said. "But it caught me."

CHAPTER 14

In which the Author explores the World of Dogs on Tarawa, particularly the world of his dogs, who grew up to be the Biggest Dogs on Tarawa, possibly because he fed them, which led him to look upon his dogs in a different light, particularly when the dogs were described as kang-kang (tasty).

One day, Vaclav, a timid green-eyed dog with white fur, given to us by Tiabo—because he looked like an *I-Matang* dog, she explained—arrived home from his reef explorations with the dog we had always referred to as the brown dog. This dog soon became affectionately known as Brown Dog, because Sylvia would not let me name her Olga. Brown Dog in turn brought her mother, a gentle long-snouted dog with black fur, known in the dog community as the neighborhood slut, and soon called by us Mama Dog, who in turn brought her most recent litter, four shrieking puppies, more pathetic than cute on account of their mangy baldness, but smart nonetheless, who quickly recognized that Sam, our cat, had claws and did not like to be trifled with. And so it came to be that we suddenly found ourselves with seven dogs and one cat, which was not ideal.

The cat was the first to arrive. He had run away as a wee kitten, proving that he was an exceptionally clever cat. I would estimate that the average life span of a cat in Kiribati is about five hours. The

I-Kiribati regard cats as useless, inedible, and harbingers of black magic. Litters are generally scooped up as soon as they are found, placed in a bag, and drowned. The I-Kiribati do not have soft and mushy feelings for the animal world. Even children, whom one would assume to be the most sympathetic to the plight of small animals, amuse themselves by flinging a kitten or puppy around by its tail until they grow bored, whereupon the animal is tossed into the current of an outgoing tide. Sam the cat, however, somehow managed to escape this fate and find his way to an *I-Matang* house, where he mewed and moaned and made such a sorry spectacle of himself that we felt obliged to let him in. He quickly made his way to the couch, clambered up, settled himself belly up, and promptly fell asleep underneath the ceiling fan. His fleas too made themselves at home.

Zeus was next. We had only recently arrived on the island and still maintained Humane Society–type feelings for dogs. That would change. Very soon I would be pleased with myself when the rocks I flung drew blood, but at the time such behavior was unimaginable. Zeus was a pitiful sight. A small puppy that had already lost every scrap of fur to the mange, he also had a belly distended by worms and nicks and cuts that were clearly infected. I should have broken his neck right there and then and put him out of his misery. But he was scrappy and personable, and when I made the mistake of giving him some bread, he looked upon me with such happy, grateful eyes that I didn't know what to do. There was no veterinarian on the island. The last one, a volunteer from Finland, had left when he more or less lost three-quarters of his right leg to a toxic infection caused by a scrape against the coral reef. The new vet had yet to arrive. When Mike wandered by one day I promptly asked him if he would like to have this dog. "He's very friendly," I said.

"Do you mean this cruel joke of a dog?" he asked. "The only thing to do with a dog like that is to crush it with a rock."

"Yes, well, I can't quite manage to do that."

"Give it time."

In the end, we decided to bring the dog to FSP, where we were sure it would grow up to be a much-loved guard dog. We named it Zeus, figuring he could use a little ego boost. Sylvia reported that Zeus had lasted exactly one hour at FSP before another dog ate him.

"You're kidding."

"No. The poor thing."

I had always assumed that the expression *It's a dog-eat-dog world* was to be understood metaphorically, but apparently there is also a literal dimension and this took some getting used to. It's a tough world for dogs in Kiribati. Contrast this with the experience of their cousins in the United States, where dogs have their own hotels, are taken for monthly pedicures, are fed gourmet dog food, and are treated with what I now regard as gag-inducing affection and deference. My mother, for instance, apparently feels that rules and discipline are only to be applied to children, whereas when her beagle jumps on top of the table and empties wineglasses in between devouring the Thanksgiving turkey, my mother gets out the camera. "She's a very independent dog," she says. Yes, well if that dog happened to find himself on Tarawa, it's safe to say that it would also find itself on the dinner table. Of course, the I-Kiribati don't have tables, but you see my point.

The I-Kiribati, particularly those from the northern Gilberts, eat dogs. I could understand why. The diet in Kiribati is so meager that now and then whenever I spied a particularly meaty person I immediately thought of a pork loin. Don't get me wrong. I had no desire to eat anyone's arm, but once you've digested raw sea worms and boiled moray eels you begin to think a little more creatively about what precisely constitutes food. Still, it was something of a gasp-inducing shock when wandering on the beach on North Tarawa I came across two men skinning a dog, preparing it for the fire. Imagine taking poor Max for a walk and all the while he is bounding along in that happy-go-lucky way of dogs on walks, and meanwhile you're thinking marinades. The dog was soon impaled on a spit— and I know I'm going to get a lot of hate mail for this—but it smelled pretty good.

Nevertheless, I could not be induced to eat an unknown dog, even though I was assured it was *kang-kang*. This is because most dogs on Tarawa are repellent to behold. Combine the mange with starvation, add in a canine social milieu that rewards feral savagery, and you are unlikely to find a blue ribbon kind of dog. Instead, what you find is a pure Darwinian dog. A tough dog.

I found this out as we tended to Vaclav. He was a puppy when Tiabo presented him to us, unbidden. "You need a guard dog," she said, and I tried not to feel slighted. "This is an *I-Matang* guard dog."

Vaclav had white fur, or at least he had some white fur. The mange had gotten him too, and so he was predominantly pink, just like us *I-Matang*. Four hours and five "accidents" later, we decided that he would be an outdoor dog. We cleaned him up and fed him the best the island could provide, fish and rice, and it was with swelling pride when we first heard him bark like a manly dog, a deep sonorous get-away-from-the-house bark.

He had had a rough go of it. Dogs on Tarawa are profoundly territorial. Vaclav found this out one day when he bravely accompanied me to the Angirota Store. It is a short walk, but a mere hundred yards from the house, a half-dozen neighborhood dogs set upon Vaclav, mauling him to shreds for having the temerity to cross their territory, and it was only through some pretty fierce and highly accurate rock throwing that I was able to save him. He limped and hobbled. He bled alarmingly from several gashes. I feared that we were going to have an Old Yeller kind of ending, but within hours he had pulled himself back together and learned a valuable lesson. It's a dog-eat-dog world out there.

Soon he made a friend. Brown Dog was roughly the same age as Vaclav, and together they prowled the reef at low tide, which in the dog community was regarded as neutral territory. Sam the cat also wandered out to the reef at low tide. He liked to go fishing. Hovering over a tidal pool, he deftly scooped out a fish, which he would then bring back into the house and play with until it died, and then he would find an ingenious hiding place for it. It was the same with geckos. Whenever he heard the soft plop of a gecko losing its grip, Sam darted with astonishing speed, clasped the gecko firmly in its mouth, no longer fooled by that devious lose-the-tail trick, and brought it back inside the house, where he mercilessly taunted it until it also died. Then he would find an obscure nook somewhere and hide the gecko. Decomposition occurs swiftly on the equator. Hours later, we would follow our noses in an exciting game of Where's the Dead Animal? Sam enjoyed this immensely.

Vaclav and Brown Dog too brought back interesting finds from the reef. Typically, they returned with skulls. On any given day, our backyard was home to a half-dozen and more dog and pig skulls, roasted an alabaster white by the sun, the bridges of the snouts splintering into barren sockets. Each day, I tossed the skulls into an outgoing tide where they bobbed like the grisly remnants of a Kurtzian (yes, him again) sacrifice, hoping that they would be carried beyond the reef before the tide turned. Each day, the dogs found new skulls upon which they happily gnawed.

We had begun to feed Brown Dog, and as a result she never left. We began to feed her because once, when she hovered a little too near Vaclav's food bowl, Vaclav's ears went ominously flat, his teeth flared, his nose twitched, he growled cruelly, and when Brown Dog still did not retreat, he set upon her with such stunning ferocity that I feared he would kill his erstwhile friend. I picked him up by the nape of the neck and decided that, what the hell, two dogs are better than one. I started buying larger fish.

Soon, Brown Dog developed into a big, fleshy, meaty dog. Tiabo was much impressed. She appraised Brown Dog with a knowing eye. "I think Brown Dog will be *kang-kang*," she said.

"Really?" I said, examining Brown Dog a little more closely. She was a good-looking dog, unaffected by the mange. "You really think she'll be a tasty dog?"

"We like the brown dogs," she said. "Fat brown dogs."

Hmm . . . I wondered. I was mighty tired of fish. Cows are large mammals, I thought. Cows have doleful eyes. Cows are presumably intelligent creatures. I would have eaten a cow, if there happened to be one within three thousand miles of Tarawa. Why not a dog? A healthy dog? A fat, brown dog? I fed Brown Dog a little *extra*. Just to preserve our culinary options.

Apparently, Brown Dog had told her mother about this fortuitous turn of events, and soon she too made her hearth in our backyard. She was a mild-mannered dog, and wise to canine life on Tarawa. She avoided trouble, kept to herself, and when I fed Vaclav and Brown Dog she perked up hopefully, but never begged. She was, however, denied a bowl of fish and rice. If there was a supermarket where I could load up on thirty-pound bags of prepared dog food, I might very well have fed this third dog, but there wasn't, and frankly, I had enough mouths to feed. Nonetheless, this did not prevent Mama Dog, as Sylvia had begun calling her, from contributing to the household's security detail.

They were good too, once Vaclav and Brown Dog had developed their barks. It was with great relish that I watched them move like unleashed hounds from hell when they gave chase to an exceedingly foolish Peeping Tom. "Get 'im, boys! Nip him where it counts."

With remarkable sensory skills, they were able to discern friend from foe. The kids still came by in the afternoons to root for twigs and *te non*. We had reached an understanding: What's on the ground is theirs. What remains on the trees stays there. Random knife-wielding men no longer traipsed near the house, but walked along the reef, just as they did when passing I-Kiribati compounds. When strangers called, they did so from the road, and if anyone approached the house, they were soon met with what began as a quizzical bark—just to let us know—and morphed, according to circumstances, into something one desperately wanted to run away from. But when two Mormon missionaries approached without a peep from the dogs, I decided that their training needed some more finessing. We didn't want Elder Jeb and Elder Brian coming around here.

Elder Jeb and Elder Brian were twenty-year-old Mormon missionaries from Utah. They wanted my soul.

"Come in," I said. "Do you want a cup of tea?"

"No, thanks."

"How about a cigarette?"

"No, really."

"Beer?"

"No, we can't."

Exactly. Caffeine, nicotine, and alcohol are three very good reasons why I will never become a Mormon. We don't even have to get into the highly colorful and fantastically ludicrous theology. To each their own, I say. But leave me alone. When I inquired if they had had any luck finding wives, they decided to move on and try their chances elsewhere. They were very nice about it, and though I did my best to be an asshole, they were never anything but polite, which has been my experience with Mormons everywhere. Still, I tried to teach the dogs to growl menacingly at anyone in pants. Only Mormon missionaries wore pants on Tarawa.

Life with the animals settled into a familiar routine. Each day I boiled a large pot of rice and carved our fish into five distinct servings. The good parts, of course, were for me and Sylvia. Sam got the blood meat, and the two dogs received the rest of the fish, head and tail included. Then one day we noticed that our yard was awash in dogs, vicious dogs engaged in some sort of barbaric ritual that involved, literally, killing each other. Brawls would suddenly break out, until the loser finally limped away to die. Whenever possible, I did my best to break it up. Standing from a safe distance, I pelted the dogs with rocks until they took their fights to the reef. But still they returned. Mama Dog was in heat.

Canine courtship is not pretty to behold. Like a teenage girl, Mama Dog wanted nothing to do with the nice guys. She was drawn to the biggest, baddest, meanest dog on Tarawa, the one who would most likely allow her to produce offspring that were themselves big, bad, and mean, and possibly, just possibly, be able to survive for longer than a month or two. If anyone doubts Darwinism, let them come to Tarawa to study the mating rituals of island dogs. The triumphant winner of Mama Dog's affections was a heinous beast that looked like the progeny of a steroid-enhanced rottweiler and a bull—not a pit bull—a bull. I hated this dog. He exuded nothing but malice. He had lost an eye in one of his brawls, and this made him appear even more menacing. I dearly hoped that someone would eat him.

A few months later, the puppies arrived. There were seven. A few days later, there were six, then five, then four. It's a tough life. I had hoped that Mama Dog would have taken her brood elsewhere, but unfortunately they all remained with us. Vaclav was very stoic about the situation. The puppies soon learned that under no circumstances should they go anywhere near his food bowl, and once that was established he simply ignored them. Brown Dog displayed a frighteningly maternal adoration for the puppies, and I desperately hoped that the new vet would arrive soon. Vaclav too was beginning to dangle obscenely. Not to mention the cat, who had begun to spend his nights fighting, and from what we could tell, managing to always lose. Clearly, it was snip-snip time.

No one took their dogs to get fixed on Tarawa, even when there was a vet on the island. Dogs were banned on Christmas Island, but on Tarawa animal control consisted of an irregular sweep by a dog-catcher armed with a long stick and a noose. This did not alleviate the dog problem on Tarawa. Nor was it meant to. The captured dogs were used to feed the prisoners.

Instead, the surplus dogs were left to fend for themselves. I had wondered about how Mama Dog was managing to feed her surviving puppies. She was a resourceful dog. A dog has to be to survive on Tarawa. I had assumed she was simply scavenging along the reef, but as I was stunned to witness, she had taken a much more proactive role to putting dinner on the table. One afternoon, as all the dogs lay slumbering in the shade, a small dog of about seven months old wandered by. Our dogs raised their heads, and determining that there was no challenge to their territory here, they went back to their snooze. Mama Dog, however, pounced on the dog. It squealed pathetically. Moments later, Mama Dog had severed its hind leg and fed it to her puppies.

If I had not already been on Tarawa for a long while, I quite likely would have felt appalled and disgusted by this act of cannibalism, but my threshold for feeling appalled and disgusted had notched up considerably since I arrived. Although in the continental world I assigned all sorts of anthropomorphic characteristics to dogs, on Tarawa I saw them as wild animals doing whatever it took to survive. What troubled me here was not the fact that these puppies were greedily slurping away at another dog, but that they might not be able to finish it all and what remained would soon stink horribly and it would be me, of course, who had to dispose of the carcass and that was not something I wanted to do on any sort of regular basis. I resolved to get rid of the puppies. I convinced four people of the superior breeding of these puppies, and one by one, whenever Mama Dog wasn't looking, I scooped up a puppy and delivered it to its new home. Then I resigned myself to feeding Mama Dog. I bought a bigger fish.

To my dismay, Mama Dog was soon in heat again and the cycle repeated itself. Her belly swelled. Her teats returned. I wondered if I would be able to drown the puppies myself. I did not think I could. There remained a residual Westernness in me that said only really nasty people kill puppies.

Fortunately, the new vet finally arrived and I made arrangements to spare the other animals from the urges and consequences of their hormonal imperatives. The cat was the first to go. Each morning he returned to the house a little more battle-scarred, and though he survived kittenhood, it seemed unlikely that he would survive as a cat unless he was fixed. I picked Sam up and carried him to the pickup truck. If you have never driven a manual-shifting car alone with an uncaged cat, I recommend that you go to great lengths to avoid the experience. I deluded myself into thinking that the cat would sit quietly in the passenger seat, but in fact moments after I started the car he found his way to the top of my head, which he used as a perch to leap toward the window, which sadly for him, was closed, causing him to experience a not inconsiderable amount of panic, which he manifested by ripping me to shreds, pausing only to relieve himself. By the time we reached the vet's office, a two-room surgery in Tanaea, I was bleeding from a number of slashes and I smelled like cat urine.

"Hi," I said. "It's nice to meet you. Welcome to Tarawa. I have a cat for you. He's presently locked in the glove compartment."

Hillary, a young volunteer vet from Britain, was kind enough to provide me with antiseptic and Band-Aids. I retrieved the cat and after he calmed down Hillary sedated him. The surgery would be done by Manibure, Hillary's assistant.

"I can see why he gets into fights. He's got big balls," Manibure noted.

"Well, make sure you get them both. I want a mellow cat."

I returned a few hours later, and found Sam, *sans cojones*, just beginning to stir.

"Here," Hillary said, handing me several needles. "You will need to give him antibiotics for the next few days."

"Um . . . Do you mean to say I have to stick a needle into this cat?"

"Yes. Don't worry. It's very simple. Just lift up the skin and inject the needle."

I tried to absorb this. I had been mauled by Sam simply for taking him on a drive. I could only imagine the abuse he would inflict on me once I stuck a needle in him. I need not have worried though. Without feline testosterone coursing through him, he offered nothing more than a meek what-are-you-doing-to-me protest, even after I accidentally punctured his skin the whole way through, sending a stream of antibiotics coursing through the air in a long, useless arc.

A few days later I brought the dogs. Unsurprisingly, they were much more amenable to a car trip. They exulted as they passed through the forbidden territory claimed by other dogs. *Ha-ha. You can't get us.*

"We got Brown Dog just in time," Hillary said. "In another day or two, she would have gone into heat."

I thanked Hillary and Manibure heartily for sparing us from that nightmare. By the evening, both dogs were bouncing about as if they had not just that very morning undergone major surgery. They are resilient, these island animals.

I soon ran into Hillary again, as was bound to happen on our small island. I asked her how she was doing, freshly arrived on Tarawa.

"Well, I am not precisely sure what it is I'm supposed to be doing. Manibure is very good and doesn't need much more training. He knows what he is doing with the pigs. So far, you are the only people to bring in their pets for sterilization. While I find Kiribati very interesting, I fear that professionally I might become a little bored."

"What was your specialty in Britain?"

"Cows and horses."

I laughed. Those animals were about as familiar to Kiribati as unicorns.

"I have just learned all these wonderful new techniques, and yet I fear I won't be able to practice here. For instance, there is this great new technique for sterilizing dogs after they have conceived, and I would be very keen to try it out, but—"

"I have just the dog for you."

"Really?"

"Yes. The only problem is she is a bit of a wanderer, and I can't be certain when exactly I might be able to take her in."

"That's all right. I can swing by your house and we can do it there."

The following day Mama Dog found herself strapped to our dining table. Hillary brought her surgical tools, and once the dog was fully sedated she set to work, skillfully incising Mama Dog's belly.

"My goodness, would you look at that," Hillary said. She was very exuberant about her work.

"It's . . . uh . . . very interesting."

"I have never seen so much fat on a dog. It's astonishing."

Mama Dog was not a fat dog. By Western standards she would probably be described as scrawny. This fat was her in-house store of energy. Darwinism at work.

"Oh dear."

"Anything wrong?" I asked.

"Yes. Quite a lot. See this?"

"Um . . . yeah." (Details omitted.)

"Her puppies died. See? They have already turned into pus. This would have killed her in a few days."

"That's not good."

"No. This is actually turning out to be major surgery. You'll give me a hand, won't you?"

For the next hour, I followed Hillary's directions—*hold this, put your finger there, pull, now stuff it all back in*. When Sylvia arrived home, she was not the least bit surprised or perturbed to find her dining table used as an operating table for a dog, though she did spend an awfully long time cleaning it afterward. I knew then that we had both made the mental leap from the continental world to the island world, where anything can happen and usually does.

A few hours later, I was amazed to see Mama Dog up and about, wagging her tail. She had just, quite literally, had her guts removed and yet she behaved as if it were just another day in a dog's life on Tarawa. Was she a freak of nature, or was this what nature produced when allowed to go its own way, unhindered by breeders? If fed and trained, it seemed to me, these were good dogs. I would wager that in a match of strength and intelligence, a Tarawa dog would far out-perform a Western dog with a pedigree.

Thanks to Hillary and the British taxpayer, I believed we had set-tled, once and for all, the number of animals making our home theirs, and so when one night we awoke to the cloying *arf-arf* of a puppy outside our window, I was in no mood to be generous. I went outside, picked up the pup, and took it to the reef, and to make my point clear, began to throw small rocks in its direction, encouraging it to skedaddle. Twenty minutes later, the puppy returned. *Arf-arf.* This continued for three sleepless nights, until finally I lost my patience and I stomped out of the house, grabbed the puppy, took it to the reef, where I had every intention of snapping the dog's neck and tossing it into the sea. The puppy was doomed one way or the other. But I couldn't do it. Yes, he looked upon me with sad, puppy-dog eyes. Instead, the following day, I picked up the little dog, walking around with it until I found a female dog with similar markings. Close enough, I thought, as I set the puppy down in front of his new mother. I never saw the puppy again.

CHAPTER 15

In which the Author describes the Behavior of
Government Officials (drunken thuggery), the Peculiar
System of Governance (Coconut Stalinism), the Quality of
Government Services (Stalin, at least, got something done),
followed by a recounting of the Interministerial Song and
Dance Competition, when for nearly Two Months all
government activities Ceased, not that anyone noticed,
followed by the Shocking Conclusion to the competition,
when the Ministry of Housing won with a dance that
Shamelessly incorporated Polynesian influences, leaving
the other Competitors to stew in their Bitter Bile.

Elsewhere in the world, governments typically confine their
activities to the defense of their nation, the education of
their youth, monetary policy, and the disbursement of pensions.
True, a few—maybe more than a few—governments have pursued
more nefarious ambitions, such as global hegemony and world
dominance in rhythmic gymnastics, but most . . . okay, many . . . all
right some—let's not get into this—confine their energy to security
and improving the quality of life of their citizens.

Not so in Kiribati. The country lacks a military force because the
I-Kiribati wisely acknowledge that no one else wants their country.
Even the I-Kiribati aren't too thrilled about having their country.
Certainly they wanted to live there, but all things being equal, they

would rather have had the British govern it. Nor does the country have any say about monetary policy, since it uses the Australian dollar as its currency. There was a brief pang of worry in Canberra that President Tito's decision to double the salaries of all government workers would lead to inflation in Australia, but then they remembered that this was Kiribati after all, with a population that could easily fit inside the new stadium in Sydney. Besides, even by doubling his salary, President Tito, the highest paid government official in Kiribati, still pulled in less than US $10,000 per annum, which didn't strike me as particularly inflated. Like us, he probably couldn't find anything to spend it on either.

The government in Kiribati also has very little to do with education. There is but one state-run school on Tarawa, the King George V High School, where government workers send their children. At any given time, half of the *I-Matangs* on the island were there to do "curriculum development" for KGV. This had gone on for several years without any discernible change in the colonial-era curriculum. The consultants, however, did swallow most of the country's education budget. The rest of the nation's children made do with church-run schools. And pensions? Few in Kiribati live long enough to collect a pension.

One can then reasonably ask what exactly does the government of Kiribati do? As far as I could tell, the government spends a lot of time drinking and brawling. No workshop on global climate change is complete until the assistant secretary of the environment has passed out in a pool of beer barf. No meeting to discuss interministerial cooperation on transport issues can occur without a climactic brawl between the principal welfare officer and the deputy secretary for transportation. And no reception for the rare visiting diplomat can be considered a success until the chairs are hurtled in a fine display of drunken carnage. The higher one is, the more such displays are expected. The vice president, for instance, decided to honor the visiting Japanese ambassador by guzzling a dozen cans of Victoria Bitter and then punching his wife as the horrified Japanese delegation looked on.

One would assume then that the government of Kiribati practices a laissez-faire approach to governance. This would be an incorrect assumption. The government of Kiribati has, in fact, emulated the North Korean model of governance. It practices what I like to call Coconut Stalinism. It controls everything. It does nothing.

On the outer islands, this was good—the do-nothing part. Subsistence living is rarely eased through diktats from the capital. But on Tarawa, indifference and inaction could be exasperating. The government owns the food co-ops, which specialize in expired tinned fish, just the thing for the fish-weary consumer. It controls the infrastructure and, as a result, rare is the stream of electricity that lasts longer than a few hours before it fizzles. Air Kiribati, government-owned, is a disaster waiting to happen. So too are the state-owned ships.

The government also manages the hospital, and I am using the word *hospital* very generously here. It is a complex of dingy single-story buildings where dogs wander through the patient wards; where flies torment the unfortunate denizens because no one has bothered to install screens on the windows—even though screening is readily available at the island's hardware store; where the emergency room lacks a sink and is therefore stained with the blood of innumerable patients; where the incinerator has failed to work, oh, for several years now, resulting in an island littered with hazardous waste; where the X-ray machine stands idle because no one bothered to order film, or general anesthesia for that matter, which means that patients undergo operations with only a local anesthetic, which just makes me shudder. In brief, the hospital on Tarawa was where one went to die.

The I-Kiribati knew this. That's why no one ever went to the hospital until they were ready to meet their maker. In the meantime, they resorted to local plants presumed to have medicinal value, healing massages, and magic to treat their ailments. Only when the tumor bulged alarmingly under the skin, or the wound turned dangerously gangrenous, or the knife could not be removed from the heart was a patient delivered to the hospital, when, of course, it was too late to do much anyway. It wasn't as if all of the half-dozen or so doctors on Tarawa were incompetent, though frankly I too was wary of seeking medical counsel from doctors trained in Burma, Nigeria, and Papua New Guinea. The United Nations, in its wisdom, sends doctors from the most medically deprived corners of Africa and Asia to the Pacific Islands. In turn, it sends doctors from the most medically deprived corners of the Pacific to staff the wards in Africa and Asia. I am sure there is a very good reason for this, but my brain is too feeble to grasp what that reason could be. But I digress. The main problem doctors faced on Tarawa was that they simply did not have the diagnostic tools, the medicine, or a clean recovery ward, to allow them to do their job. Sylvia spent two years trying to donate hospital equipment, for free, gratis, as a gift from the American people, training included, but failed to do so because the secretary of health, a doctor himself, could not bring himself to sign on the dotted line. He was a busy man, attending conferences around the world sponsored by the United Nations, the World Health Organization, and other groups that believe the best way to help the Third World is to lure away the few people in those countries who have the power to do something and bring them to a swank hotel in Geneva, where they can . . . where they can do what exactly? The program usually emphasizes "networking opportunities."

For a long while, I assumed that the government was irredeemable, that its ministries were staffed entirely by idle sycophants with no greater ambition than to fritter away every foreign aid dollar that arrived in the country. This, however, turned out not to be the case. The ministries were indeed ambitious. They each had a goal, a drive to succeed, a desire to be the very best that they could be, and they were staffed accordingly. Academic credentials mattered not. Nor did experience. The critical skill a potential employee brought to their ministry was their ability to dance.

Every year on Independence Day, the ministries competed for the honor of winning the Interministerial Song and Dance Competition. This was the highlight of the holiday, and ministries spent months preparing. In the evenings, the *maneabas* on South Tarawa rumbled to the sounds of hundreds of ministerial workers singing and dancing into the small hours of the morning. Costumes were prepared; long grass skirts and pandanus brassieres for the women, matching lavalavas, intricate armbands and crowns that looked to be inspired by the Statue of Liberty for the men. As Independence Day neared, all semblance of official government activity ceased. For a month, each team, consisting of a hundred or more participants, fasted from dawn to dusk. The consumption of alcohol, remarkably, was forbidden. More remarkable still, sex too was prohibited. The dancing spirits—and how they loomed over the participants—demanded purity.

This struck me as a great sacrifice to make for the spirits. In a country like Kiribati, where most people struggle daily to ensure that they have enough to eat, there is little room for asceticism. A vegan, for instance, would very soon be a dead vegan in Kiribati. Even a less militant vegetarian is unlikely to survive on an atoll. In Kiribati, one eats what is available when it is available. And for a government worker to spurn alcohol seemed to me the height of self-denial, surpassed only by the repudiation of sex. The I-Kiribati struck me as a lusty people. Their conversations were laced with sexual innuendo, and in the months preceding the arrival of our dogs, rare was the night when returning from an evening out we did not stumble across a lusty couple coupling in our backyard, seeking an escape from the public forum that is I-Kiribati home life.

"Fasting I can understand," I said to Sylvia. "And the no-alcohol rule strikes me as a pretty good thing. Most of these guys could use a little drying out. But clearly, this no-sex injunction is going to be hard for the dancers."

"Clearly," Sylvia replied, "you haven't been talking to the women here about their sex lives."

That was true. I was under the impression that to inquire about a woman's sex life was a cultural faux pas of the first order, one that would very likely get me killed by an enraged husband.

"And now that I think about it," Sylvia continued, "don't start asking a woman about her sex life. She'll believe you have designs on her, and this will get back to me—everything does, you know—and I'll be expected to bite your nose off."

This was also true. Biting off someone's nose was an acceptable way to display jealousy. I had initially assumed that the large number of people sporting disfigured noses was the result of leprosy, but in fact it was simply the mark of a jealous encounter. Men bit the noses off women, and women bit the noses off men. This did not necessarily mean the end of the relationship. There were many noseless couples in Kiribati. There was, it seemed, a dark side to the sex lives of the I-Kiribati. I asked Sylvia what she knew.

"Have you heard of dry sex?" she asked.

"Isn't that from the *Kama Sutra*?"

"It's when a woman stops lubrication. This is done by inserting a mixture of coral and herbs into her vagina. It's the preferred form of sex for I-Kiribati men. They claim it increases their sensation."

"No."

"Yes."

"I was under the impression that only occurred in places like tribal Pakistan."

"Here too. And just like tribal Pakistan, kidnapping your bride is an acceptable form of courtship here."

"I had no idea."

"That's because you're a man, and an I-Kiribati woman won't talk to a man about that sort of thing. Did you know that Kineita kidnapped Beita?"

Beita worked at FSP. Kineita was her husband. Their marriage struck me as the very model of conjugal bliss. They were affectionate. Kineita was a respectful, doting husband. They had a precocious two-year-old son.

"Beita was in love with another man," Sylvia continued. "She wanted to marry him, not Kineita. But Kineita apparently couldn't take no for an answer, so he kidnapped her and held her for two weeks until she *agreed* to marry him."

That seemed odd to me. "Why didn't her family or the other guy rescue her?"

"What do you think Kineita was doing to her for those two weeks? He was having sex with her. That shamed her family. And the other guy wanted nothing more to do with her. She had no choice but to marry Kineita."

"And yet she seems pretty happy with him."

"She is. He is a Seventh-Day Adventist. He doesn't drink and he doesn't beat her."

That made him quite the catch in Kiribati, I realized. And he had job security. Kineita, it turned out, was also a fine dancer. He would be representing the Ministry of Education, where he worked in curriculum development.

WITH THE COMPETITION LOOMING, the ministries began to finalize their lineups of singers and dancers. Some took a rather expansive view of who constituted a ministerial employee. The Ministry of Environment, for instance, had talent-spotted Bwenawa and Tiabo, excellent dancers both, and so invited the FSP staff to participate under the banner of its ministry. FSP did environmental work; ergo FSP fell under the Ministry of Environment. This greatly excited the staff. Sylvia too was invited to dance. It was felt that the novelty of having an *I-Matang* woman doing one of the sitting dances would score extra points with the judges.

"I know I should do it," she said. "It would be a cultural experience. I should have cultural experiences. That's why we're here, right? But I really don't want to spend the next four weeks in a *maneaba*, staying up until 3 A.M., learning how to do a sitting dance. Is that bad of me?"

"No. I am sure there will be other opportunities for you to wear a grass skirt and a pandanus bra."

I, of course, was pleased that Sylvia had declined to dance. She too would have been expected to make the sacrifices necessary to ensure a visitation from the dancing spirits. And those sacrifices were not ones I wanted to share in. Nor did I particularly want to see Sylvia's body inhabited by the dancing spirits. They spooked me. I felt deeply uncomfortable whenever I saw a dancer overcome by the spirits. It begins with uncontrolled yelping and wailing, followed by tears, and ends with the dancer tumbling to the ground, where she flaps like a fish until she passes out. Spectators nod approvingly while she is carried out of the *maneaba*. It was like watching a schizophrenic have an epileptic fit. I found it deeply unsettling. I wished the spirits would just leave these dancers alone.

The I-Kiribati, however, are disturbingly eager to be swept away by the dancing spirits. Each day, the FSP staff staggered into the office after a long night of dancing practice. They were exhausted, malnourished, and not at all excited about the prospect of working. Instead, the one-hour lunch break turned into a three-hour nap. At exactly noon, the mats were unrolled and the staff settled into a group snooze, save for Bwenawa, who was banished to another room because he snored.

"What can I do?" asked Sylvia.

There was nothing Sylvia could do. All of Tarawa had been swept into the tumult of the Song and Dance Competition. From dawn to dusk, the starving, sex-deprived sleepyheads that made up the dancing teams listlessly staggered through their days. At night, every sizable *maneaba* on the island thundered to the sounds of hundreds of people belting out the tunes of the ancients. I thought it was wonderful—an entire month free of "La Macarena."

Finally, Independence Day arrived. Sylvia and I had been invited to view the proceedings from the grandstand, which was quite the honor for FSP, never mind that the grandstand was a cement slab of questionable structural integrity. We were told to arrive at 7:30 A.M. sharp. Typically, I don't celebrate anything at 7:30 A.M. Typically, I am not even conscious at 7:30 A.M. But there was a good reason for the early start. Gathered on what was optimistically called a field were hundreds of schoolchildren arranged like Nazi regiments attending the Nuremberg rallies. In the foreground stood the police, with twenty lucky officers displaying the country's military might. This consisted of twenty muskets of a type last used during the Boer War. Each was fastened with a bayonet. There wasn't any ammunition for the guns. It had run out. In 1908.

I liked the fact that the police force in Kiribati was unarmed. Elsewhere in the Pacific, island armies amuse themselves by staging coups, or instigating civil wars, or pursuing lucrative opportunities in the drug trade and otherwise behaving like schoolyard bullies who happen to have M-16s. In Kiribati, however, the greatest ambition of a police officer was not to carry a musket, but to be selected for *Te*

Brass Band, the police marching band. They stood beside their comrades in arms, waiting, as everyone else was, for the president and the vice president and the other blah-blah-blahs to finish with their speeches. There were many speeches. There were long speeches. There were honors given. Meanwhile, the sun rose ever higher. The field, which was a slab of barren white coral, began to sizzle and it was not long before the participants arraigned on the field began to droop.

The first to fall was a police officer. He dropped his gun, swayed, and crumpled to the ground. He was immediately scooped up by two men with a stretcher, who carted him off to a spot alongside the field, where a canopy had been raised to offer shade. The next to pass out was a schoolgirl. She too was whisked off to the shade. By the time the speeches ended, eleven people had succumbed to heat exhaustion. It was only 9:30 in the morning. Did I mention that it's hot in Kiribati?

Led by *Te Brass Band*, which played with so much gusto that they would have been the highlight of any Octoberfest, the remaining participants began to march. The I-Kiribati have a great affection for marching. This too was a legacy of English colonial rule. I always found it curious to see which habits and traditions remained after the English departed. Very sensibly, the I-Kiribati wanted nothing more to do with cricket, which is quite likely the most mind-numbingly tedious game ever devised. Sadly, corned beef was a keeper. And so too was marching. Bedecked in traditional garb, the students stomped in formation around the field. Quick-time, slow-time, a goose step here, a wiggle there, they demonstrated their expertise. The audience greatly enjoyed this display of the country's martial prowess. They were tumbling over each other with laughter. The I-Kiribati have a very appealing way of diluting their pomp with a healthy dose of silliness.

By the afternoon, the festivities had moved to the Kiribati

Protestant Church *maneaba* in Bikenibeu, which was one of the island's larger *maneabas*. It was standing room only as the Inter-ministerial Song and Dance Competition got under way. I tried to think of an American equivalent to the competition. I strained to imagine the Department of Defense dressed up in grass skirts and lavalavas, preparing to dance against the dreaded Department of Health and Human Services. I struggled to imagine Madeleine Albright in a snug-fitting pandanus bra. But I couldn't quite grasp the image, which is perhaps just as well.

Each ministry had a hundred-plus singers, including the ministers themselves, and as they sang you couldn't help but feel excited. Percussion was provided by what appeared to be an upturned bookcase. A half-dozen men pounded the instrument with the palms of their hands. An emcee pounced around the *maneaba*, beckoning the singers to greater heights. The dancers were languid and fluid, with highly stylized and suggestive gesturing of hands and eyes, balanced by a sensuous undulating motion in the hips, a movement accentuated by long grass skirts. Unlike the women, men are allowed a greater range of movement in their legs, and they were charged with maintaining the pulse of a dance through a choreographed stomping of feet and clapping of hands. Every gesture was significant. There is no free-form dancing in Kiribati. But there is rhythm, and watching the dancers it was clear that the I-Kiribati have got rhythm. Except, of course, those who were carried off by the spirit. They cried and fluttered and bellowed, until they collapsed unto the *maneaba* floor for a good shake. Extra points.

When it was the Ministry of Environment's turn, Bwenawa took to the floor. He was their emcee. He shimmied. He swooned. He led his singers up the scales and then down again. He went to the men for the low bass. He gestured toward the women to give him some treble. With his thick mane of billowing hair, he had become the Leonard Bernstein of Kiribati. I turned to the dancers. Tiabo was beginning to get teary-eyed. She was quivering. Don't pass out, I thought. It makes me uncomfortable. But the spirit eluded her, and she remained upright.

Afterward, I asked Bwenawa how he thought they did.

"Not very good," he said. "But we enjoyed ourselves."

As we spoke, the Ministry of Housing had taken to the floor. They were slick. The male dancers were a little more buff; the female dancers a little more lithe. The thatched bras were a little snugger. The grass skirts hung a little lower on the hips. They sashayed. They swayed. Suggestively.

"Stop staring, you lech," Sylvia said.

"Maybe you should have danced after all," I countered.

When they had finished with their evocative dance they blew kisses to the *unimane* judges. The audience let out a collective gasp. And then the audience began to giggle. In Kiribati, giggling is more an indicator of discomfort than amusement.

"That wasn't I-Kiribati dancing," Bwenawa said. "That was more like Polynesian dancing," he went on, clearly disgusted.

The judges had wandered off to confer in private. They were gone for a long time. In the meantime, tension rose. There were more than a thousand people gathered around the *maneaba*, each with firm opinions about which ministry deserved the coveted prize. When the judges returned, they announced their decision. The Ministry of Housing had won. The singers and dancers from the housing ministry cheered. There was muted applause elsewhere.

And then the tension broke. There was yelling. There was shoving. There was pandemonium. I didn't understand what was happening. My I-Kiribati language skills had not advanced to the point where I could understand the finely crafted insult. But clearly, a lot of people were upset with the decision. Sylvia and I drifted to the periphery of the uproar, where we found the secretary of education thoughtfully observing the commotion. I liked him. Unlike most in the government, he was devoted to preserving I-Kiribati culture from the encroaching influence of the continental world.

"Hi," I said. "How's the curriculum development going?"

He laughed. *I-Matang* humor.

I asked him what he thought of the judges' decision.

"It was a bad decision," he shook his head. "That wasn't I-Kiribati dancing. In I-Kiribati dancing every gesture means something. It is very specific. But what the Ministry of Housing did was like the dancing in Tahiti." The secretary of education began to undulate. "It's not the Kiribati way." He paused for a moment. "But the girls were very nice to look at, eh?"

In which the Author goes deep inside the mind of the Novelist and expounds—for the benefit of future generations—on what it takes to produce Literature, the noblest Art, to which many are called and few chosen.

Moving on . . .

In which the Author flies Air Kiribati, Lives, Explores the island of Butaritari, famed for Merrymaking, followed by some thoughts on what it means to be Marooned, since the Author had a lot of time to ponder what it Means to be Marooned, because, frankly, Air Kiribati is not one of the world's More Reliable Airlines.

The longer we spent on Tarawa the more Sylvia and I came to realize that to live on Tarawa is to experience a visceral form of bipolar disorder. There is the ecstatic high, when you find yourself swept away in a lagoonside *maneaba* rumbling to the frenzied singing and dancing of hundreds of rapturous islanders. And there are the crushing lows, when you succumb to a listless depression, brought about by the unyielding heat, sporadic sickness, pitiless isolation, food shortages, and the realization that so much of what ails Tarawa, the overpopulation and all its attendant health and social problems, need not be as bad is it is. It was after one such low that I found myself surprisingly amenable to Sylvia's suggestion that we fly Air Kiribati to Butaritari, one of the northern Gilbert Islands. We were to accompany Te Iitibwerere, a local theater troupe that Sylvia had hired to produce message-oriented plays on the importance of green, leafy vegetables and the proper treatment for diarrhea, among other topics not typically explored on Broadway. And so we found ourselves at the airport, where despite our more sensible instincts, we were checking in for a flight on Air Kiribati.

Truthfully, I would have preferred to visit a city, some place with an old town. Despite illusions to the contrary, I was a creature of the city. I was not immune to the lure of comfort, convenience, and options. I liked the hum of a metropolis, the energy that emanates from hundreds of thousands of people tightly confined, by choice working and living among crowds, and I particularly enjoyed the corner respites, the cafés, bars, and restaurants that encouraged lingering and merriment. A perfect day would be spent perusing bookstores and the finery of brick town houses in a city's old quarter, dawdling in a café and contemplating the listings of plays and films I probably wouldn't see, having a couple of beers at a friendly neighborhood bar, enjoying dinner at a restaurant with sublime food and easy atmosphere, and returning to a charming hotel, confident that the electricity would be on and the water running. Also, it would be fall. I would wear a sweater.

Alas, Air Kiribati didn't offer weekend packages to Copenhagen. Instead, we would be flying the *wanikiba*, or flying canoe, to Butaritari, an island that intrigued us because it was lush and verdant, which was unusual in Kiribati, and its people had a reputation throughout the islands for being exceptionally languorous and easygoing. This excited our curiosity. It is difficult to convey exactly how hard it is to acquire such a reputation in Kiribati, where energy conservation is a quality long cultivated and, as far as we could see, already perfected. Also, Butaritari was known for merrymaking, and this finally sold us on the island as our destination. Each island in Kiribati is known for something—Maiana for white lies, Tabiteuea North for settling disputes with knives, Onotoa for frugality, Abemama for oral sex (I kid you not)—and spending a week idling and carousing seemed like an appealing way to learn a little more about Kiribati. But we had to fly Air Kiribati to get there, and it says much about my willingness to explore an island where the lack of a functioning sewage system did not affect the overall quality of life that I checked in for the flight without the assistance of heroin.

After bowel movements, the state of Air Kiribati was the favorite topic of conversation on Tarawa. *Did you hear about when the plane ran out of fuel midair and had to glide in for a landing*, someone will say. Or . . . *about when the engine died*, or *about when the pilot passed out mid-flight*, or *about when they forgot to turn the beacon on at the airport*, or, my favorite, *The pilot let me fly the plane*. Distressingly, these were not mere rumors. I had never been so uneasy about boarding a flight. It did not help that the shoeless airport official was not pleased with my weight. The expression on his face, which just moments earlier had revealed only benign indifference, contorted into something approaching a scowl. As I stood on a rusting, antiquated scale, fulfilling my role in a preboarding ritual meant to instill anxiety in travelers, I watched the creases on his forehead burrow deeper, saw his eyes recede in a squint of deep concentration, and listened to the strange clucking noises emanating from his mouth. "Tock, tock, tock," he said. He seemed personally affronted by my weight. And, I must add, I am not a fat man.

Indeed, standing on the scale, I was startled by how much weight I had lost—twenty-five pounds—with absolutely no effort at all on my part. I was fit when I arrived on Tarawa, so this wasn't a loss of excess baggage. This was a withering away, and I had once been proud of my iron gut. The Tarawa diet is the ultimate weight loss plan—hookworm, roundworm, dash of salmonella, hint of dysentery, season with cholera to taste—results guaranteed, except for women. Sylvia lost not a pound, which confirmed for me that when challenged, women have a much stronger constitution than men. This makes sense, of course. Life in Kiribati has a strong Darwinian cast to it, and men, except for one brief glorious moment, are pretty useless from an evolutionary perspective and can therefore be allowed to wither, whereas women are hardwired to survive. The "weaker sex" moniker may apply to the bench press, but Nature isn't a gym rat.

And I nearly lost a few more pounds when I contemplated the plane we were about to fly. This would be an old Spanish prop plane that predated Franco. It tilted ominously, exuding an air of exhaustion. As the airport official clucked and fretted over our small, featherlight backpacks, I watched the pilot stand on a stepladder and tug at a wing until it aligned with the other wing. Then I smoked eighteen cigarettes. Even Sylvia asked for a cigarette. Sylvia doesn't smoke. She's from California.

I did not want to cause a scene, but walking across the tarmac I did feel it was my duty to highlight to the members of Te Iitibwerere that the two engines were connected to the wings with *masking tape*. Really. They regarded this as very funny, and I knew then that the I-Kiribati would remain forever unfathomable to me. It was explained to us that the masking tape wasn't actually connecting the engines to the wings, but merely covering up the parts of the plane that were corroded through with rust, and strangely, as I regarded the swaths of masking tape elsewhere on the fuselage, I didn't really feel that much better.

The interior of the aircraft, a CASA, resembled that of an aging, decrepit school bus, complete with benches, though it was not nearly so large or comfortable. As we taxied, I hoped that someone was restraining the dogs, pigs, and children that usually occupied the runway. Pigs, let it be said, are stupid animals, though, as we discovered earlier, they do make landing a plane on Tarawa a uniquely interesting experience. Once we were in the air, a cool breeze was felt inside the cabin and it would have been pleasant had it originated from an air-conditioning unit. Clearly, more masking tape was needed. Two men, wiser than I, sought comfort on top of the luggage that was strewn haphazardly in the back of the plane, and as the engine coughed and sputtered and the aircraft trembled, I found myself envying them their alcoholic stupor. The Pacific Ocean below appeared placid and lush and impossibly vast, like a blue universe unraveling toward infinity. It seemed presumptuous to fly over something so expansive and grand as the Pacific Ocean in a contraption so pitiful as ours, and I thought it ominous that when we began to descend we could see in the near distance the island of Makin, a small atoll traditionally regarded as inhabited by the spirits of the I-Kiribati no longer residing in the temporal world. Missionaries, however, dispute this.

Landing on a rock-strewn strip cleared of coconut trees was exactly as I expected it would be. Terrifying. The passenger door jammed, and we scrambled out through the rear cargo door and soon we began to feel like Martian invaders. *I-Matang I-Matang*, said a chorus of tiny voices. But they quieted when I bared my teeth, and the youngest even scattered into the bush. Parents in Kiribati tell their children to behave or otherwise an *I-Matang* will devour them, which has led to the wonderful result that the younger segment of the population believes *I-Matangs* to be cannibals. I, of course, did nothing to dissuade them. Literary endeavors, which I imagined myself to be engaged in, were not enhanced by an audience of children clustered by the windows, watching raptly as I silently pleaded for a thought. In Kiribati, solitude was granted only to the wicked.

With Te Iitibwerere we piled into the Island Council Land Rover, which was dented and scratched and had the words *With the Compliments of the People's Republic of China* stenciled on the door. The Land Rover was driven by the island clerk, who is referred to as the island "clark," an anglicization that reminds the visitor that this is a Commonwealth country, where, just like in England, pronunciation has little to do with spelling.

"How many cars are there on Butaritari?" I asked the clerk.

He pondered this for a long time. "Three," he finally replied.

"How many cars work?" Sylvia asked.

"One."

We barreled down the island's one, lonesome dirt road toward the main village. There were two guesthouses on the island. Te Iitib-werere were staying in the government-owned guesthouse, but we knew enough about the sensibilities of the government of Kiribati to choose the privately owned guesthouse, a tidy cinder-block house of three bedrooms notable for its enigmatic living room. On one wall, a mural depicted a bare-breasted young maiden kneeling as a supplicant to a can of Foster's lager. On another wall was a glow-in-the-dark crucifix, above which hung the flag of the Kiribati Protestant Church. Obviously, we had stumbled across an avant-garde depiction of the duality of human nature, and I made a note to re-create this scene one day and sell it as an installation piece for an enormous sum to Charles Saatchi, the British art collector—known for his rather expensive view on what constitutes art. A cow carcass? An empty room? *How much did you want for that?*

Evening light descended, and as we walked through the village the air itself began to assume pink and blue hues. The dinner hour approached and fires were lit and the smoke settled over the village as a fine mist, capturing the soft light of sunset. The homes we passed were traditional structures of coconut wood platforms raised on stilts with a triangular roof thatched with pandanus leaves. These huts, called *bua*, were set on family compounds around which chickens, pigs, and dogs combated for scraps. The youngest children were naked and the oldest women, reverting to custom at twilight, were bare-breasted. Others, both men and women, wore wraparound lavalavas and T-shirts. A toothless old man, a respected village elder, greeted us warmly while bedecked in a frayed T-shirt that read *Shit Happens*, which seemed particularly apt in Kiribati.

The blue of the lagoon darkened, blending into the sky, and the small islets that rose from the reef were no longer distinguishable from the clouds neatly bisected by the horizon. Our perceptions were blissfully focused on the evening songs and the beauty of a dying sunset, when we stumbled upon a haunting example of the detritus of World War II. On a small beach, rippling waves lapped at the skeletal remains of a Japanese seaplane, destroyed when the Americans attacked in 1943, liberating the island from the Japanese, who had occupied the island since December 1941. Small boys threw stones at the rusting hulk, as no doubt their fathers had done before. Further, a small shrine consisting of a stone slab on which a rising sun was painted commemorated the Japanese losses.

Dusk quickly turned into night, too quickly for us as we staggered back to the guesthouse in pre-moon darkness. There was no electricity on the island. Kerosene lanterns swayed from the rafters of wood and thatch dwellings, casting figures and objects as shadows flickering through incandescent orange firelight. Dogs awoke from the torpor of the day. They were fighting somewhere nearby and we heard staccato barking and one dog yelping and then only whining and silence. Dogs were eaten on Butaritari, but regrettably, demand did not keep up with supply, and so, as on Tarawa, we walked carrying large rocks.

Back at the guesthouse, we were greeted by Edma, the matronly woman who prepared the meals. She was very thoughtful. No doubt, she believed that as *I-Matangs* we would prefer to eat *I-Matang* food, which in Kiribati took the form of fat-enhanced corned beef, served straight out of the can atop a bed of rice. This meat product was regarded as a great delicacy in Kiribati, and I believe that we left Edma befuddled with our request to eat only what the island could provide, she thinking undoubtedly that we were peculiar for wanting the food that the I-Kiribati would prefer to avoid, having eaten fish and breadfruit every day of their lives. But we didn't care. Nothing could induce us to eat canned corned beef, which is vile and repellent and gag-inducing.

Later that night, it occurred to us why the handful of cinderblock houses on Butaritari were used solely for storage and daytime entertaining. As we watched the geckos flit across the walls, gorging on clouds of insects, we realized that the windows were without screening. The brick walls trapped the heat of the day and nothing stirred the stagnant air. Rats scurried around us. This bothered Sylvia. Tantalizingly, there was an unoccupied *bua* outside. We contemplated it, but then noticed that the house dog was in heat, attracting a dozen or so male dogs who ceaselessly mauled each other for the privilege, and so we remained indoors, sweltering, frequently bitten by carnivorous mosquitoes, and not at all amused by the resident rodents. "But at least there are no cockroaches," I noted brightly. Sylvia needed cheering up.

Fortunately, there was also daytime Butaritari. We had a couple of days until Te Iitibwerere was scheduled to perform in the villages and so we toured the island on our own. Our wanderings kept us primarily on the lagoon side of the atoll, where nature offered such an alluring scene of idyllic paradise that one can understand why in the nineteenth century seamen abandoned their ships and their lives and became beachcombers. At low tide, the lagoon retreated, leaving a vast expanse of barren and desolate mudflats, where the ocean beyond shimmered like a mirage. But at high tide, with the clear azure water again lapping gently on a sandy beach that held not a single footprint, the scenery evolved, and as we stared into infinity, perhaps suffering from a mild case of sunstroke, it occurred to us that the essence of life is derived from the color blue—liquid blue, pale blue, deep blue, shades of blue separated first by the breakers that cascaded on a distant reef and then by the horizon. It is quite possible to spend hours doing nothing but floating like driftwood in water as warm as the tropical air, stealing glances at solitary mangrove trees rising brazenly from the lagoon, and the wall of coconut trees leaning over the shoreline offering a shady respite.

Of course, just as we were convinced that we had returned to Eden who should show up but a brightly banded sea snake. This snake's claim to fame is that it is the most venomous creature in the world, and its presence as we snorkeled over an old fish trap was not entirely welcome. Like many, I regard snakes as a tangible expression of evil, and I would be very pleased if evolution saw fit to attach large flags to the slinking reptiles, just so we would always know where they were. Perhaps I was still shaken from my time as a landscaper, when in the backyard of a family's home I experienced an epic conflagration between an angry copperhead and an unforgiving weed whacker. I have ever since been wary of things that slithered. But the sea snake wasn't slithering, it wasn't even swimming, it just floated in the warm water, drifting contentedly, and I remembered that to be bitten by this, the most lethargic critter in the world, is to be guilty of being very, very stupid. The only instances I had heard of sea snakes biting involved people sticking a finger down its throat or instigating coitus interruptus among amorous snakes, and I don't think the human gene pool has suffered greatly from the results. Even Sylvia, clearly sun-drunk, declared that she found the snake "pretty." Then she began talking to the fairy terns. "Pheeet-pheet," she called to them. A lagoonside beach on Butaritari is like that.

The great pleasure of Butaritari was that with a population of just three thousand, the atoll was as close to pristine as possible. The reef positively exuded health and at low tide the odors emanating from the reef shelf held none of that fetid stench of decomposition, rubbish, and shit that so marred everyone's existence on Tarawa. One morning, we left the guesthouse and wandered off in search of an oceanside beach where only some good snorkeling would interrupt hours of resplendent nothingness. We headed toward Ukiangang, a village close to the western end of Butaritari. The road drifted away from the lagoon and toward the middle of the atoll, where breezes did not reach. By mid-morning, the sun was unrelenting. As we walked past the few *bua* on this part of the road, we saw the inhabitants slumbering in the shadows, waiting for the intensity of the sun to lessen before emerging. Sometimes a child's voice could be heard, notifying all who could hear that *I-Matangs* were walking past. Otherwise, it was still.

It was clear why the people of Butaritari were regarded as lazy by the rest of the country. The relatively abundant rainfall had made life on the island comparatively easy. Unlike the central and southern Gilberts, which experience little rainfall and much drought, Butaritari enjoys a true wet season. Subsistence living therefore requires much less work. On most atolls, which offer one of the Earth's harshest environments, only the coconut palm tree thrives. But on Butaritari, we walked past trees laden with breadfruit, pandanus, bananas, and papaya, as well as many small gardens. There was such an overabundance of fruit that much of it was allowed to drop uncollected, something unheard of elsewhere in Kiribati. And both the lagoon and the ocean were teeming with fish. I had always thought the term "subsistence affluence," an expression used by international development–types, to be an oxymoron, but on Butaritari, where the cash economy has little relevance, it seemed appropriate.

As we neared the taro pits outside Ukiangang, we turned off the main road and followed a slender bush trail up a northward-jutting peninsula. No one seemed to live on this stretch of land, and so we dropped our anti-dog rocks. After hiking some distance through the bush, we were greeted by an ocean intent on asserting its dominance over the atoll. The waves broke heavily on the reef, a continuous roar punctuated by the cracking sound associated with nearby lightning or artillery fire. The reef extended a mere fifteen yards or so before plummeting into the depths, and waves carried the height and power of ocean swells before breaking, sending frothy chaos barreling toward the rocky shore. Idling on the ocean surface just beyond the breakers were fisherman in small, traditional outrigger canoes, rising and falling with the waves, seeking the evening's dinner.

We searched for a small bay or inlet, the likely launching point for the canoes, hoping to find calm water where we could don our snorkeling gear. After making our way through an ankle-twisting landscape of narrow crevices and slippery boulders, we came across a small bay framed by a golden beach where dozens of canoes rested under canopies of thatch. Venturing into the turquoise water, we swam among coral and fish of dazzling color. An incoming tide taunted us by spitting into our snorkels and hurling us perilously close to the boulders that cropped up in the most inconvenient of places. We turned to swim back to the beach, when suddenly we found ourselves surrounded by dolphins, a school of twenty-some intent on displaying a playful form of perfection, gleefully leaping into the air, twisting and turning, before falling back into the sea, and as they swam around us they seemed as happy to see us as we them, which could not possibly be true.

TE IITIBWERERE, the theater troupe we had traveled with, were the island equivalent of Hollywood stars. True, they didn't have any money, nor did they live in fancy houses, and they weren't stalked by paparazzi and autograph hounds, and Botox and personal trainers didn't figure very prominently in their lives, but in the entertainment world of Kiribati they were stars. On Butaritari, they were to perform plays in each of the island's villages. They were five women and one man, whom we will call Lothario as he was then married to one cast member and dating another, which added a certain frisson to their performances. They were staying in the guesthouse adjacent to ours, a government-owned cinder-block house that looked very much like a chicken coop. It lacked beds, running water, and a generator, and it was more abundant in rats than our guesthouse. It did, however, have the benefit of being perched atop a seawall overlooking the lagoon. On Butaritari the hours between dusk and dawn pass slowly and quietly, unless, of course, you are traveling with both your wife and your mistress, and so on most evenings we attached ourselves to the troupe. Around sunset, a fish would be cleaned and a bottle that once contained soy sauce but now brimmed with sour toddy would be passed around. A guitar was strummed and they would sing under the expanding white light of a rounding moon and a million stars. Bright is the moonlight on an equatorial atoll.

"Okay," Tawita said, finishing a sweet tune and turning to me and Sylvia. "Now it's your turn. You must sing."

I dreaded this. It often happened that we were asked to sing. The I-Kiribati are unself-conscious about singing. This is because they have the voices of angels. When I sing, however, small children begin to cry, dogs whimper, and rats scurry to the water and drown themselves. Sylvia, who is ravishingly beautiful, possesses a formidable intellect, and whose very existence illuminates my life, sings like a distressed cow. Entire villages scatter into the bush when we sing together. I tried to explain this to Tawita, but she was having none of it. "You must sing. Do not be shy."

And so we did. We sang Bob Dylan's *Tambourine Man*. We sang it just like Bob, with raspy, nasally voices and a peculiar sense of harmony. *Heeey Mr. Tambourine Man/ Play aaa song fer me/ I'm nooot sleepy and there is no place I'm goiiiiing tooo.*

The theater troupe drowned themselves in the lagoon before we could finish. Actually, they didn't do that. Rather, they drowned in tears of laughter. It began with a snicker that turned into a titter which led to guffaws and soon the group was convulsing in hysterical laughter.

"Stop!" Tawita cried. "That was very bad."

"Yes," I said. "We are aware of that."

"You must never sing again," she said.

"That is how we prefer it."

During the days, Te Iitibwerere guided us through the formalities of the *maneaba*, which functions essentially like a town hall, a community center, a church, a Motel 6, and the U.S. Senate, but with more dignity. A *maneaba*, typically built with coconut wood, thatch, and coconut fiber rope, can be upward of a hundred feet long and sixty feet high, and it is here that just about everything of consequence occurs. Kiribati is a deeply conservative country, and inside the *maneaba* etiquette is important. As an *I-Matang* accustomed to a culture that no longer has much place for formality and tradition, I paid attention. There were rules, Tawita explained. Women, for instance, must never reveal their thighs. Breasts, fine. Thighs, no. Shoes must be taken off before entering a *maneaba*, and it is considered bad form to sit with legs outstretched, pointing your blackened soles at those across. Sitting cross-legged is best, but since you can be sure that once inside a *maneaba* you will not be leaving for at least a couple of hours, you soon find yourself quietly stretching and unknotting, here and there daring an outstretched foot. A hat must never be worn inside a *maneaba*, and on some islands hats must be removed even if you are simply walking past a *maneaba*. If biking, you should dismount and walk. "Also," Tawita continued, "what is it called when you make a stinky from your backside?"

"A fart," I offered.

"Yes. You must never fart inside a *maneaba*."

We absorbed this, and as we entered the *maneaba* in the village of Kuma we rehearsed our speeches. We would have to introduce ourselves in I-Kiribati, and we were determined to get it right. Since I-Kiribati has no relationship to the languages we speak, learning it could only be done by rote memorization, which gives a teacher an opportunity to create mischief. Sylvia's staff enjoyed recounting the time when one of her predecessors, a particularly humorless woman, asked them to help her with a speech she needed to make welcoming the Minister of Environment to a workshop. Instead of bland niceties, they had her say, "I would like to see your penis." She felt encouraged by the laughter and continued on with ever more lurid statements. "I think it is very big," she said. I respect I-Kiribati humor. I like its bawdiness.

As we settled in the corner of the *maneaba* reserved for visitors, a woman offered us young coconuts, which are refreshing and nutritious and impossible to drink without slurping loudly. The entire village was soon congregated inside the *maneaba*, and after an *unimane* welcomed us to Kuma, we were asked to introduce ourselves. Following custom, which requires that you share your name, your father's name, and his home island, I stood up and said, in I-Kiribati: "Greetings. I am Maarten, son of Herman of Holland."

"Aiyah, aiyah," the village responded. "We welcome Maarten, son of Herman of Holland."

I liked the sound of that. Maarten, son of Herman of Holland, had a medieval ring. True, it wasn't as evocative as say Vlad the Impaler, but still, Maarten, son of Herman of Holland, suggested trouble.

After a few more words, Sylvia followed: "Greetings. I am Sylvia, daughter of Joe of California."

"Aiyah, aiyah. We welcome Sylvia, daughter of Joe of California."

"You know, darling," I said, "California is part of the United States now."

"Yes," she said. "For the time being."

One by one, the theater troupe followed. Now that we all knew each other, the play could begin. One would think that childhood diarrhea and respiratory infections would be difficult subjects for a play, but Te Iitibwerere carried it off brilliantly, possibly because diarrhea and respiratory infections are the stuff of everyday drama in Kiribati, but perhaps also because storytelling and songs are still the primary transmitters of knowledge in Kiribati. There are no I-Kiribati writers. Although the people of Kiribati are fairly literate, there is nothing to read beyond what their church provides, which means that nearly all knowledge of themselves is transmitted orally. Thus the plays about the runs. In New York, plays examine the ennui of contemporary life; in Kiribati, plays explore the art of rehydration. The audience laughed knowingly and nodded thoughtfully, and Sylvia was very pleased. It is one thing to sit in an air-conditioned office in Washington, poring over thousands of pages of buzzword drivel—"disseminating knowledge over the Internet"—and it is another thing all together to be in a village on the far side of the world, watching people get the health care information they need in a clever, effective, low-tech, real-world kind of way. If this had been a World Bank health program, a gazillion dollars would have been spent on consultants and first-class air travel, culminating in a report issued four years later recommending that Kiribati build a dam.

While the actors and the elders traded another round of speeches, lunch was brought to the center of the *maneaba*, where it remained for a very long time. There were flies, big flies, and they swarmed around the food. A half-dozen women languorously swept their hands back and forth over the assorted plastic plates, which elsewhere are called disposable, but here will be used to the end of time. There were more speeches. Sylvia was thanked for her $20 contribution to the preparation of the meal. There were songs sung heartily. There were garlands placed upon our heads, crowns of flowers. Talcum powder was sprinkled on our necks, Impulse deodorant sprayed under our arms. And finally we could partake of the meal. Ah . . . one last speech. An elder, a gentle moon-faced man, explained that we hadn't been expected until the following day—it happens, there is but one radio phone on Butaritari—and so would we please excuse the humbleness of the meal. No worries, we said. It would no doubt be delicious. It was not.

Have you ever wondered what an eel the size of a python tastes like? No? Well, I can attest that it is the most wretchedly foul-tasting victual ever consumed by a human being. Slimy, boiled fish fat that could only be swallowed because, as was the custom, the entire village was silently watching us consume this meal, and they would likely be offended if we let the gag reflex do its work. For ten long minutes, the village did nothing but silently watch us eat. A few of the men were shaving. With machetes. These are tough people. It's very *kang-kang*, we said, as another dozen flies settled on the sliver of eel we held in our hands. And then finally, the village elders, the men, the children, and the women, in that order, partook of the meal, and with the center of attention elsewhere, I began to quietly place the contents of my plate behind me, donating it to the mangy dogs that circled the *maneaba*.

And then we danced. The exuberance of the I-Kiribati for dancing cannot be overstated, as we had already witnessed with the Interministerial Song and Dance Competition. But it is *te twist* that inspires a certain madness in the I-Kiribati. No matter what time of day or night a *maneaba* function occurs, there comes a moment when the village generator is brought to life, feeding energy to a Japanese boom box, and with startling rapidity all the old ways recede, replaced instead with the throbbing atmosphere of an outdoor disco devoted not to the nurturing of sexual tension, but rather to the propagation of shameless silliness. It is the pinnacle of bad form to refuse an offer to dance *te twist*, and as the most exotic guests, we were often asked to dance, Sylvia by good-looking young men and me by the village aunties. To the sounds of Pacific pop and the ubiquitous "La Macarena," we twisted, flailed, bumped, and grinded. As we danced, someone thoughtfully sprayed us with Impulse deodorant and showered our necks in talcum powder. My dancing aunt goaded me into ever greater displays of silliness, and just as I settled into a series of moves that closely resembled the movements of a chicken surprised to have lost its head, women from every corner of the *maneaba* rushed at me like linebackers, grasping onto me with ferocious bear hugs. These were strong women. Though I was not quite as substantial as I once I was, I was by no means a small man, and yet they flung me around like a rag doll. Later, outside the *maneaba*, members of the theater troupe told Sylvia that this was a fairly risky, though not unheard of, method used by women to display their partiality toward someone.

"You should have hit them," Tawita said to her. "Some women would have bit off their noses if they had done that. You should at least demand mats and bananas."

"Are you kidding?" Sylvia replied. "Did you see how they threw him around? I'm not getting involved. They can do what they want with him."

ON BUTARITARI, we felt like we had discovered the true end of the world, where just beyond the horizon ships were known to sail over the rim of the Earth. Such illusions were easily cultivated staring into the blue void, realizing that behind you there was only a slender ribbon of land separating the ocean from the lagoon. Yet, as we rode up and down the atoll on borrowed bicycles (one with a chain that preferred to be elsewhere, the other without brakes, which mattered not on a flat island), watching the men fishing and the women tending gardens and the children playing or shyly staring at us from the heights offered by the coconut trees that they climbed with such ease, it sometimes seemed as if the rhythms of life were focused solely on Butaritari, and that the larger world, the world of continents and great cities existed only as faraway dreams. But the larger world had descended upon Butaritari, of course. When Robert Louis Stevenson visited, in 1889, the island had been reduced to a dissolute kingdom, governed by liquor, guns, murderous traders, and besieged missionaries. Stevenson, though, was soon enough reduced to the timeless lamentations of the *I-Matang* on an atoll: "I think I could shed tears over a dish of turnips," he wrote in a letter. And elsewhere: "I had learned to welcome shark's flesh for a variety; and a mountain, an onion, an Irish potato or a beefsteak, hàd been long lost to sense and dear to aspiration." Where else but in Kiribati has deprivation remained so constant?

The most profound visitation of the outside world during the modern era occurred with the arrival of World War II. The Japanese had initially garrisoned Butaritari with troops shortly after their attack on Pearl Harbor in 1941. The island, and particularly Tarawa, formed part of Japan's defensive periphery around their conquests in East and Southeast Asia. In 1943, the U.S. Marines destroyed the Japanese forces in what came to be known as the Battle of Makin.

After the war, the missionaries returned and Butaritari reverted to English colonial rule, but unlike elsewhere in Kiribati, where America and Americana fails to resonate, Butaritari retains a strong affection for the United States. As it happened, our stay coincided with the anniversary celebrations commemorating the Battle of Makin. These were to be conducted in the village of Ukiangang, and on the appointed morning we trudged the two miles from our guesthouse, eager to see the festivities. We got there just in time to see the marching competition. Between the school and the great *maneaba*, Ukiangang has a clearing that approximates a village square, and here dozens of children were marching in formation—left-right-left-right—round and round the square, past the painting of a plump and benevolent G.I. greeting islanders emerging from their shelters, and past hundreds of giddy onlookers, who dissolved into laughter whenever the march master issued his orders—

"Huuahh ehhh, huuaahh uhhh"—with Monty Pythonesque exaggeration. It seemed everyone was bedecked in T-shirts connoting America. Monster Truck Madness said one. My Parents Went to Reno and All I Got Was This Lousy T-Shirt said another. Mr. Shit Happens was there. And once again I was amazed at how clothing moves around the world. The stories those T-shirts could tell. One old man, wearing a frayed U.S. Marine Corps T-shirt approached us and sang a flawless rendition of "The Battle Hymn of the Republic." He sang it the whole way through, Tripoli to Montezuma. He did not speak another word of English otherwise.

With the midday heat, events soon moved into the shade offered by the village *maneaba*. Mostly it was traditional dancing, and as the dancers fluttered and swayed and undulated I was reminded again how achingly beautiful I-Kiribati girls are, thinking, boy, she's going to be something when she's older. And then I looked at those who were in fact older and began to wonder what exactly was going on with the I-Kiribati girls between the ages of sixteen and twenty that prevented all but a very few from becoming beautiful women, until it occurred to me that the past few months in Kiribati hadn't actually done wonders for my beauty either. And then a group of boys marched into the center of the *maneaba* and they looked like trouble. They wore droopy shorts. And bandannas around their heads. They glowered menacingly. Someone turned on a boom box and inside this *maneaba*, in the village of Ukiangang, on the island of Butaritari in the Gilbert Islands, Vanilla Ice was heard. *Ice Ice Baby*. The boys danced with that skippity-hop-look-I-have-no-shoulders thing that Vanilla Ice made his own. I glanced at the *unimane*. These were men who could recite their genealogies back five hundred years and more, who knew how to read the water and the sky, who knew how to build things as large as a *maneaba* without a nail, who knew, in short, how to survive on an equatorial atoll on the far side of the world. What on earth would they make of this sudden intrusion of the most appalling song ever recorded—something far, far worse than anything recorded by Yoko Ono—a song that I daresay represents all that is vile and banal in Western civilization? I am saddened to report that the *unimane* were delighted by *Ice Ice Baby*. They smiled and nodded in time to the music, gleefully watching their grandsons prance about like junior varsity pimps.

End this madness now! I felt like yelling. *Trust me! It's for your own good!* But I held my tongue and said a silent prayer fervently hoping that this was the beginning of nothing.

OUR STAY ON BUTARITARI was to have lasted a week, but as we feared and half expected, it would be extended indefinitely. Air Kiribati, it was announced on the island's lone radio, would not be making its weekly flight between Tarawa and Butaritari. No one seemed to know when the service might resume or, more troubling, why the flight had been canceled in the first place. Sometimes, months pass before a flight returns to an outer island. And so we waited. And brooded.

There is no romance in being marooned on an outer island. You are stuck, deprived of options, and it is then that your anxious westernness reappears, something we had thought we had long since discarded. We began to feel profoundly bothered by Third World inefficiency. We railed against indifference and incompetence, the two dominant governmental traits. Sylvia worried about deadlines and lost time at work. I . . . did not. Nevertheless, we sulked like petulant children, refusing to budge from the guesthouse, preferring instead to escape into our books.

As the days passed, the island began to feel stagnant and immobile, nothing seemed to move or change, except our perceptions, which no longer regarded languid and indifferent Butaritari as the idyllic paradise of our imaginations. The smiles and stares we received from people were no longer regarded as charming and friendly. We knew that we were the objects of much curiosity, and we began to feel like circus freaks cast into a crowd to provide amusement. When we sat in front of the guesthouse reading our books, dozens of people gathered to watch us read. Our smiles became frozen and plastic grins. The beauty of the island was lost on us. The trees seemed aloof and mocking, the sea a barrier separating us from our lives. We had lost, temporarily, our sense of fatalism and our appreciation for the absurd.

The plane did eventually arrive, five days later, excreted from the clouds on a day that saw tempestuous winds bend the coconut trees straddling what was euphemistically called a runway, and rain showers that struck the earth with the vehemence of machine gun fire. The Air Kiribati representative, whom the night before we had found sprawled on the road, having misjudged, or perhaps judged perfectly, the amount of sour toddy it takes to induce total inebriation, conducted the preboarding weigh-in with bleary-eyed avarice, allowing all excess luggage on board and pocketing the fees, which would undoubtedly be put toward the afternoon sour toddy. The pilot, Air Kiribati's lone woman, which may or may not mean something, did draw the line when she felt the plane shudder as a motorcycle was squeezed on board. When the doors were finally closed, the air was redolent with the odors of overheated bodies, ripe bananas, and raw fish. Soon the cracks and fissures that punctured the body of the aircraft would allow a cool and cleansing breeze inside the cabin. It would be the worst flight of my life, and I can think of only one reason why I didn't wholly succumb to panic and nausea. We were going home.

CHAPTER 18

In which the Author recounts the Battle of Tarawa, which is now forgotten in America, because America is a Today kind of country, sometimes a Tomorrow kind of country, but rarely a Yesterday kind of country, and it does not linger on the deaths of soldiers past, which is not possible on Tarawa.

I t is often said that Americans have no sense of history. Ask a college student who Jimmy Carter was and they will likely reply that he was a general in the Civil War, which occurred in 1492, when Americans dumped tea into the Gulf of Tonkin, sparking the First World War, which ended with the invasion of Grenada and the development of the cotton press. Actually, I would be impressed with that answer. The more likely response is *Who the fuck cares?*

Elsewhere in the world, people are a little more knowledgeable about American history. They know, for instance, exactly what year it was when the CIA overthrew their government. In the United States, however, history is largely paved over, abandoned, and relegated to textbooks so shockingly dull that they could only have been written by politically correct creationists whose sole objective was to offend no one. And it's not just the textbooks, of course, where history has been washed out. The land has been settled for more than ten thousand years; Europeans have been traipsing about since the fifteenth century, which by any measure, is a very long time ago. Yet, outside of

Boston and—I can't think of anyplace else—one is hard-pressed to find a building that predates the twentieth century. In Europe, every town has a memorial commemorating the townsmen who lost their lives in the two world wars. In America, every town has a Wal-Mart. Only on the Great Plains does one find the telling remnants of lives lived and lost, the abandoned homesteads that creak with forgotten stories, and the only reason those boards still stand is that the landscape is so bleak and foreboding that no one else wants to build there ever again. Frankly—and I mean no offense to the good people of North Dakota—I can't believe you haven't all left yet.

Even on the acres where momentous events have occurred, such as a Civil War battlefield where the outcome changed the course of history, the site has typically been gussied up, dusted off and varnished, with the result that the visitor sees nothing. At Manassas, for instance, I saw a freshly mowed field, a quaint farmhouse, a lovely stone wall, but mostly I saw a great place for a picnic. I did not see a battle that cost the lives of thousands. It was too *clean*.

Contrast this with Tarawa, where nothing is clean. Generally, this bothered me. There are few sights more dispiriting than a long seawall built with discarded junk—cars, tires, cans, oil barrels, et cetera—slicing through an emerald lagoon. This was the best that could be done with the detritus of the *I-Matang* world. On the continents, a broke-down car soon becomes a forgotten broken-down car once it is towed to someplace unseen. On Tarawa, though, nothing disappears. If nature can't consume it, it remains on the island, most often right where its working life came to an end. This includes the relics from the Battle of Tarawa, one of the bloodiest engagements fought during World War II.

The Japanese admiral charged with defending Tarawa had predicted that a million men and a thousand years of battle would be required before his soldiers could be dislodged from the atoll. The Second Marine Division needed three days. The Battle of Tarawa was fought on the islet of Betio, which is less than one square mile in size. On November 21, 1943, the U.S. Marines approached Betio under the morning sun. They misjudged the tides and their landing vehicles could not traverse the reef and so they waded five hundred yards in the open and suffered a 70 percent casualty rate in the first wave of attack. There were 4,300 Japanese soldiers on Betio, as well as several hundred Korean laborers, and over three days all of them were killed except seventeen soldiers who surrendered because they were too injured to fight on and could not find within themselves the strength to commit suicide. The Marines lost 1,113 soldiers. Corpses are still found when new wells are dug. There is also unexploded ordnance. Now and then a bomb is discovered. Shipping containers are moved from the port and stacked high around the bomb to direct the explosion up. And then—*boom*.

The remains of this battle exist today as untended features of the land- and seascapes, devoid of the solemn pomp that usually attends war ruins. On land, laundry hangs from antiaircraft guns. The turret of a small tank lies discarded like junk in a clearing where pigs and chickens feed. Bunkers are used as trash receptacles and toilets. The Japanese big guns remain encased by sandbags, now petrified, and in their shadows volleyball is played. On the reef, the detritus of battle endures as nautical hazards. Oceanside, the reef is littered with tank traps, ammunition, the remains of a Japanese Zero, and a B-29. Each relic marks where someone died and someone killed, and the lack of sanctity granted these vestiges of war does not allow you the distance to pretend otherwise.

If there is one indelible image from the Battle of Tarawa, it is a photo of dozens of dead Marines bobbing in the shallows just off what was called Red Beach II. I often launched my windsurfer from Red Beach II. Just twenty yards from the beach lies a rusting amtrac. At reef's edge are the brown ribs of a ship long ago grounded, where

Japanese snipers once picked off Marines wading and swimming and floating toward a beach that offered nothing better. A little farther I directed my board over the wings and fuselage of a B-29 Liberator. Clearing the harbor entrance, I confronted the rusting carcasses of several landing vehicles. Near the beach was a Sherman tank, with children playing on the turret.

The Battle of Tarawa is an inescapable part of daily life on the island. I frequently found myself on Betio, pursuing a rumor that fresh fruit could be found at a particular store, when I would stumble across an antiaircraft gun or a cement bunker or a tank turret and I would think, *Oh that's right, 5,500 men were killed here.* After a while, it just sort of seeps into you that Tarawa was the site of unimaginable violence and that it ought to be remembered. It bothered me that among my American friends and acquaintances only one had any knowledge of the Battle of Tarawa, and he happened to be a Marine. Perhaps it's because I had to been to Bosnia. Once one sees a park transformed into a cemetery, one understands that battles ought to be remembered.

There are a few memorials commemorating the battle on Tarawa. In the 1960s, Navy Seabees began work on a causeway linking Betio to the rest of Tarawa. It was to commemorate the Battle of Tarawa. They never finished it. Another war arrived and they were sent to Vietnam. Instead, the Japanese finished the project and today it is called the Nippon Causeway. There are two other memorials on Betio. One is a Shinto shrine honoring the Japanese and Korean dead. Every month a Japanese worker from the port project cleans the memorial, wiping it down and clearing trash and brush. It is always meticulously clean. The other memorial sits in front of the Betio Town Council building. It is a time capsule shaped like an obelisk. No one prunes the weeds here. There is a flagpole, but there is no flag. The memorial reads:

"Follow Me"
2nd Marine Division
USMC

Battle of Tarawa
November 20, 1943

To our fellow Marines
who gave their all!
The world is free because of you!
God rest your souls

1,113 killed   2,290 wounded

The Central Pacific Spearhead
To World Victory in World War II
Semper Fideli

On the other side, it reads:

Memorial to sailors, airmen,
chaplains, doctors, and especially to
Navy Corpsmen

30 killed   59 wounded

Sealed November 20, 1987
Camp Lejeune, N.C., U.S.A.
To be opened November 20, 2143
From our world to yours
Freedom above all

Sylvia had grown up next door to a survivor of the Battle of Tarawa. She didn't know this at the time; he had died shortly after she left for college. It was only after Sylvia's parents had mentioned to his widow that their daughter was now living on Tarawa that she learned that for all those years she had lived beside a veteran of the battle. No one knew. The former Marine never talked about it. His widow mentioned that in the years after they were married, he often woke in the middle of the night, screaming, terrified, haunted by the experience. But he never talked about it. Not even the survivors care to remember the Battle of Tarawa. And so all that remains of the battle are the ruins, slowly dissipating on a reef in the equatorial Pacific, just a short distance from the Nippon Causeway.

CHAPTER 19

In which the Author begins to hear rumors of Lurid Happenings in Washington, and suddenly he Regrets his Situation, his Location, and Wishes only to have access to a tabloid newspaper, a television, an Internet connection, but he is Denied.

The reading situation had become desperate. I'd read through every book we'd brought. I had read all of Mike's books. I had trudged through the scraps left by previous FSP directors. I read a biography of the last days of the Romanov family. I read *Dune.* Then I read it again. I like my entertainment not too serious, not too stupid, sort of like this book.

But there are only so many times one can read a book. I am quite certain that I am the only man in the Pacific to have read *All the Pretty Horses* three times, which might be why in my own prose I found myself writing sentences that were approximately four pages long, describing the sad yet inevitable descent of a leaf. More troubling than the dearth of books, however, was the utter absence of newspapers and magazines. In Washington, I had been a certifiable news junkie. Sundays just didn't feel complete until I had burrowed through forty pounds of newspaper. I even read *Parade.* Each weekday, I began my morning with the *Washington Post,* the *New York Times,* and, because I respected their coverage of events in Slovenia, the *Financial Times*. From the debate on health care to the governor's race in West Virginia to recent events in Mali, I was *informed*.

Alas, on Tarawa I lived in a state of ignorance not known to westerners since the advent of papyrus. I often found myself approaching other *I-Matangs*. "I'll trade you my December 1978 *Scientific American*—it's about this new thing called computers—for your March 1986 *Newsweek*. I'd like to relive Iran-Contra for a spell." At noon, I religiously tuned in to the English-language news summary on Radio Kiribati. I had grown very fond of its opening jingle—the theme from *The Good, the Bad, and the Ugly*—but the news broadcast itself made for a compelling argument on the importance of a free and independent media. Inevitably, the government-controlled broadcast would begin with something like: *The recent power outages have proven to be a boon for shops selling kerosene lanterns.* And then it would cut to Radio Australia. *In Wagga Wagga today . . .*

The bimonthly newspaper was no help either. It contained a World Focus page, where the government printed what it thought were the most important global news issues of the day. "Precious Rock Keeps Diana's Name Alive" was a typical headline. The I-Kiribati might not have been aware that the Cold War had ended, or even that there was such a thing as *cold*, but thanks to the government of Kiribati they were well informed about all things Diana. I no longer cared much about Princess Diana. She's dead. Let it go. But the government would not let it go, and so every two weeks we would learn yet another profoundly inconsequential detail about the life and times of Princess Diana.

I eventually confined my hunt for news to the shortwave radio my father had thoughtfully given to us as a parting gift when we left for Kiribati. Unfortunately, it says much about the extreme isolation of Kiribati that I couldn't call up much beyond Radio Bhutan. Occasionally, I caught five minutes or so of the BBC before it faded into the ether, and I must have caught it on London's night shift, since the programs I found were of the "Gardens of Wales" and "Folk Songs of Bolivia" variety. I had nearly resigned myself to living in an entirely news-free world, when I heard a snippet that suddenly made me ravenous for news and commentary and rumor, causing me to pathetically spend the small hours of the morning scanning the shortwave radio dial, wishing again that my world was occupied by CNN and *Time* and Sunday newspapers and, in particular, tabloids. I was desperate for any info regarding a woman named Monica.

I have long had a weakness for spectacle, and I'm willing to go to great lengths to consume its delights. It filled me with despair that I was missing out on the fun of a sex scandal enveloping the White House, particularly this sex scandal. The deliciousness of it. Its luridness. Its breathtaking stupidity. Now and then, in the small hours before dawn, I caught Voice of America. Inevitably, it was transmitting America's Top Forty Countdown, confirming that America's propaganda arm believes insipid banality to be the best way to capture hearts and minds abroad. If they must go lowbrow, I thought the Clinton sex scandal offered some opportunities. But sadly, VOA declined, preferring instead to inform the world that America can best be understood through the Backstreet Boys and Mariah Carey.

Eventually, I discovered that if I turned to a particular frequency at exactly 6 P.M., I could catch approximately five and a half minutes of BBC's *Newshour* before it faded into static. A newsreader presented a summary of the day's happenings—revolution in Indonesia, a crashing global economy, trouble in Argentina. Do get on with it, I thought. This was followed by analysis. But even the BBC felt that the Clinton sex scandal was of sufficient global import to merit a lead story, and so for the one and a half minutes that remained until I lost reception, I listened to—and I don't want to make too much of this, after all I am an adult, sophisticated, not at all puerile, really—a BBC correspondent by the name of, ahem, Judy Swallow, explain the day's events. *All of America today is talking about a cigar and a stained blue dress . . .* and then there was static. What cigar? What's so important about a cigar? What's so significant about a blue dress? Stained with what?

It was maddening.

In an effort to obtain more information, I decided one day to subscribe to *The New Yorker*. I knew, of course, that it would be months until I saw a magazine, but I figured that if someone was putting each issue in the mail, a few would eventually reach Tarawa. I was willing to wait. True, by the time the magazines reached me, they would have been terribly dated. But it still would have been fresh for me. I knew nothing. There weren't more than a few dozen homes on Tarawa with telephones, and we, lucky us, lived in one of them. And so I called the international subscriptions department of *The New Yorker*.

"Hi. I'd like to subscribe to *The New Yorker*, please."

"Name?" said a faint voice through the static.

I gave her my name.

"Phone number?"

"28657," I said.

Pause.

"I need more numbers, sir," said the voice on the line.

"Um, I don't have more numbers. I'm calling from a small country, a very small country."

"The computer won't let me continue until I fill in all the spaces."

"How many more numbers do you need?"

"Five."

"Then make it 28657-00000."

"Address?"

"P.O. Box 652, Tarawa, Kiribati."

"I need a street name, sir?"

"There are no street names. There's only one street here."

Pause.

"The computer won't let me continue until I put in a street name."

"Okay. Put in Main Road."

"All right, sir. You said Tara-something. Is that a city?"

"It's an island."

"I need a city."

"There are no cities on this island."

"The computer won't let me—"

"Put in Bikenibeu."

"Bikeni-who?"

"B-I-K-E-N-I-B-E-U."

"Okay. State?"

"Ma'am, there are no states here. There are no cities. There are no streets. There are only islands."

"I need a state, sir. The computer won't let me—"

"Put in T-A-R-A-W-A."

"Country?"

"Kiribati."

"Kiri-what, sir?"

"K-I-R-I-B-A-T-I."

"Sir, it's not showing up in the database."

"It's an independent country. It's been a country for almost twenty years. Surely *The New Yorker*'s database of independent countries has been updated in the past twenty years."

"It's not showing up in the database, sir. Is there another name I could try?"

"Try Gilbert Islands."

"I'm showing Ocean Island, Gilbert and Ellice Islands."

"Ocean Island hasn't been called Ocean Island in seventy years. It's called Banaba."

"Bana-what?"

"And the Gilbert and Ellice Islands are two separate countries now. The Gilbert Islands are part of Kiribati, and the Ellice Islands are now called Tuvalu."

"Tuva-who?"

"Never mind. Let's go with the colonial name."

"All right, sir. Let me repeat the information. The address is: P.O. Box 652, The Main Road, Bikenibeu, Tarawa, Ocean Island, Gilbert and Ellice Islands. Telephone number 28657-00000. Is that correct?"

"Yes. I mean no. How much exactly is it going to cost me for you to send *The New Yorker* to the wrong island in the wrong country?"

"Let's see. You're not in Europe?"

"Nope."

"And you're not in Asia?"

"No."

"And you're not in Latin America."

"No."

"Okay. Then you're in Other."

She offered a chin-dropping figure. Already, the phone call alone was costing me the equivalent of the gross domestic product of Kiribati. I might have gone ahead with the subscription if I had been an English colonial officer stationed on Banaba in 1910, but I wasn't, and I thought it imprudent to spend big bucks on a magazine that wasn't at all confident that Kiribati existed.

Denied a magazine subscription, I turned to the other *I-Matangs* on the island. Most of them were Australian. "What have you heard?" I'd ask. "What's with the blue dress?"

The Australians would inevitably begin "Americans are so puritanical . . ."

"Yeah, yeah, yeah," I'd say. "Whatever. Now, what do you know?"

They knew nothing.

"I'll see what I can find out," Sylvia offered. "I'm meeting with an English consultant tomorrow." While not quite as obsessive as I was, Sylvia was notably curious about recent affairs in Washington. This was her president after all.

"Well, I asked her about the cigar," Sylvia said the following day.

"And?" I asked, positively drooling for the lowdown.

"She wouldn't say. But she was really blushing."

"Blushing? You mean this is blush-worthy news? What on earth did Bill Clinton do with a cigar? This is killing me."

I imagined what it must be like in America. The Clinton Sex Scandal 24/7 on television. Newspapers with screaming headlines. Rumors on the Internet. Magazine pieces on what it all meant for America. Salivating Republicans. How I wished I was there. Instead, I found myself at reef's edge, under the white light of a million stars, watching the night fishermen scour the reef for octopus, as I worked the knobs of my shortwave radio, longing to hear nothing more than a Jay Leno monologue.

In which the Author discusses the foreign Aid Industry, whose emissaries, the Consultants, arrive monthly, air service permitting, peddling Models of Sustainable Development, which have worked very well in Africa, followed by some thoughts on the Red Menace on Tarawa, the sinister agents from China, whose Evil Plottings were Subverted at every turn by the Author's Beguiling Girlfriend, who engaged in the Black Arts of Spy Craft, the Perilous Game, a game that she did not master; which led to some false information being sent to Washington, possibly leading to Unforeseen Consequences in U.S.-Sino relations.

I decided to diversify from fiction writing. Now and then, I passed my scraps of art to Sylvia for perusal. She was very positive. "Um . . . this is very . . . descriptive," she said after reading a passage describing a tree, which had taken me six weeks to write. But when she declared, in as encouraging a manner as possible, that my protagonist, my hero, read like a "caricature of a gargoyle," I knew it was time to spread my wings. I began to edit papers for the local foreign aid industry.

In one week of editing a "feasibility study" I earned more than twice what the average I-Kiribati earned in a year. The study, funded by the Food and Agricultural Organization in Rome, recommended going forth with a plan to transform Butaritari into small-farmer plots for growing market vegetables, which would then be sold to middlemen on Tarawa, called "marketers," who would sell the vegetables to the co-ops, who would then sell them on to consumers on Tarawa. It must have looked like a sensible thing to do over an espresso in Rome. Of course, how one transports perishable vegetables from an island that lacks electricity and refrigerators was never quite addressed. By air? By boat? Had the authors actually set foot on Kiribati? Nor were the implications of the *bubuti* culture mentioned. What is the point of working harder to earn more money, when at the end of the day you will be obliged to turn over your profit to anyone who asks? Nor did the study find it problematic that for the scheme to break even, a consumer would have to pay approximately $10 for a single tomato. No, the authors concluded, this is a good plan. Let's fund it.

Whatever. I soon learned that the greatest beneficiaries of *I-Matang* aid were the *I-Matangs* themselves, and I was excited to finally get a piece of the pie myself. It had been an awfully long time since a dollar had come my way. In some alternate universe, I had credit card debts and student loan payments, but that universe was a long, long way from Tarawa. No one was calling me here to remind me that a payment was due. I had vanished from that world and I gave it no further thought.

Still, even though we had absolutely no need whatsoever for extra dollars pride compelled me to, at least now and then, bring in a paycheck. I did what I could to help Sylvia with her job. Indeed, on Tarawa I was known as the FSP husband. But here and there I enjoyed the sight of a check with my name on it. And so I edited.

This gave me an interesting perch from which to observe the foreign aid industry in Kiribati. To this day, I remain baffled by the UN. I could never figure out what they did. Every few months, Air Nauru would deposit another batch of fashionably dressed UN staffers, who would then spend most of their time on the atoll bitching about the I-Kiribati. "The people are so dirty," said a Nigerian woman, tossing a Hermès scarf around her shoulders. She was on Tarawa to improve the plight of women in Kiribati. "How could you possibly live here?" asked the Frenchman with the tasseled loafers, after he was told that no, he could not have a club sandwich. He was in Kiribati to help the children.

Watching the parade of consultants that descended on Tarawa became the equivalent of watching the evening news for us. We knew what the chattering class back home was talking about simply by noting what causes the consultants represented. One day, for instance, a team of antismoking specialists arrived in Kiribati. I had the good fortune to spy upon them in the bar of the Otintaii Hotel, where they were meeting with officials from the Ministry of Health, grim-faced men who nodded politely as they were told of the tobacco industry's evil designs for Kiribati and who, the moment these sullen but healthy Western people departed, opened up their tins of Irish tobacco and rolled their cigarettes with pandanus leaves and had a good laugh as they began an evening of serious drinking. They were aware, no doubt, of the 1996 figures on causes of morbidity in Kiribati, which included 99,000 cases of influenza (which killed close to 2 percent of the population in 1983), 15,000 cases of diarrhea that were serious enough to be reported (including 4,500 cases of dysentery, primarily among children), and 44 new cases of leprosy. There were no statistics on smoking-related diseases and deaths. There was no reason to collect such data. No one lived long enough to be mortally embraced by lung cancer and emphysema.

There was, it seemed to me, considerable dissonance between the health care concerns of westerners and the realities of the Pacific. Diarrhea and acute respiratory infections, for instance, killed nearly 10 percent of children under the age of five. But glamorous people don't die of diarrhea. Elizabeth Taylor doesn't hold fund-raisers for people with the runs. And so the money goes to AIDS, and not childhood diarrhea. So be it. If donors want to give money to fight AIDS rather than diarrhea or malaria, by far the greater killers in the developing world, I certainly won't emit a peep of protest. I thought that the wisest thing one could do to prevent AIDS in Kiribati would be to take one banana and one condom to the Marine Training School, where I-Kiribati men are taught how to crew freighters, and explain that when in port you really shouldn't visit prostitutes, but if you must, use a condom because otherwise you will die. Here's a condom. Here's a banana. Here's how it works. Total cost of program? Approximately $1. Lives saved? Innumerable.

Foreign aid donors think differently, however. Instead of pursuing a simple prevention program, three-quarters of the country's doctors and most of the senior nurses were sent to Perth, Australia, where they attended a five-week-long conference on AIDS counseling—not prevention, not treatment, but counseling. Total cost? $100,000. Lives saved? None. I could only imagine a doctor talking to an I-Kiribati woman infected with AIDS by a husband returning from his tour at sea. *How's your self-esteem?*

The I-Kiribati, however, were largely indifferent to the presence of foreigners in Kiribati and the work they did. The only way consultants could get anyone to show up for a workshop in which they would explain the proper way to live on an atoll was to pay what were euphemistically called "sitting fees," or bribes. On the outer islands, the volunteers were generally thought of as the village pets, amusing diversions that entertained the villagers with their strange ways. On Tarawa, the *I-Matang* presence was still sparse enough that people would gawk and giggle whenever one was sighted. Or perhaps it was just me that they gawked and giggled at. Nevertheless, I think it fair to say that the presence of a few foreigners in their midst was hardly a concern for the I-Kiribati. Until the Chinese arrived, that is.

Seemingly out of the blue, a new Chinese Embassy was constructed. It was white with a red tiled roof and impenetrable reflecting windows. It looked like an ungainly cross between a Beverly Hills mansion and a Taco Bell franchise. In front there was a glass-enclosed display featuring a tableau of industrial images under the peculiar headline "China: Friend of the Environment." The embassy was constructed entirely by workers flown in from the People's Republic of China, using tons of rock taken from the shoreline, which is actually not so environmentally friendly, as it furthers erosion, and erosion is no laughing matter on an atoll.

Soon the library on Tarawa—a one-room building I sometimes visited to peruse their collection of vintage *National Geographics*, a remnant, as was the rest of their modest collection, of the colonial era—began to display with suspicious prominence the latest issues of *China Today, Beijing Review, China Pictorial*, and *China's Tibet*.

I wondered what the Chinese were interested in. What on earth would compel them to open an embassy in Kiribati of all places? No one builds embassies on Tarawa. Even the two countries that did have embassies barely filled them with staff. Australia had four diplomats. New Zealand only one, and he was also assigned to several other countries.

The government of Kiribati soon announced that it had agreed to buy an airplane, the Y-12, from China. Every aviation specialist in the Pacific thought Kiribati should buy a Twin Otter, which are reliable and safe. The entire region was flying Twin Otters, ensuring a nearby supply of spare parts. Instead, the government bought a Chinese airplane for what was universally regarded as a wildly inflated price. Clearly, there was some funny business going on, but what? Selling one airplane to an impoverished nation hardly struck me as worthy of a new embassy.

The government then announced a plan to send I-Kiribati girls to Hong Kong, where they would work as servants for $400 a month, minus rent and meal costs. Who knew that China was suffering from a labor shortage? The prospective employer could choose the girl of his choice after viewing his options on videotape. As details of the contract emerged, which stipulated that the girls would have no recourse should they be unhappy with their employers, popular disgust with the plan forced the government to abandon it.

Still, procuring unwilling prostitutes, which was among the Red Army's more financially rewarding sidelines, did not strike me as an activity necessitating an embassy. It was only when the government announced that it had agreed to lease land to China so that they could construct a satellite tracking station that it began to make sense. The Chinese Embassy declared that the tracking station would only be for civilian-use satellites, but many found this hard to believe. Why did the Chinese prevent customs officials from examining the shipping containers they brought in to build their satellite tracking station? Why would the government of Kiribati allow them to get away with it?

Once the Chinese began construction of the station in an isolated grove in Temaiku, the rumors flew. The Chinese were bringing in guns. A boy had seen a Chinese man board a bus with a gun. The embassy had an armory. A submarine had emerged just beyond the reef in Temaiku on a moonless night and supplied the tracking station with mysterious goods, presumably guns. It did not help that the Chinese, and sometimes there were dozens of them, kept completely to themselves.

"I am scared of the Chinese," Tiabo told me. "They are bad people. They have guns."

"I don't like the Chinese," Bwenawa said. "They don't believe in God. They do not care about the I-Kiribati people. And they have guns."

Even Radio Kiribati felt obliged to comment. Rumors that the Chinese are bringing in guns are false, it declared. To prove it, several *unimane* would be allowed to tour both the embassy and the satellite tracking station.

The *unimane* declined. We do not know anything about such things, they said. We want the *I-Matang* to go inside. The Chinese, however, would not allow *I-Matangs* inside their embassy and tracking station. Only elderly I-Kiribati men were welcome.

"I am very worried," Bwenawa said. "We know that China has enemies, and I am scared of what would happen to Tarawa if China goes to war. Will those countries attack Tarawa? It has happened before."

China's enemy, or strategic partner depending on the week, happened to be quite busy nearby. On Kwajalein Atoll in the Marshall Islands, the United States was preparing to test its new missile defense program. An intercontinental ballistic missile would be fired from Vandenberg Air Force base in California. Shortly thereafter, an interceptor would be fired from Kwajalein. As the date approached, more and more Chinese arrived, and from their curt bearing, I assumed they were from the Red Army. Once the test was conducted, they left again. Clearly, the tracking station in Temaiku was a spy station.

Sylvia and I decided this needed investigating. We approached the tracking station by bicycle, stealthlike. Just in front of the building, on the beach, were massive piles of discarded Styrofoam, deposited there by the Chinese as they finished the construction of the station. In the days that followed, the Styrofoam would travel down the atoll, befouling it, until the ocean took it forever. *China: Friend of the Environment.*

The station itself was nothing much to look at. It looked like a rural school with single-story buildings and tin roofs. The most striking feature was the massive satellite dishes. The complex was surrounded by a barbed-wire fence. Just outside the gate, we got off our bicycles.

I looked at Sylvia.

"I think we should," I said.

"Are you sure?" Sylvia asked.

"Yes. We must."

"You're right. It's necessary."

"*Free Tibet now!*" we shouted.

And then we pedaled like hell before they shot us.

SHORTLY THEREAFTER, Sylvia was dispatched to the Federated States of Micronesia, where she would donate the hospital equipment that the government of Kiribati had declined to accept. With Sylvia traveling—and oh, how I envied her—I decided to have my fish and rice at the Otintaii Hotel, which offered a deceptively impressive menu, though in fact it could rarely scrounge up anything more than fish and rice. There, I discovered a veritable Chinatown. I passed the time guessing who represented Chinese officialdom and who was there to buy I-Kiribati passports, a lucrative sideline for the government of Kiribati, particularly in the months leading up to Hong Kong's absorption by China. The Hong Kong Chinese were easy to spot. The men display flash, and the women, unaware of local cultural mores, display flesh. The differences between a Shanghai merchant and a Beijing lackey were more subtle, but the shoes gave everything away. The bureaucrats wore plastic sandals; the merchants genuine imitation leather.

I was sitting by myself when a young Chinese man asked if he could join me. There were no other seats available. He sat down, and though his English was halting and my Chinese nonexistent, we got to talking. He was an engineer, a recent graduate from Beijing University, and he was on Tarawa to help finish the Chinese Embassy. "I want to build the most beautiful building in Kiribati," he said. He was affable. I found it curious that he got his degree at Beijing University. Only the country's elite studied there, the children of the Communist Party's leaders. I asked him about the demonstrations in 1989, when thousands of students, particularly from Beijing University, demanded reform.

"They were misguided," he said. "China is a very great country."

He looked deeply uncomfortable.

"What about the massacre in Tiananmen Square?" I asked.

Before he could respond, an older Chinese man, clearly someone of authority, walked over from the next table and pointedly put out his cigarette in the ashtray in front of me, all the while staring at the young engineer.

"Excuse me," the engineer said. "I have found another seat."

I spent the rest of the evening alone.

When Sylvia returned, I told her about the incident. Obviously, the Chinese smoker was a political officer. I also updated her on the latest rumors. There was a second submarine. More guns had been spotted.

"Oh good. More information to pass on," she said.

"Pass on to whom?" I asked.

"The American ambassador to the Marshall Islands."

"Excuse me? You're informing the Americans about the Chinese on Tarawa?"

"Uh-huh. I met with her in Majuro and told her everything I knew."

"Not knew. *Heard*, as in rumored."

"Whatever. She wrote it all down, and asked me to keep her updated."

This was an interesting project for Sylvia to pursue. Of all the guidebooks to the Pacific, only one mentioned Kiribati. And in that guidebook, FSP was described as a CIA front. This had outraged Sylvia.

"I thought you were going to send a letter to that guidebook," I said.

"I am."

"But now you're spying for the U.S. government."

"Yes: But it's a secret."

Some months later, when the American ambassador arrived on Tarawa to attend Independence Day celebrations—had another year passed already?—Sylvia offered her the latest intelligence on Chinese activities in Kiribati. More submarines. Where the Secret Room was in the embassy. The strength of their defenses around the tracking station. The payoffs to the government to keep quiet. The spike in Chinese activities whenever the Americans tested their missile defense system. Sylvia was thorough. She was also undeterred when the source of the rumors regarding the submarines and the guns turned out to be an *I-Matang* prankster.

"So what?" she said. "You agree that the Chinese are using the satellite tracking station to spy on what's happening on Kwajalein?"

"I do."

"And you agree that the Chinese are corrupting the government?"

"I do."

"And you agree that the Chinese are the biggest polluters on Tarawa?"

"I do, though I don't understand what that has to do with anything."

"Well, I don't like it," she said. "And if I can make their lives a little more difficult, then I'm happy to do it."

Beware the wrath of the roused environmentalist. Which is perhaps why not long after we left Tarawa, four American F-16s did a few low-level flyovers above the satellite tracking station. Which may have led to the Chinese taking down an American spy plane off the southern coast of China. I'm not saying these events are connected. But I'm not saying they're not.

In which the Author shares some thoughts on what it means to Dissipate, to Wither Away, Dissolute-like, and how one becomes perversely Emboldened by the inevitability of decay, the sure knowledge that today, possibly tomorrow, the Body will be unwell, which leads to Recklessness, Stupidity even, in the conduct of Everyday Life.

I am not sure when it happened, but at some point during my time on Tarawa I stopped wearing a seat belt. I saw nothing unusual in having the pickup truck filled with gas from a pump that was smoking, delivered by an attendant who himself was smoking. The sight of three-year-olds piled precariously on speeding mopeds no longer filled me with wonder. Body boarding in bone-crushing surf was an activity to be savored. Digging flies out of ever-deepening cuts became a thoughtless little habit. Four-day-old tuna? How 'bout sashimi? Six cans of Victoria Bitter? Why not? And hey, smoke 'em if you got 'em.

I'd become immune to disease, not physically, but psychologically. Nothing fazed me. "Do you remember that consultant from New Zealand?" Sylvia asked. "The one who was here to train the police force? Well, his office just sent a fax. Apparently, he's in the hospital with cholera and leptospirosis. They thought we should know."

"What's leptospirosis?"

"Something to do with rat urine."

"Well, he shouldn't have had the rat urine . . . Hey, I found some fresh sea worms for dinner."

I took it all in stride. Cholera, leptospirosis, hepatitis, leprosy, tuberculosis, dysentery, hookworms, roundworms, tapeworms, mysterious viral diseases, septic infections, there were so many diseases to contend with on Tarawa that it was best to ignore them altogether. Beyond boiling drinking water, there wasn't much that could be done. What happens happens, I thought. It could always be worse. That's what I told Sylvia when she was felled by dengue fever.

"I feel like I'm dying," she said. "Every bone in my body hurts."

"You're not dying," I contended. "Unless its hemorrhagic dengue fever."

"There's no cure for that."

"No there isn't. But at least it's not Ebola. Just relax. You'll probably feel better in about two weeks."

And she did.

On Onotoa, in the far southern Gilbert Islands, it seemed perfectly normal to have a meal of salt fish in a *maneaba* where fifty-odd shark fins were drying in the rafters. Afterward, I went swimming. When I did come across a shark in the shallows above the reef, I just smacked the palm of my hand hard on the surface of the water, and off it swam. Sharks had become an irritant, nothing more.

Flying Air Kiribati also ceased to fill me with dread, even after the CASA wrapped itself around a coconut tree while attempting an emergency landing on Abaiang. I'd traveled to Abaiang on a homemade wooden boat, just for fun, and as I stared at the CASA with its sheared wing, I thought, *Ah well, at least we still have the Chinese plane.*

At a funeral, I had a generous helping of chicken curry. In front of me lay the corpse. It was the custom in Kiribati to lay out the body of the deceased for three days before burial. Kiribati is on the equator. I had seconds.

Somehow, two years had passed since we first set foot on Tarawa, and in those two years I had become, in my own peculiar way, an islander. Certainly I was an *I-Matang*. But the world from which I'd arrived had become nothing more than an ever-receding memory. Sylvia too had adjusted to Tarawa. When I cut her hair, she no longer cringed in fear. She too had lost her vanity. When she took the electric razor we borrowed to shave my head, she was no longer troubled when her haircuts made me look like a skate-punk with unresolved anger issues. I, of course, couldn't care less. No hair, no lice, I thought.

One day, she arrived home and declared: "I ran over another dog today."

"What's the tally now?" I asked.

"Four dogs and three chickens."

"Didn't you run over a pig?"

"No," she said. "That was you."

Shortly after she'd arrived on Tarawa, Sylvia swerved to miss wandering dogs. It was instinctual. But Tarawa is a small island, where every speck of land is occupied or used, and to stray from the road's narrow lane was to risk the lives of humans, and no dog was worth that. And so now, like me, if she couldn't brake safely, she simply ran over the dog. Perhaps she felt bad about the first dog, but by the fourth dog, she took it as she did any other bump on the road.

When her staff at work declared that one of the rooms in the office was haunted by malevolent spirits, Sylvia did what any manager wise to the ways of Kiribati would do. She organized an exorcism. Unsure whether the spirits were Catholic or Protestant, Sylvia had both a priest and a minister cast out the offending spirits. The staff were satisfied.

We found that we no longer had much in common with the

newer volunteers and consultants to arrive on Tarawa. Every six months or so, another dozen *I-Matangs* arrived on Tarawa, replacing those whose contracts had ended, or more commonly, those *I-Matangs* who had been broken by Tarawa. The newcomers seemed dainty to us, naïve and ill-prepared for island life. Whenever I saw a newcomer, I had only one question: "Did you bring any magazines?"

"I've got a *People*," one said.

"Can I have it?"

The world on those pages, however, seemed utterly foreign to me. Instead, I found myself asking Bwenawa, "So, tell me a little more about this Nareau the Cunning character."

Whenever possible, we traveled to North Tarawa or to one of the outer islands. The threat of being marooned no longer troubled us. In fact, we welcomed it, because if one can ignore the heat, and the scorpions, and the awful food, the outer islands of Kiribati are about as close to paradise as one can reasonably ask to experience in this life. I have mentioned the color in Kiribati, and I will mention it again. There is no place on Earth where color has been rendered with such intense depth, from the first light of dawn illuminating a green coconut frond to the last ray of sunset, when the sky is reddened to biblical proportions. And the blue . . . have you *seen* just how blue blue can get in the equatorial Pacific? In comparison, Picasso's blue period seems decidedly ash-gray.

I admired the outer islanders. Though they had cloth, kerosene lanterns, and metal fish hooks, they survived on the atolls largely as their ancestors had, without any outside help at all. I was struck by how resistant to change these islands were. Inevitably, the handful of Western-style cinder-block buildings that were built on the islands for one grand purpose or another, stood derelict and forsaken, abandoned in favor of the customary wood and thatch homes and meeting places that were so perfectly suited to the equatorial climate.

Traditional singing and dancing existed not for the benefit of package tourists, but as ways to amuse and engage the people themselves once dusk put a definitive end to the day's work. The lagoons were clean, untampered with by clogging causeways and indestructible trash, and on the turquoise surface, men fished in skillfully crafted sailing canoes. It is no wonder that 85 percent of the thirty thousand people living on South Tarawa claim one of the outer islands as their "home island." There remains a way of life on those islands that exists in very few places now. It is a way of life I greatly respect.

Even on the outer island though, the continental world intrudes in strange and inexplicable ways. Whoever unleashed Vanilla Ice on Butaritari ought to be severely punished. And no punishment would be too cruel for the miscreant who brought in "La Macarena." But it is these glimmers of a world beyond the village that causes outer islanders to voice the lamentations of provincials everywhere—*we're bored*—and many, too many, have chosen to depart their islands for the flickering lights of South Tarawa, where inevitably there is a relative or two whom they can *bubuti*. Every month, more people arrived on South Tarawa and more children were born. But the island did not get any bigger. The water did not become more abundant. And with too many people living on too little land, South Tarawa was becoming a filthy, noxious hellhole.

But it was our filthy, noxious hellhole. South Tarawa had become our home. We knew how to live here, on an island that had fallen off the map. Like the I-Kiribati, we had become fatalists. We no longer believed we could control our world. Each day was marvelously odd. One day I might be snorkeling with an enormous eagle ray, and the next I might be clutched over with stomach pain as the parasites that had made my intestines their home threw a party. A day might be wonderful or terrible, but it was never, ever boring. When I woke up in the morning, my first thought was always, *What now?* I am quite likely the world's laziest adrenaline-junkie, and so living on Tarawa worked well for me. I didn't have to do anything. Shit just happened on Tarawa.

And so when Sylvia's contract ended, we weren't sure what to do. Sylvia could have held on to the job until the end of time. She reported to no one except her donors. She had some good projects. The FSP staff were quite likely the most motivated people in Kiribati. She liked the job. As for me, well, the book wasn't really working out. I learned that contrary to what they say, books do not write themselves. I thoroughly explored that avenue. Every day I said, *All right, book, go write yourself.* But the book wouldn't budge. Instead, it asked me for a story. But I didn't have a story, which, of course, is a problem when writing a novel.

This setback didn't trouble me. Tarawa has a way of shattering professional ambitions. Of course, my professional ambitions could have been shattered by a hummingbird's feather. Nevertheless, when your world is reduced to a sliver of land smack-dab in the middle of the Pacific Ocean, your aspirations tend to change. Once, I wanted to be a foreign correspondent for *The New York Times.* Now, I aspired to open a coconut with the same panache as the I-Kiribati.

We *could* continue to live here, I thought. I could teach. I could suckle at the teat of the foreign aid industry. There was plenty to do. More important, there was still much to experience in Kiribati. I had plans to do some long-distance windsurfing. I was fairly certain I could reach Abaiang. Maiana would have been more difficult, but I'd already found someone to accompany me in a boat. I wanted to learn how to build an I-Kiribati sailing canoe. I wanted to explore more of the outer islands. Abemama's distinction for quality oral sex, for instance, needed further investigating. Perhaps now and then, to escape island fever, we could travel, Air Nauru permitting, to a larger land, such as Samoa.

"If we stay any longer," Sylvia cautioned, "we'll never be able to go back."

That was quite likely true. Any longer in Kiribati and the culture shock that was sure to inflict us upon our return would almost certainly prove to be fatal. When we first arrived on Tarawa, we laughed at the stories of the I-Kiribati who had traveled abroad, usually no farther than Fiji. One spent a week in a hotel room after she couldn't figure out how the elevator worked. Another sustained severe injuries when he tried to navigate an escalator. One man who had traveled to Hawaii returned complaining bitterly of the cold. Now, as I contemplated going back to the distant shores of the United States I found myself a little more simpatico to the plight of islanders cast off in the great big world beyond the reef. Frankly, I was more than a little intimidated myself by the thought of having to weather the peculiarities of the continental world. On Tarawa, I understood life. Food came from the ocean; water from the sky. Coconuts were good for you; stand underneath a coconut tree for too long, however, and you would get conked. Tides determined the day's activities. Taboo areas were to be avoided. There is always time. It had all become very manageable. I understood this world . . . well, most of it in any case. To leave the islands was to set forth for the unknown. We would be adrift in the continental world.

Of course that world had air-conditioning and restaurants and bookstores. There were doctors. There was ample electricity. Lots of water, too. And toilets. Lots of toilets. And there were family and friends. No one had come to visit us in Kiribati. Those who had the time lacked the money. And those who had the money lacked the time. There's the conundrum of American life in a nutshell. During our absence, we missed innumerable weddings, a couple of funerals, and the births of our first nephews and nieces. I thought of the handful of long-term *I-Matangs* in Kiribati and realized that all of them had, either by choice or default, become severed from their old lives. The isolation in Kiribati is unforgiving.

It was the sudden appearance on Tarawa of one such long-term *I-Matang* that finally compelled us to make our decision. Half-Dead Fred had arrived. For twenty years he had eked out an existence on Tabiteuea North. I had heard of Half-Dead Fred, of course, just as I had heard of Banana Joe and a few of the other *I-Matangs* who resided on the outer islands much as the beach-combers who preceded them had. The government of Kiribati, however, had decided to expel the foreigners who had overstayed their visas. Half-Dead Fred had overstayed his by nineteen years. He had arrived those many years ago from the Marshall Islands, where he had been working for a defense contractor. One day, as an Australian might say, he went walkabout and ended up on what is quite likely the most traditional of islands in Kiribati, where he found himself marrying a procession of young brides, who provided him with land where he could cut copra. Life moved along in its usual helter-skelter fashion and suddenly two decades had passed. And after twenty years on the Island of Knives he was told that it was high time for him to return to the United States, which he had not seen since disco was king.

Half-Dead Fred was staying with Mike. Everybody stayed with Mike. If you ever happen to find yourself in the equatorial Pacific needing a place to stay, just head on over to Mike's house. Bring him something to read, ideally a surfing magazine, and you can stay until you grow old. This seemed to be what Half-Dead Fred would have preferred. The government wanted to expel him to the Marshall Islands, but the Marshall Islands correctly pointed out that Half-Dead Fred was not Marshallese and that according to international law deportees could only be deported to their country of origin. The government of Kiribati, however, was not too keen to shell out the money for a plane ticket to the United States. And there matters remained until, miraculously, Half-Dead Fred's father was found living in Florida, and he agreed to spring for the airfare.

Air Nauru, as usual, was not flying. It had been impounded in Australia—again—for declining to pay its bills. In the meantime, Half-Dead Fred lingered on at Mike's house, which is where I found him one afternoon, enraptured by Mike's computer. Mike, like everyone in Kiribati, was resourceful. One year he might get his hands on a hard drive. Three years later, he'd find a monitor. A year or two later, he'd get word that some westerner was soon to arrive on Tarawa and he'd fire off a telegram listing all the goods he desired that were unavailable on Tarawa, which is to say pretty much everything invented since the wheel. This is how Mike ended up with a video game called Doom, or was it Gloom, or possibly Boom. Anyway, as I walked in I saw Half-Dead Fred hunched in a chair spellbound by the imagery on the computer.

Half-Dead Fred had earned his moniker. He was so wasted in appearance that in comparison a cadaver would seem plump and rosy-cheeked. Tall and gangly with a long salt-and-pepper beard, Half-Dead Fred looked much as I imagined Robinson Crusoe would look had Robinson Crusoe been marooned for a few years longer. He wore a pair of shorts that anywhere else would have long been discarded or put to use as rags. He was shirtless and barefoot. Then again, I too was shirtless and barefoot. So was Mike.

"How long has he been like that?" I whispered to Mike.

"Since the power came back on."

"That was five hours ago."

Mike nodded.

"Does he talk?" I asked.

"Oh yes," Mike said. "When the power's off he doesn't stop talking. Of course, what he says doesn't make any sense. But he does talk."

We stood watching him. It was strangely riveting. Half-Dead

Fred hadn't even acknowledged the presence of others in the room, so entranced was he with discovering the tools that would allow him to rescue the princess locked in a dungeon by a nefarious wizard in cyberworld. I could think of few things more discombobulating. Twenty years on an island in the world's most remote island group, where every day was occupied by fulfilling one's basic subsistence needs and where one had to constantly watch one's back, because this was the Island of Knives after all, and then to suddenly find oneself deeply ensconced within the alternate reality of a video game.

"Is he mad?" I asked Mike.

"As in crazy? No, I don't think so. But *sane* would be a little too strong."

For some reason I found the sight of Half-Dead Fred staring determinedly at a computer screen more than a trifle disturbing. I wasn't sure why. I couldn't quite grasp the source of my discomfort, until I realized that what I was looking at was . . . *me.*

This would be me, I realized, if I remained in Kiribati any longer, a dissolute man untethered from his own land, a foreigner who has adapted to the queer realities of island life, but a foreigner always, disconnected from the world beyond the reef, and possibly even from his own mind. Half-Dead Fred was my future.

"Let's go home," I said to Sylvia later that evening.

"It's time, isn't it," she said.

"Yes. It's time to go home."

TWO MONTHS LATER we found ourselves at Bonriki International Airport, our necks sagging under the weight of a dozen shell necklaces, our heads crowned with garlands, our luggage weighed down with a half-dozen mats. We had spent much of the previous week in the island's *maneabas* attending one farewell party after the other.

They take goodbyes seriously in Kiribati, quite likely because they tend to be permanent. When people leave the islands, they don't come back. At the airport, it seemed as if half of Tarawa was on hand to see us off. Of course, every time an airplane arrives on Tarawa half of the island shows up simply for the novelty of it. Nevertheless, we were touched by the number of people on hand. The FSP staff were there, of course, and so too were their families. The tears flowed freely. I bought everyone a round of coconuts.

"We have come to think of you as family," Bwenawa said, "but now it is time for you to return to your families in the *I-Matang* world. We will remember you. You are good *I-Matangs*. And you must remember us here on the islands under the sun."

We most certainly will, we said.

We walked across the tarmac toward the airplane, and as we climbed the stairs we turned to see all those people gathered behind the fence, no longer exotic strangers, but friends. We waved a last good-bye and entered the aircraft, Nauru's Boeing 737, where we were immediately walloped by a bracing gust of culture shock.

Air-conditioning.

Settling into our seats—plush, comfortable seats that reclined at the push of a button—was a journey in itself. The plane took off with a satisfying roar and as it turned southward toward Fiji we had our faces pressed to the windows, straining for that last view of Tarawa before it receded forever a nanosecond later.

"Well, we did it," Sylvia said. "We've lived at the end of the world."

"Yeah," I said, gazing at the blue magnitude of the Pacific. "Do you think they'll have cheeseburgers in Fiji?"

In which the Author expresses some Dissatisfaction with the State of his Life, ponders briefly prior Adventures and Misadventures, and with the aid of his Beguiling Wife decides to Quit the Life that is known to him and make forth with all Due Haste for Parts Unknown...well, not entirely unknown, though fatherhood was new, causing the author to share a page or two of Exuberantly Gloopy Prose on how wonderful, really and truly, it is to have a Little Island Boy.

T he urinal spoke to me. This had never happened before. True, there had been occasions when toilet bowls had spoken to me. Don't do shots, they said. Particularly tequila shots. I listened, and no toilet bowl has ever spoken to me again. But this was the first time a urinal had spoken to me. It made some comments about my manhood. "Ha-ha," it continued, "just kidding." The urinal called himself Norm. Norm had a television show. Norm wanted me to watch his television show. It aired weekly on the ABC network. When I finished, Norm quieted. Then someone else approached the urinal. Norm the urinal began to talk again.

I returned to my seat at the Childe Harold, a bar in Washington D.C. I had met Sylvia there for an afterwork drink.

"The urinal spoke to me," I told her.

"What did it say?"

"It said its name was Norm. It asked me to watch his television show on the ABC network."

"What did you say?"

"I said, 'Norm, I piss on you.' "

Sylvia looked at me oddly. "You're not adjusting very well, are you?"

"I am too."

"You have to accept that bathrooms are an acceptable place to advertise television shows. That's how it's done here. This is our home now and we have to adjust."

Sylvia was wearing a shell necklace. She carried a purse made from pandanus leaves. Her shirt said "Stop Toxic Hazardous Waste in the Pacific." In the two months since we had returned from Kiribati, Sylvia had yet to reveal so much as her ankles to the world at large. Before Kiribati, she wore short-shorts and miniskirts. She was often referred to as the leggy blonde. Now, the Taliban would have been proud of her modesty. Sylvia was not a model of adjustment. I pointed this out to her.

"I am adjusting," she said. "It's just that I find shopping to be so . . . *hard.*"

The shopping mall. The American shopping mall. It frightened us.

After we left Kiribati, we had spent some time traveling around the Pacific. Fiji seemed to us a vast country. Its capital, Suva, felt like a megalopolis to us. We rarely left our hotel room as we were too busy marveling at this strange new wonder called air-conditioning. On the islands of Vava'u in Tonga we met yachties who reveled in their escape from civilization. "This is the end of the world," said one. There were hotels, restaurants, cars, whale-watching tours, tourists, and twice-daily flights to Nuku'alofa. None of the yachties, or cruisers as they insisted on being called, had ever sailed to Kiribati. In Vanuatu, we stood on the rim of an active volcano and saw dawn emerge, and then flew to Port Vila, where we fattened ourselves up on French bread and cheese and smoked salmon and the most delicious steaks it has ever been my good fortune to eat.

Nevertheless, despite these forays into the world beyond the reef, we remained utterly unprepared for America. It was a shocking experience. From the moment we landed, we began to quiver. Driving on the L.A. Freeway in our rental car, we were honked at, cussed at, gestured at, and moments away from being shot at. I could not understand how anyone could drive faster than thirty-five miles per hour. I tried accelerating up to forty, but it seemed dangerously fast to me, and I slowed down.

We had decided to return to Washington, D.C. This was a poor decision. What we should have done was move to Hawaii and slowly ease ourselves back into America. A couple of years in Hawaii, and then maybe we'd be ready for Key West. Instead we moved to the capital of the most powerful country on Earth, where we immediately felt like yokels from another planet. "Would you look at that?" I'd say to Sylvia. "I think that there is what's called a limooosiine. Golly. Sure is big. Must be some real important folk inside."

Once we'd found an apartment, I made a foray to the supermarket around the corner for provisions. Two hours later, when I had failed to return, Sylvia went out to look for me. She found me staring blankly at a display of maple syrup. My shopping cart was still empty.

"Did you know that there are thirty-two different varieties of maple syrup?" I said.

"Well, just choose one," Sylvia said.

"But which one?"

This stumped her, as it had stumped me. Confronted by so much, how does one choose? Regular or low-fat? The gourmet syrup from Vermont or regular old Aunt Jemima? Glass bottle or plastic? Fortunately for us, someone else eventually selected a bottle of syrup, and we decided that if it was good enough for her, an experienced American consumer, then it was good enough for us. Then we moved on to the butter section. Did you know that there are forty-three different kinds of butter and margarine? By the time we finished our shopping, winter had arrived.

Eventually, we had to go to the mall. We both needed new shoes and a new wardrobe. I was perfectly happy with my flipflops, but once we arrived in Washington, I noticed that people hurriedly crossed the street when they saw me approach. Even though the thermometer said it was 78 degrees, I found it excruciatingly cold, and so I walked around with several layers of tropical shirts and socks with ingeniously cut slits to accommodate my flipflops. So attired among the besuited Washington throngs, I discovered that I elicited the kind of reactions typically reserved for gun-toting crackheads.

Inside the mall we fell silent, our chins dangling below our knees. Before us were acres of climate-controlled, Muzak-enhanced retail space devoted to satisfying every consumer desire. It was breathtaking. We had become accustomed to no options whatsoever, and suddenly we were in a shopping mall, an *American* shopping mall. Bloomingdale's or Hecht's? Khaki or denim? Loafers or laces? All around us, people confidently walked into stores and made purchases. We moseyed around as one might do on the moon, feeling awed and bewildered. The dragon ladies at the makeup counter eyed us wearily. I was in tattered shorts and a flower print *Bula* shirt I had picked up in Fiji. Sylvia's T-shirt promoted the nutritional value of *bele*, a weed that can survive on an atoll. Flip-flop, flip-flop, we wandered around the mall. And then we wandered right on out of the mall. It was too much. Taking pity, my mother solved our fashion problems by shopping for us. She has very strong opinions on how a man should dress and, having no other options, I obliged her. It was Sylvia who drew the line at the cravat.

Once I had shoes, I set about getting a job. I had hoped that after two years, the credit card people and the student loan people would just forget about the past and let things slide, but this turned out not to be the case. "Remember that nice meal we had in Annapolis three years ago?" I said to Sylvia. "Well, after three years of interest and late fees and finance charges, that meal is going to cost me $1,500." This did not please Sylvia. On a piece of paper she added our rent, our monthly grocery bill, utility costs, and various miscellaneous expenses, and divided it in two. "This," she said, circling the figure, "is what you need to earn each month. Not a penny less."

Fortunately, due to a terrible misunderstanding, I soon found myself working as a consultant to the World Bank. I am not exactly sure what it was that led the World Bank to believe I had any expertise in infrastructure finance. I had never even balanced a checkbook. I hadn't even tried. There is not much reason to balance a checkbook when your checking account rarely tops the three-figure mark. And so, to the Third World countries who had the misfortune of working with me on their infrastructure projects, I wish to apologize. I was just kind of making it up as I went along. I hope you understand. I needed the paycheck.

It was a large paycheck too. A large, tax-free paycheck. I was grateful to the World Bank. I understood what they were doing. They were alleviating poverty one consultant at a time. To earn this generosity, I played a game of pretend. I pretended to feel comfortable in a suit. I pretended to know what a derivative was. I pretended to be aware of the Asian financial crisis. *What Asian financial crisis?* I thought. The only financial crisis I was aware of was my own.

At a luncheon hosted by the chief economist of the World Bank, I was seated beside the Minister of Infrastructure from Haiti. He described how painful privatization would be for his country. Thousands of people would lose their jobs. Many more would find themselves destitute. I nodded sympathetically.

Yes," I intoned. "It will be painful, but necessary."

That was my mantra at the World Bank—*painful, but necessary.* Privatization will lead to greater efficiency, which will lead to greater productivity, which will lead to an increase in capital, which will lead to more investment, which will lead to wealth and prosperity for all. I absorbed this like an infant absorbing the strange new world he finds himself in. I sat at my desk like a sponge soaking up the conversations in the corridor, internalizing the e-mail traffic, trying to decipher what my boss was talking about. *Painful, but necessary.*

It took many months, but eventually drinking water straight from the tap no longer seemed like a provocatively dangerous thing to do. Wearing shoes began to feel natural again. Restaurants ceased to be intimidating. After we got married, Sylvia and I honeymooned in Brittany. When a business trip took her to Brussels, I joined her for a long weekend in Amsterdam. We vacationed in the wine country of Sonoma. Somehow, inexplicably, by small increments, we became part of the cosmopolitan class. We lived well. We traveled comfortably. We read the right newspapers. We subscribed to the right magazines. Conversations alighted upon the IMF's role in Turkey, the cuisine of Andalusia, market reform in China, the animal life of Zambia, and where to find white asparagus. We were adapting to millennial America.

At the World Bank, my coworkers and I discussed the pressing issues of the day. Which airline has the best business class, Singapore Airlines or British Airways? Which stock should I buy, Nokia or Qualcomm? Where should I buy a suit? Burberry's or Brooks Brothers?

On a trip to the Middle East—business class, via a rest stop at the Park Lane Sheraton in London, with an automatic upgrade to suite—I spent two weeks at the InterContinental Hotel in Amman, Jordan, ostensibly to help organize a conference on infrastructure finance. I had little to do beyond ensuring that the PowerPoint projector worked correctly. The most pressing task was composing a birthday greeting to King Abdullah on behalf of the World Bank and the senior government officials attending the conference. It took the better part of a day before the French-speaking Moroccan, the robed Saudi clutching his prayer beads, and the jittery Syrian agreed that the felicitation was sufficiently flowery for the occasion.

When the conference ended I traveled to the south of the country to visit Petra, the golden city in the canyon. I had long fantasized about going to Petra. I had always envisioned approaching it after a hard journey across the desert, guided by Bedouin tribesmen, pressing on in the blazing sun, resting at the occasional oasis, where we would water the camels and pass the time discussing *The Thousand and One Nights*. Instead, I barreled through the desert in a chauffer-driven black Mercedes. I was with my boss, a Persian who often reminisced about the caviar served in the first-class section on Iranian Airlines before the revolution, and a professor from the Harvard Business School. They were engaged in an animated discussion about the deal Goldman Sachs had made to finance a new power plant in Qatar. We passed through Palestinian refugee camps. In the desert, young boys herded their goats. We were overtaken by an enormous white Cadillac with Saudi plates. Above, a squadron of military helicopters hovered near the Israeli border. It felt so odd passing all this life in a chauffer-driven Mercedes, and suddenly it occurred to me that I had become what I once loathed—a grossly overpaid consultant dithering in the sun. I was wasting my time. As you may have gathered, I am generally amenable to wasting time, but not like this. I felt like I was perpetuating a fraud, and while I can't say that I felt any particular moral outrage, I did appreciate the ridiculousness of my situation, and if I was going to live a ridiculous life, I could do better.

Sylvia too had since become dispirited with life in Washington. For a long while, she had simply absorbed the sights, sounds, and realities of life in the most important city in the world. She was like an automaton. She had some distant memory of this world, but it felt like a long-forgotten dream. Confident now that she understood life in Washington, she began to form opinions. "This sucks," she would declare after another day of forging partnerships, promoting synergy, attending conferences, disseminating knowledge on the Internet, producing vapor. In Kiribati, she had worked with the tangible. In Washington, she worked with the gaseous. How exactly will a link on a corporation's website improve the lot of the two billion people living on less than a dollar a day? Presumably, they don't have broadband access. Quite likely, they don't even have electricity.

One evening, returning home after an excruciatingly long day, which was devoted solely to massaging the prose written by a non-native English-speaking economist into something approaching coherence, I was pleasantly surprised by a proposition put forth by Sylvia.

"Would you be inclined to move to a small island in the South Pacific?"

"Oh yes please."

And that is how two years after we returned from Kiribati, we once again found ourselves on a distant island, enveloped by the familiar blue waters of the Pacific.

AND SO AFTER A YEAR in Vanuatu, we found ourselves in Fiji, where Sylvia worked as the Regional Manager of FSP. I had decided to write a book—this book, as a matter of fact, and this time I would finish it. (Note to editor: Really.) Life in Fiji, as one can imagine, was very interesting. For instance, there was a coup recently, which was very exciting, though frankly, I think a lot of people in Fiji would be happier if the military traded in their guns for a good horn section.

Life in Fiji, however, became particularly interesting once Sylvia discovered that she was pregnant. Determined to be both the best husband and father that I could be, I read every book I could get my hands on. Every evening I prepared heaping platters of grilled fish, potatoes, spinach, pasta, followed by bowls of fruit and jugs of ice cream. I consulted my book. "Okay. It says here that in month four protein is important. We're having steak tonight."

"It's ninety-five degrees," Sylvia said. "I don't want steak."

"Immaterial."

Soon, though, Sylvia was spending her evenings baking. Sylvia is not by nature a baker. She's more a sauté kind of person, but some strange physiological impulse had kicked in and the house became redolent with the sweet aromas of carrot cake and banana muffins and chocolate chip cookies. I encouraged this. Packages from oversees arrived containing baby onesies and Sylvia spent a long time folding and unfolding and becoming more than a trifle weepy. "Aaaaw . . . it's so cute," she said, drying her eyes. Her belly ballooned in a very interesting fashion. One day, after I mistakenly added five garlic cloves to the pesto I'd prepared, rather than the one clove the recipe called for, Sylvia announced that the baby was kicking mightily, and what a strange and wondrous thing it is to put your hand on your wife's belly and feel your child moving like an agitated Mexican jumping bean.

Shortly before the baby was due, we met with Morgan and Catherine, English friends of ours with two island-born children of their own.

"You will need help with the baby," Catherine remarked.

"I think we can manage," I said. "I've been reading a book."

"Have you now?" Catherine said.

"Yes. Very diligently. It said that infants sleep eighteen hours a day. That leaves just six hours for parenting-type activity."

"You poor man. May I ask when was the last time you held a baby?"

I thought for a moment. "1986."

"I see." For some reason, Catherine began to laugh very hard.

"I figure that for the first few days, we will just let the baby do his own thing, you know, get comfortable outside the womb, and then we'll mold him so that he adapts to a more civilized routine."

"Yes, quite. That sounds very sensible."

I UNDERSTAND NOW why Catherine laughed so hard. Four months have passed since Lukas was born. The books were wrong. Lukas does not sleep eighteen hours a day. More like eighteen minutes a day, in eighteen-second intervals. I can count on one hand the hours I have slept in those four months. And it is the strangest thing: I don't mind at all.

Lukas is a handsome, happy baby, who for some unknown reason, has decided that he has no need for sleep. The world is too full of wonder. He has spent his first Christmas in a Fijian village. He has grown very found of the mynah birds nesting on the roof and as a result I have called a truce with the pugnacious creatures. He knows that his hands are for waving in a most charming manner. He knows his legs are for thrusting determinedly back and forth, because if a baby is going to walk, he needs to exercise. He knows that he can now trust his parents to bathe and change and burp him, though it was rough going at first. He knows mummy is for lunch. He knows that daddy is where we go to spit up lunch. He knows how to smile. He can play an epic game of peek-a-boo.

He has also swum in the Pacific Ocean. One day, we took him to Pacific Harbor on the southern coast of Viti Levu, the main island in

Fiji. Few tourists go to Pacific Harbor. The weather is too unreliable. And so we had the beach to ourselves. It was a dazzling South Pacific day. A few miles distant lay Beqa, a mountainous green island offering postcard contrast with the blue of the South Pacific. Lukas was in his swimming diapers. We put a T-shirt on him, as well as a hat, and with him on my shoulder we waded in. He took to it immediately, kicking and splashing as I twirled him through the balmy water. He was happily giggling, until suddenly he stopped. He tensed. His face puckered up. He pooped.

"I can't believe he's doing this," I said, grimacing as I extended him outward.

Sylvia laughed. "He's our little island boy."

ᕙ◯◯ BIBLIOGRAPHY

Crocombe, Ron. *The South Pacific*. Suva: University of the South Pacific, 2001.

Davidson, Osha Gray. *The Enchanted Braid: Coming to Terms with Nature on the Coral Reef*. New York: John Wiley and Sons, Inc., 1998.

Grimble, Arthur. *A Pattern of Islands*. London: John Murray, 1952.

Koch, Gerd: *The Material Culture of Kiribati*. Berlin: Museum fur Volkerkunde, 1965.

Macdonald, Barrie: *Cinderellas of the Empire*. Canberra: Australian National University Press, 1982.

Mason, Leonard, ed.: *Kiribati: A Changing Atoll Culture*. Suva: University of the South Pacific, 1985.

Maude, Henry Evans: *Of Islands and Men: Studies in Pacific History*. New York: Oxford University Press, 1968.

———: *Tungaru Traditions: Writings on the Atoll Culture of the Gilbert Islands, by Arthur Francis Grimble*. Honolulu: University of Hawaii Press, 1989.

Stevenson, Robert Louis: *Tales of the South Pacific*. Edinburgh: Canongate Books, 1996.

Talu, Sister Alaimu, et al: *Kiribati: Aspects of History*. Suva: University of the South Pacific, 1979.